Aspects of English
Editor: John Sinclair

Reading Children's Writing

Aspects of English
Editor: John Sinclair

Language and Literature
An Introductory Reader in Stylistics
Edited by Ronald Carter

Reading Children's Writing
A Linguistic View
John Harris and Jeff Wilkinson

Reading Children's Writing

A Linguistic View

JOHN HARRIS and JEFF WILKINSON

Department of English, Sheffield City Polytechnic

with contributions by:

RONALD CARTER   NICOLA COUPE   MICHAEL HOEY
PAM MORGAN

London
ALLEN & UNWIN
Boston   Sydney

Allen & Unwin (Publishers) Ltd,
40 Museum Street, London WC1A 1LU, UK

Allen & Unwin (Publishers) Ltd,
Park Lane, Hemel Hempstead, Herts HP2 4TE, UK

Allen & Unwin, Inc.,
8 Winchester Place, Winchester, Mass. 01890, USA

Allen & Unwin (Australia) Ltd,
8 Napier Street, North Sydney, NSW 2060, Australia

First published in 1986

British Library Cataloguing in Publication Data

Harris, John
    Reading children's writing : a linguistic view.
—(Aspects of English; 2)
1. Written communication   2. Linguistics
I. Title   II. Wilkinson, Jeff   III. Series
808'.042   P211
ISBN 0-04-407021-7
ISBN 0-04-407022-5 Pbk

Library of Congress Cataloging-in-Publication Data

Harris, John, 1942–
    Reading children's writing.
(Aspects of English)
Bibliography: p.
Includes indexes
1. English language – Composition and exercises –
Study and teaching – Addresses, essays, lectures.
I. Wilkinson, Jeff.   II. Title.   III. Series: Aspects
of English (London, England)
PE1404.H36 198   808'042'0712   85–11092
ISBN 0-04-407021-7 (alk. paper)
ISBN 0-04-407022-5 (pbk. : alk. paper)

Set in 10 on 11 point Times by Mathematical Composition Setters Ltd
and printed in Great Britain by Biddles Limited, Guildford, Surrey

Series Editor's Introduction

This is a series of books about language, mainly English, from a practical point of view. Each volume deals with an important area of current interest and presents new material against a background of established scholarship. The authors are all experts in their subject, and in each case have written because they have something to say. The books are intended to appeal to serious readers who have a general or professional interest in language. Anyone with more than a casual curiosity about the sounds, structures, vocabulary or variety of English will find profitable reading in the series. For teachers and students, the books are intended as useful textbooks in their subject areas. Some indeed are provided with guidance for use in self-study or as course books. Some provide coverage of a subject by collecting and editing contributions by several different authors, offering a variety of approaches. Some present a personal, innovative point of view in familiar territory.

It is not assumed that the reader already has a comprehensive command of modern linguistics. Linguistics, the study of language for its own sake, is a subject which many find abstract and inaccessible. Although the books are substantial contributions to linguistics, they are written with attention to the needs of a broader readership than the community of academic linguists. Different traditions of linguistic study put the emphasis of the work at various points between *theory* and *description*. At the theoretical end the centre of interest is now highly formalized. A set of abstract statements gives the broad outline of how a language is organized – the main categories that are used, the types of rules allowed, and so on. The nineteen sixties enjoyed a period of intense theoretical work led by Noam Chomsky, and since then many linguists have returned to the job of description, of providing detailed accounts of the workings of individual languages.

As part of the inevitable reaction to a concentration on theory, people began to study areas which had been relatively neglected. For example, connected texts and spoken discourse, rather than individual sentences, became prominent during the nineteen seventies. The study of variety in language contrasted with the uniformity which was a useful simplification in formal theory. More recently still, the study of vocabulary is growing to match the more abstract realms of semantics. The return to an interest in description does not reject theory – in fact it poses questions which lead to a constant review of theories – but it means that fresh approaches can be developed in most areas, and this series of books will chart some of the important developments.

PROFESSOR JOHN McH SINCLAIR
University of Birmingham

8 March 1982

Contents

Notes on Contributors

JOHN HARRIS is principal lecturer in the Department of English and co-ordinator of the Language Development Centre at Sheffield City Polytechnic. He has taught in primary and secondary schools as well as in a college of education. In addition to teacher training and in-service work he teaches on the writing skills component of the BA English studies at Sheffield. His main research interest is in children's writing development and he has written several articles on this subject including *Writing Development 8-13* (with Stan Kay; Rotherham Metropolitan Borough Council, 1981).

JEFF WILKINSON is senior lecturer in the Department of English at Sheffield City Polytechnic. He is involved in both teacher training and in-service work on aspects of language development and works on the linguistics component of the BA in English studies. His main research interest is in children's writing development at transition from primary to secondary level.

RONALD CARTER is currently lecturer in English studies at the University of Nottingham. He has taught both in schools and in a college of education. His interest in linguistics and education is reflected in several articles and in *Linguistics and the Teacher* (Routledge & Kegan Paul, 1982) which he edited. He has also written on literary subjects, notably on W. H. Auden and has edited two books on stylistics, *Literary Text and Language Study* (with Deirdre Burton; Edward Arnold, 1982) and *Language and Literature* (Allen & Unwin, 1983) which was the first book in the *Aspects of English* series.

NICOLA COUPE is lecturer in English and Education at Newman College in Birmingham. She has taught in infant and junior schools and has a particular interest in children's writing development. Formerly a member of the Schools Council Communication Skills Project team, she has also an interest in the description of children's oral competence. Currently involved in teacher training and in-service work she has continued her interest in children's writing from her initial involvement in a survey, conducted at Westminster College, Oxford, into the structural organization of the language of school-aged children.

MICHAEL HOEY is currently lecturer, English Language Research, University of Birmingham. Before moving to Birmingham in 1979 he worked for several years at Hatfield Polytechnic with Dr Eugene Winter where he was particularly concerned with the development of the writing competence of science and engineering students. His main teaching and research interest is in written discourse. Publications include *Signalling in Discourse* (ELR, University of Birmingham, 1979) and *On the Surface of Discourse* (Allen & Unwin, 1983).

PAM MORGAN teaches English at the Jack Hunt School in Peterborough. She is particularly interested in language development in the area of special needs and is also keen on drama. At present she is working on an M.Litt. at the University of Birmingham, investigating the organization of children's writing in the secondary school.

Introduction

Children's writing has recently become the focus of considerable attention both in Britain and North America. As is to be expected with a subject of such complexity, many perspectives are reflected in the recent literature, some pedagogic, some psychological and some linguistic. This book offers a different perspective that is, nevertheless, complementary to much of the existing work. The focus here is on text organization which is an area of linguistic study that has developed dramatically over the last decade. It is not an analytical approach that has been applied systematically hitherto to children's writing. Yet it is an approach which we believe has much to offer.

A second innovation is that all the chapters that offer descriptions of organization do so through detailed analyses of pieces of writing by children of either top junior or lower secondary ages. This phase of schooling has been selected for two main reasons. It marks a stage of development at which children begin to move towards making a range of conscious choices in their writing, to developing different styles and suiting styles to purposes. It is also a time during which children change schools and the effect of moving from primary to secondary school may involve quite radical changes in the types of writing expected. It follows then that the book is addressed to teachers at both primary and secondary levels; it is also addressed to student teachers and to all who are interested in the description of language-in-use, in particular those linguists who are interested in text structures and in the applications of linguistic description to teaching.

The book is organized sequentially and it is likely that most readers will prefer to read it in this way as the argument progresses. Initially we present a description based on recent research data and official reports of the state of writing in schools, concentrating on the context of the work rather than the products or texts themselves. We then look at how texts can be described and how descriptive approaches relate to developmental features. Subsequent chapters describe in detail organizational features of narrative and non-narrative writing. Organization is shown also to be central to an understanding of children's use of vocabulary. Chapter 7 argues the case for teachers' responses to children's work needing to be based on a principled framework and offers suggestions as to what this might be, looking, for example, at issues such as the use of 'time' and 'tense' in narrative writing. Chapter 8, based on a seminar discussion, provides a case-study of how children's texts can be 'read' taking a text organizational perspective and also considers implications for classroom practice. Aspects of this are then explored further in the final chapter.

However, in a book of this nature there is no inevitable order for reading and we have borne this in mind by making each chapter self-contained. Teachers may prefer, for example, to start at Chapter 8 with an example of 'readings' of children's writing, going from there to the detailed exposition of organization in Chapters 3 to 7 and then fitting these notions into a classroom context by reading Chapters 1, 2 and 9.

Linguists will find that Chapters 3 to 6 expound recent descriptive approaches to text organization including treatments of cohesion and vocabulary study that are innovative. Each of these chapters also shows how analysis is crucial to the diagnosis of children's writing problems. Although the examples used are of children's writing the approach adopted is by no means restricted to such data, and has applications to a wide range of texts both literary and non-literary.

All the papers in this book are original and our thanks are due to the contributors for their ready co-operation in the process of revising and editing the material. We wish also to acknowledge a special debt of gratitude to Michael Convey, now a member of Her Majesty's Inspectorate, who was initially a co-author of the book. He was much involved in the early planning including the convening of the seminar on which Chapter 8 is based and has continued to take an active and encouraging interest in the progress of the book. Finally our very warmest thanks must go to Liz Couldwell, secretary at the Language Development Centre, Sheffield City Polytechnic, whose ability to produce accurate typescripts from our illegible drafts with cheerful patience at all times has been quite exemplary.

JOHN HARRIS
JEFF WILKINSON
Sheffield, 1985

Reading Children's Writing

1 Children's Writing in School – the Context

JOHN HARRIS

Writing in the world outside school is not something that happens willy-nilly. It occurs because there is a purpose to be fulfilled, whether this be social or personal; it is addressed to a readership of some sort; its successful achievement requires a complex range of abilities being harnessed to the task. The form of the writing, moreover, will be radically affected by the constraints of readership and purpose. These points are obvious enough. Yet they need to be borne constantly in mind since it might be inferred from a survey of practice in schools that these basic factors are often, if not universally, overlooked. This, it should be emphasized, is not to argue that writing in school should necessarily reflect the full range of types of writing found outside school. But it does suggest that some rethinking is needed about the contexts and purposes for writing in school. Traditions of practice become established and it may be that, without it being full appreciated, these traditions neither reflect what teachers themselves know to be useful nor what can be demonstrated from a variety of perspectives to be helpful to pupils.

An illustration may add substance to the argument. I have often at the beginning of in-service courses on writing asked teachers to make a brief list of their regular writing activities and to indicate how they approached each task. As might be expected, the activities typically recorded range from the informal to the highly formal and from tasks requiring only a few words to those requiring many thousands. Each task varies in the way it is approached and, consequently, in the time spent on it. A selection of items from a typical list might look something like this:

Task 1	Shopping list
length:	50 words approx.
readership:	self
time spent:	5 minutes
degree of formality:	low
approach to the task:	jotted on back of envelope during/after consultation.

Task 2   Completing holiday booking form
length: 300 words approx.
readership: travel agent
time spent: several hours
degree of
formality: high   .
approach to
the task: careful noting of details beforehand − filling in form
                   itself − checking entries − getting partner to check
                   again to eliminate possibilities of error or ambiguity.

Task 3   Consultative paper on implementation of language
                   policy in school
length: 5,000 words approx.
readership: Head and rest of staff (in the first instance)
time spent: about ten days intermittently
degree of
formality: high
approach to
the task: initial notes and directed reading − outline(s) − first
                   draft in rough − revised − first typed draft circulated
                   to two close colleagues for comment − revision of
                   draft incorporating criticisms − final typed draft −
                   typescript proofread − duplicated and sent out.

This illustration shows that teachers in their own practice of writing have good instincts. They naturally vary their approach according to the purpose and the readership of the writing. The process also can be seen to differ according to the status of the writing. As competent writers the teachers know how best to approach each task and how to call upon other agencies that can help them to fashion, when necessary, a finished text that serves appropriately and efficiently its communicative function. When we look at practice in schools, however, the evidence suggests that teachers do not relate their own experiences of writing to the school context. And it is this evidence that now needs to be looked at in some detail.

Over the last decade several useful, if limited, descriptions of practice at both primary and secondary level have come from a range of sources such as Department of Education and Science (DES) surveys and reports and from several research projects. Nevertheless, there is a great need for a full investigation of the practice of teaching writing in our schools. The most recent and the most comprehensive survey at secondary level is the Writing Across the Curriculum Project conducted by the Scottish Council for Research in Education (SCRE, Spencer, 1983a and 1983b). However, no survey comparable in scope has been conducted in England, nor one at primary level. It should also be noted that several of the research projects have been designed to describe development and, therefore, have been concerned more with products than with the contexts and the processes by which products emerge (see, for instance, Britton *et al.*, 1975; Wilkinson *et al.*, 1980). Other justifiably well-regarded contributions to the literature on children's writing are primarily concerned to identify good practice and do not attempt a general description (see, for instance, Rosen and Rosen, 1973; Protherough, 1983). Bearing in mind, then, the limitations outlined above, I shall describe the evidence as answers to questions that are crucial to the context and practice of writing in school — questions, incidentally, which teachers frequently raise themselves in discussions of children's writing as an initial stage in rethinking their own practice.

How Much Writing do Pupils do?

The overall impression is that pupils are required to undertake a vast amount of writing. The Secondary Survey (DES, 1979) talks of 'the often formidable amount of writing carried out by many of the more able and average pupils' in the pre-examination years at secondary level. The report cites individual examples of the amount of writing required in different subject areas. A personal favourite is of a pupil from the lowest stream in a school who produced 11,000 words while doing a course called 'Planning for Life'! The report further suggests that such vast amounts of writing were a uniform demand over the 400 schools surveyed. Within this vast amount the most commonly found types were notes and essays.

At primary level there are two sets of specific data available — the Bullock report (DES, 1975) and the Oracle study (Galton *et al.*, 1980) — as well as the more grossly quantified evidence of the Primary Survey (DES, 1978). There is broad agreement between the two sets of specific data about the amount of time per week spent on language activities, which is over six hours. Within these six hours, Oracle found that writing of all types occupied more than five hours while Bullock put the figure lower at just under four hours per week. However, the Oracle study investigated all writing activities and within this differentiated between creative writing (stories, poems and personal anecdotal writing) and all other forms of writing. Creative writing, surprisingly, accounted for just under 9 per cent of a pupil's total time, other forms just over 20 per cent, while Bullock investigated writing occurring within the domain of English as a subject. Separate sets of data record the amounts of time spent on topic work but the amounts are not subdivided into the reading (library research) and the writing that are normally the staple activities of this sort of work in primary schools.

It is worth mentioning, in passing, that it is clear from the evidence of the SCRE report that teachers hold writing in high esteem – an attitude widely held also by society in general. Protherough (1983) also reports that an inquiry based locally in the Hull area found that both teachers and pupils regard writing as highly important both for reasons of prestige and as an indicator of educational achievement. This high esteem is, no doubt, reflected in the time devoted to writing.

The first point, then, is clear enough. Pupils at both primary and secondary level are expected to spend a significant proportion of their time in school writing, whether this is interpreted as 'own words' writing or dictated notes.

What Types of Writing are Pupils Expected to Master?

The most challenging finding of the SCRE report (Spencer, 1983a) is that 75 per cent of the total volume of writing in the pre-examination years at secondary level consists of four types:

(1) Copied notes
(2) Dictated notes
(3) Fill-in-the-space answers on worksheets
(4) Short answers of one sentence or less.

Of these, the first two account for 50 per cent; the last two for 25 per cent. As the report points out, these types of writing serve a very limited range of subject-learning purposes, that is:

> to aid memorization of subject content;
> to store information (for revision purposes);
> to allow the teacher to check on learning of subject content.

However worthy these purposes may be they are but a few of the wide range of purposes available for writing and it may be argued that they are not necessarily best served always by the short-burst type of writing described. Other purposes are ignored. Without attempting a comprehensive list one might add such purposes as:

> developing the reflective type of thinking and expression that is pro-moted much more readily by writing than by talk (see, for instance, Olson, 1977; Bereiter, 1980);
> the exploration through writing of feelings, experiences, attitudes and opinions;
> developing mastery in O and A level type essay writing.

Although the Secondary Survey does not present detailed statistical evidence, its impressionistic comments are in accord with the findings outlined above.

At primary level there is little precise evidence available about the types of writing expected. The Primary Survey reports that 'in virtually all classes children undertook some form of narrative writing'. This might be based on personal experience or incorporate imaginatively constructed events. Topic writing was found to be extensive but often amounted to no more than copying out extracts from reference books, confirming the findings of the Bullock Committee four years earlier. The narrow range of types of writing attempted is also suggested by this comment in the Primary Survey:

> It was rare to find children presented with a writing task which involved presenting a coherent argument, exploring alternative possibilities or drawing conclusions or making judgements.

The conclusion to be drawn from the evidence is that at primary level narratives (personal and fictional) and topic work (frequently copied from sources) form the staple diet of writing for many children. At secondary level the major portion of the 'vast amount' of writing noted above is short-burst writing often of copied or dictated notes.

Who are the Readers and What is the Purpose?

The answer to the first part of the question is simple enough: it is the teacher. Some writing is not looked at at all, particularly, it would seem, dictated notes which are for the pupils' own subsequent use, though the Secondary Survey suggests that these notes may often be inaccurate factually and/or incoherent in expression. Most writing, however, is scrutinized by the teacher who sets it either to check on the accuracy of the information, to correct spellings or, mainly in the context of secondary English work and creative writing lessons at primary level, to make some form of personal evaluation often as an oral comment rather than a written one. (The topic of teachers' responses is explored in detail in Chapter 7.)

There is evidence that some pupils at secondary level sometimes ask parents or peers to read through work prior to handing it in. At primary level it is customary practice for writing to be displayed on classroom walls or mounted in folders for pupils to read at their leisure, though whether it is actually read as much as is supposed is doubtful. I have noticed that it is often displayed too high up on the walls to be readable.

What then of the purposes of writing? In subject areas at secondary level the purposes are clear enough, according to the SCRE evidence.

Most teachers see the main objective of writing as ensuring that pupils record and memorize information; secondly, as providing a means of assessing whether pupils have understood information; thirdly, as giving opportunities for practising the types of writing demanded by the subject and in public examinations. To these can be added – since writing tasks may quite legitimately have more than one purpose – that teachers see writing as allowing for the diagnosis of pupils' strengths and weaknesses in writing and as providing opportunities for pupils to clarify and organize their thoughts. These purposes, it should be stressed, are those described by teachers. How far they match up with the evidence presented above relating to the high preponderance of short-burst writing is another question entirely.

The same survey, interestingly enough, took evidence from pupils on what they perceived to be the purposes of writing. Nearly half saw it as helping learning in some way; a third regarded it as providing a correct record of information for subsequent reference; nearly a quarter were unsure or vague about the purpose of being set written work. Many teachers of English at both secondary and primary levels would argue that the purposes of writing of an imaginative or personal nature have to do with the personal growth of the pupil by encouraging the sharing and shaping of experiences and also with the exploring and developing of the resources of language for expressing emotions and creating literary artefacts such as poems, stories and playscripts. How far pupils themselves are aware that these are the purposes of creative writing (to use the flag of convenience) is to be doubted. Cowie (1984), for example, reports the findings of a small-scale questionnaire that pupils at top junior level were often unsure why they were asked to write stories and they were completely foxed about being asked to write poetry – even if they enjoyed doing it!

Who Sets the Writing?

Although at primary level it is most common for teachers to set a writing task, the Primary Survey indicates that children did some writing on subjects of their own choice in just over half the classes observed. What proportion of the total volume of writing this amounted to is not recorded. It would also, of course, make a lot of difference as to how we interpret this information if we knew whether the personal choice was exercised in creative writing or in topic work where it might mean a total lack of guidance and control over the feasibility of the task attempted by a pupil.

At secondary level there is little evidence of self-initiated writing. There is a generally accepted premise that pupils write to the instructions of their teachers who often indicate in some detail the expected content, as we shall see in the next section. Again a likely exception would be pre-examination work in English lessons, but there is no hard evidence to draw upon.

How is the Writing Task Introduced?

The SCRE report states that at secondary level 'there was little indication that many teachers tried to create circumstances prior to writing in which pupils could think out or talk out what they were going to write, nor that many efforts were made to stimulate a strong motivation to write.' However, it is clear that some teachers give a lot of thought to the structuring of the content of the writing prior to requiring pupils to do it. Explanations and questioning of the class are the most usual forms of preparation. Reading from a textbook or worksheet is also common. There is evidence of some discussion prior to writing between a teacher and an individual pupil but none, in the surveyed schools, of discussion among pupils.

The same report also states that 'there was little evidence of any major effort to develop or explain the skills and strategies with which pupils could approach the particular problems of the writing they were about to do.' Guidance in the form, usually, of brief oral instructions was offered on the type of writing, the content to include and how to organize it. A typical example is provided by the Secondary Survey:

> Write an essay on the Great Exhibition of 1851. The following points may help, but credit will be given for original work:
> Who organised the exhibition? The building itself – Fears concerning the whole idea – Fears concerning the building – Who visited the exhibition? – How – What was unusual about this day out? – The things the visitors saw (great detail here) – Popular material – Gimmicks – What did these ideas tell of progress? – Any shortcomings? – Foreign exhibits – Reflection of the era – Your own ideas

The evidence available for practice at primary level is much more fragmentary. The Primary Survey states that in four-fifths of the classes observed the children's own experiences frequently provided the basis for language work. Re-telling of stories (fictional, historical and biblical) was another common activity. But there is no indication of what activities or instructions typically precede the task of writing. Bennett *et al.* (1984) in their study of the learning experiences of six- and seven-year-olds report that 'language tasks frequently had extended preambles involving the discussion and elaboration of the stimulus, the revision of key vocabulary and the reiteration of the teacher's rules for writing (referring to neatness, grammar, use of word-books and spacing, for example)'. Certainly an impressionistic view of creative writing at primary level is that much care is lavished on the quality of the stimulus and that frequently this is followed by a wide-ranging class discussion related to the stimulus. There appears, however, to be an arbitrary cut-off point for the discussion which indicates that the time for writing has come. There is, then, no attention paid to the writing *qua* writing. So far as topic work is concerned it is probably a reasonable assumption since so much of it is reported as being copied from source materials that little preparation or instruction precedes the actual writing.

What Account is Taken in School of the Process of Writing?

There is virtually no evidence about how teachers perceive of, or plan for, the process of writing. The SCRE report notes that 'despite the apparent expectation of many of the teachers that some writing should be redrafted, the researchers found during the project very little evidence of pupils making advance notes for or tentative drafts of writing and none at all for any major redrafting of an extended piece of writing (involving, for example, significant changes in content, structure or style)'. Writing, then, in which the first formulation is also regarded as the finished product appears still to be the norm at secondary level. Again, one may wish to except literary writing, particularly poetry, in the context of the teaching of English, though there is no firm evidence to support this.

At primary level there is no relevant research evidence on this question except for a brief mention in Lunzer and Gardner (1979) that a very small percentage of time is spent in deliberation prior to writing. It may well be that recent interest in the writing process (see, particularly, Graves, 1983) has influenced practice at primary level. My own impression, however, gained from many visits to schools and extensive in-service work is that allowing scope for planning, drafting and revising written work is the exception rather than the norm. Increased availability of word-processing facilities in schools may bring about a change, since it is one of the great benefits of processors that text can be extensively revised at all sorts of levels from individual words through to resequencing of long stretches of text prior to printing out.

How is Writing Taught?

The evidence in the Primary Survey does not specifically highlight how (or if) writing is taught. It does, however, mention that spelling was taught in a majority of lower junior classes from published materials that were not necessarily related to a pupil's own needs or writing problems. At upper junior level nearly all the classes surveyed were taught spelling in this way. It is, incidentally, interesting to read in this and other reports that the use of course-books for teaching English language abilities is still widespread – a practice that many believe to have disappeared decades ago!

The SCRE team did investigate the question of who teaches writing by asking pupils about their experiences. In general the pupils reported that their English teacher or their primary teachers had taught them about writing. About 20 per cent said that no secondary teacher had taught them about writing and most of the pupils also stated that they were not aware of having been taught how to proceed with most of the written tasks they were set. The concern, it appears, is almost universally with *what* needs to be written (the content), not with *how* it needs to be written (form and organization).

Conclusions

It will be immediately obvious that one important question has been omitted from the list of questions about writing; how is it marked and/or commented upon? This is an aspect that is addressed at length in Chapter 7 and elsewhere in the book. Its omission here should not be taken as in any sense indicating a low estimation of its importance.

The purpose of this chapter has been to establish with a minimum of comment a general description of what sorts of writing go on in schools and how writing is approached. When all allowances are made for the variable quality of the evidence – and it is worth stressing again that there is an urgent need for a full-scale investigation of practice – it has to be admitted that the picture that emerges is not encouraging. It would appear that in many schools traditional practices of writing go unchallenged and unchanged and that these practices are, in fact, at variance with what teachers themselves do when they are writing.

Subsequent chapters offer descriptions of some of the linguistic organizational demands of the types of writing practised in school and highlight the problems that even the more able pupils find with these. The all-important question of how competence in writing can best be taught is addressed in the final chapter. It is, therefore, inappropriate at this stage to offer any quick and easy solutions. However, the evidence surveyed does provoke some important questions about writing in school which it may be useful to spell out.
Can we justify:

(1) the apparently narrow and not necessarily clearly focused range of writing normally practised in schools?

(2)   the amount of copied writing as helpful in any way to learning to write?

(3)   the little regard that appears to be paid in practice to the actual processes of creating a text?

(4)   the scant evidence of any 'teaching of writing' other than correcting spelling and punctuation errors?

(5)   the concentration in subject teaching on content at the expense of offering pupils positive help in mastering the intrinsic demands of specific types of writing?

(6)   the widespread use of short-burst writing, particularly at secondary level, when this is obviously an inadequate preparation for the types of writing required in many public examinations and later in higher education and many trades and professions?

Suggested Further Reading

Beard, R. (1984), *Childrens Writing in the Primary School* provides a sound introductory discussion of both practice and research relating to children's writing over the last two decades.

Spencer, E. (1983a), *Writing Matters – Across the Curriculum* reports on the most recent investigation into the practice of writing in schools at Secondary level. Although the investigation was carried out in Scottish schools, the findings should not be regarded as localized.

Thornton, G. (1980), *Teaching Writing* is brief, but wise and probably the best introduction to current thinking about writing in schools.

2 Describing Children's Writing: Text Evaluation and Teaching Strategies

JEFF WILKINSON

Linus: You know what I like about Saturdays, Marcie? There are no 'D minuses'! You can go outside, and kick a football or run around, and you won't get leaped on by a 'D minus'.
Marcie: What are you going to do when Monday comes again?
Linus: I'll be back inside where the 'D minuses' can't get me.
Marcie: You're weird, sir!

Peanuts by Schulz
(United Feature Syndicate Inc, 1983)

Throughout the primary and secondary school range, pupils perceive a written response to their work as an assessment of a finished product. 'What did you get for your story?' is, therefore, a much more likely question for them to ask of each other than 'What did she think of your story?' In fact, a response to writing is seen, by both the teacher and the pupil, as a way of evaluating the merits, or otherwise, of a completed activity. What I want to argue is that assessment should place more emphasis on the communicative process between writer and reader.

Not only are pupils, it would seem, writing for a large amount of the time they spend in school, but they are also producing written work which, by and large, they see solely in terms of the achievement of a good, bad or average grade. Rarely is the act of writing perceived as being genuinely communicative (a dialogue between writer and reader) but dominated by the ultimate examination goal:

I really tried with that work. All weekend, I wrote pages. And I got a C. That's what I'd get for it at CSE I was told. What's the point of writing your heart out for C.

Louise, 16 (*The Guardian*
Tuesday, November 25 1980)

Writing seems, all too often, to be geared to the examination system or to be nothing more than straightforward copying (project or topic work lends itself, particularly, to this form of task). So, from the pupil's point of view, writing lacks specific purpose and, from the teacher's point of view, there is the danger of misinterpreting a piece of writing because the specific circumstances of its production have been ignored. Brodkey (1983), looking at a text produced by her eight-year-old son, convincingly illustrates this point by drawing attention to the false assumptions that can be made about the errors in any written work if no account is taken of the circumstances of the writing (that is, type, purpose, audience, and so on): 'We lack experience in reading children's writing, but we also lack experience in thinking about it . . . we lack much needed information about the who-what-where-when of child writing' (Brodkey, 1983, p. 328).

A profitable approach, therefore, to the linguistic study of children's writing might be to consider it in relation to its use. Many intuitive assumptions can, indeed, be clarified by the application of a principled linguistic framework. In fact, much that has been written recently on language variety (Wallwork, 1969; Gregory and Carroll, 1978; O'Donnell and Todd, 1980; Crystal, 1984) has already contributed a great deal to outlining a linguistic model for the identification of language use in all its diversity (for example, spoken and written forms, accents and dialects, register variation, attitudes to notions of correctness, and so on); and such features may be useful in creating a recognition of the need for pupils to develop writing competency in a wide range of situations.

Above all, it is necessary to develop as precise a way as possible for describing those features of a text which might best facilitate its improvement, and certainly it is the increasing interest in the scientific study of language over the past few years that has led many teachers to consider the value of such an approach for investigating the nature of the writing process in school. Beard (1984) acknowledges the possible areas for development:

> Linguistics can provide insights into the nature of language, its variety and development . . . Children's writing evolves from the use of this structure and related teaching and learning processes are inevitably bound up with it. Any decisions in the classroom on the setting or marking of children's writing, or on ways of improving spelling, for example, will inevitably carry with them assumptions on the nature of this structure and the ways in which it may mature. Such assumptions will need to be critically assessed and perhaps modified if teaching opportunities are to be maximised. (Beard, 1984, p. 6)

Working from a broad perspective of language and how it operates in use (in relation to types, purposes, audiences, and so on), several linguists have become increasingly interested in describing those language features of children's writing which are specifically seen to relate to its production in particular situations, and which would be of assistance to teachers both in the identification, and subsequent development, of specific writing skills.

Much of the previous research, however, into the linguistic description of children's writing has focused only on the grammatical structure of texts, and has concerned itself with identifying 'norms of linguistic maturity'. A consideration of grammatical patterning, therefore, has been pursued irrespective of context (La Brant, 1933; Schonell, 1942; Harrell, 1957; Sampson, 1964); and much time has been devoted to the classification and counting of certain grammatical features – in particular, sentence structure.

Harpin's research (1973, 1976) is perhaps the most widely known study which considers, and makes use of, this particular approach in some detail. His work concentrates on describing the syntactic development of children's writing in the primary school range, essentially focusing on such features as sentence/clause length and subordination as indices of measures of progess towards maturity in language competence (in other words, the older the child, the more complex his language becomes).

While acknowledging the usefulness of subordination features and clause complexity as an indication of language development in writing (justified by the consistency of the findings mentioned in both the work of Harpin and previous researchers), I would, however, suggest that too much emphasis has in the past been placed on the description of such language elements as 'potential adult forms' (Hunt, 1966; Gannon and Czerniewska, 1980) and not enough on what children are doing as they write. Attention has too often been drawn to what *should* be there, rather than to what is actually happening when pupils put pen to paper. Recent research into grammatical structure in children's writing (Kress, 1982; Perera, 1984) provides a much more effective insight into the particular demands that learning to write makes on a child. This is not to argue that Harpin ignores this aspect entirely (for instance, he notes the different grammatical demands that different types of writing make on pupils); he does not, however, make it one of his central concerns.

Describing the language features of children's writing, therefore, is not simply a question of noting how often a child uses a particular linguistic item, but also a question of identifying its function in the writing situation. Writing development is then much more realistically and revealingly seen as an increasing ability on the part of the pupil to handle a variety and range of language features which may vary very much from situation to situation. A developing competence in handling increased clause/sentence length and grammatical complexity might well be an accurate reflection of a growing confidence in writing skill; but such confidence also needs to be reflected in descriptions of what children are specifically *doing* with language in particular situations. The danger arises when, for example, grammatical patterning in a text is seen *solely* as a yardstick for identifying where the child is in relation to some kind of 'adult model' of how writing ought to be structured. Syntactic maturity becomes an end in itself, and writing purpose is ignored.

For example, Gannon and Czerniewska, in describing the written work of secondary school children (1980, pp. 109–131), concentrate on the syntactic patterning of such writing. However, much of what they have to say about its grammatical structure is couched in ways which imply a comparison with some kind of 'adult template' (irrespective of situation, purpose, audience, and so on): 'In an eleven-year-old's work this whole sentence reflects considerable maturity' (p. 110); '*there* shows a stylistic device advanced for this age' (p. 115); and 'a serious grammatical error appears to have arisen because the child has attempted a sophisticated syntactic form' (p. 119). There is almost a feeling of contempt for the child's adventurousness. After all, compare how children usually set about learning a language – commonly, by making mistakes (see Brown, 1973). The writing children produce is solely matched against this 'mature adult model'; and this is the norm then set which the pupil must somehow strive to achieve. Hunt (1966), in noting the gradual increase in the number of subordinate clauses used by children in their written work as they increase in age and maturity, compares such achievements with the model to be acquired – that used by 'the superior adult writers who produce articles for *Harper's* and *Atlantic*' (p. 58).

I am not, I hope, giving the impression that subjective judgements as to the effectiveness or otherwise of a text are inadvisable; only that such judgements need to be related more precisely to, and supported more effectively by, the function and situation of the actual writing produced. If this is not done, we are in danger of equating 'syntactic complexity' with maturity, exclusive of any situational constraints.

On the one hand, this can lead to a misunderstanding of how language is actually being used in any particular instance. For example, Gannon and Czerniewska look at a story produced by eleven-year-old Anna, from the point of view of the complexity of its grammatical structures. Having established that the 'normal' order for elements in clause structure takes the form of Subject–Verb–Object–Adverb, they then identify her use of 'Out came 8 little mice' as an example of a 'sophisticated syntactic form' because of the inversion of its normal clause elements. Yet such inversion is very often the norm in stories that children both hear and read from a very early age. So, as Brodkey (1983) effectively comments, it is not that grammar is unimportant, it is simply that it is not enough.

On the other hand, a view of maturity as the increasing ability to handle syntactic complexity can also lead to the production of teaching materials which concentrate on the development of such structures in children by means of a series of graded exercises which give pupils practice in the manipulation and reordering of syntactic elements. Fraser and O'Donnell (1968) produced a course (called *Control and Create*) to develop the writing skills of secondary school pupils, which would seem to follow such principles. Essentially, it aims to teach ways of organizing language on paper by means of a series of exercises (graded progressively in terms of syntactic complexity) which purport to make pupils consciously aware of the potential variation possible in grammatical structures – an interesting and stimulating approach, perhaps, but, because the situations are not contextualized, the language remains unrelated to any communicative purpose. For example, several exercises seek to explore ways of combining simple sentences in a variety of increasingly complex ways:

> The sentences 'Samson was a man of great strength' and 'Samson was the scourge of the Philistines' can be organized in several different ways: (1) 'Samson was a man of great strength *and* he was the scourge of the Philistines': (2) 'Samson, *who was a man of great strength*, was the scourge of the Philistines'; and (3) 'Samson, *a man of great strength*, was the scourge of the Philistines'.

Whilst it is acknowledged that many structures may be more complex and, by implication, more mature than others, the differences in function created by different grammatical patternings are never explored.

A similar approach can be found in more recent language textbooks for schools: for example, Cleland's series on language development for primary school children, *English for Primary Schools* (1976), where, again, sentence-combining exercises in de-contextualized situations form a regular part of the activities suggested in each part of the books in the series. For example:

> Use *and*, *but*, or *because* to join each pair of sentences.
> (a) The harvest was poor. The summer had been cold and wet.
> (b) Sandra went out to play. She could not find any of her friends.

Neither approach seeks to relate grammatical patterning to the particular function or use such items might serve in any actual situations. For instance, in the example from the series *Control and Create*, it would have been useful to consider, perhaps, the functional differences between using a co-ordinate clause with 'and' (see Leech and Svartvik, 1975, Section 387, for a description of equivalence) and the relative clause, 'who was a man of great strength'. Similarly, Cleland seems to be offering 'and', 'but', and 'because' only as synonyms, and does not pursue their possible operations as 'contrasts of meaning':

for example, 'and' illustrating simultaneous events or cause–and–effect or chronological sequence (see Harpin, 1976, p. 68).

If such approaches to the linguistic development of children in general, and of children's writing in particular, are to be effectively pursued, it might reasonably be expected that activities centred on the manipulation and re-organization of grammatical structures be more contextually based (see Chapter 9 for a description and discussion of some of this type of work). Any theory, therefore, for the linguistic description of school-based writing needs, by identifying a text's purpose and audience, to consider the relationship between the form of that text (for example, its grammatical structure) and its function (its meaning in relation to its situational adequacy).

With this particular perspective in mind, therefore, I would now like to apply such observations to the description and discussion of a particular piece of writing. A junior class of ten- to eleven-year-olds was asked by their teacher, after much discussion based on their own memories of events and on personal anecdotes, to write about an accident that they had either heard about or been involved in. This is the particular account that ten-year-old Adrian produced:

> One day there was a accident and There was a crash around around-about and one of the cars and you get minorer Peter went walking down with him and collide and the car was a crash and there was three crashes on the moterway and The car was surt of a ambulance and It was a black car and The was not very good.

The teacher's response to this piece of writing was one of genuine despair, but concern: 'I don't really know where to start with this one', she said; and I think it would be true to say that much of her assessment of it stemmed from an 'error analysis' of the text, primarily in terms of spelling and punctuation (that is, replacing what is not there, rather than considering what the child is actually doing). Approaches such as that used by Gannon and Czerniewska (although, perhaps, based on more explicitly identified linguistic criteria) would similarly offer, it would seem, a description of mistakes in relation to an adult norm. I make no excuses, at this stage, for selecting a text which on the surface would appear to be more problematic than most, because it seems to me that its problematic nature stems directly from viewing the text in precisely this way – as writing to be corrected so as to conform to the reader's concept of an acceptable piece of written work. What I want to suggest is that any linguistic theory that tries to account for the occurrence of certain features in children's writing needs to be explicit; but such a theory must also be sensitive to not just the writing in its finished form, but also to the process that has made the child write in the way he does. This description needs to account meaningfully for such texts in a way that will be practically useful for teachers both from the point of view of their initial evaluation, and also from the point of view of subsequent development. Such an approach would appear to be one which considers those linguistic features of the text *as a whole* which contribute towards or, in fact, impede the communicative process between writer and reader.

In presenting a description of the grammatical structuring of Adrian's writing, some initial insight is gained into the nature of the writing task set and how Adrian has approached it. The text itself consists of eleven free clauses combining to produce (it would appear) one sentence, which is, in fact, the whole text (see Kress, 1982, for a very useful and relevant investigation into the child's early concept of sentence as a textual, rather than a syntactic unit). Adrian's only use of a final stop may well relate to his concept of the story 'as a whole unit'. Each clause is attached to the next by the use of the same linking word, 'and' (with the exception of 'you get minorer' followed by 'Peter went walking down with him'). Most of the uses of 'and' would appear to indicate no immediately logical connection between one clause and the next (producing almost the impression of a noting of random thoughts), except for, perhaps, 'Peter went walking down with him *and* collide', where the function of the action verbs indicate, in their ordering, some kind of chronological sequence: that is, 'and then' (Harpin, 1976, p. 69). There is no indication of any kind of subordination in the text. Clause structures regularly consist of the same sequence of elements (Subject–Verb–Object: five times; Subject –Verb–Object–Adverb: twice; Subject–Verb–Adverb: once; and Adverb–Subject–Verb–Object: once, where the adverb is placed initially because of story-telling convention: 'One day'). Of these structures, three are of the 'there was . . .' kind; and two are of the 'it was' type.

On the basis of the description of such grammatical features, it would be relatively simple to form some kind of assessment of Adrian's stage of development, utilizing a 'syntactic complexity/maturity' model. Convey and Wilkinson (1977), provided with the data-base of the writing of a whole school from infant to lower secondary on the topic of 'Me', analysed the grammatical structures of the written work using Harpin's criteria, and suggested stages of writing development in terms of the use of certain identifiable structures (for example, verb types, use of prepositions, elements of clause structure, subordination, and so on), at certain age levels. In particular, they noted the frequency of the use of 'there was. . .' and 'it was. . .' types of structure in the writing of first-year infants, along with a distinct preference for using verbs with a form like 'I like playing'; 'she went riding'; (note Adrian's use of 'Peter went walking' in this respect).

The noun groups in Adrian's writing predominantly consist of one word only in subject position (for instance, 'it' and 'Peter'), and in object position usually occur with 'a' or 'the'. The only introduction of any kind of word prior to the headword in the noun groups is the use of 'black' in 'a *black* car'. Prepositional groups are mainly of the kind indicating *place*: for example 'around aroundabout' and 'on the moterway'. Convey and Wilkinson's research, likewise, acknowledges the frequency of occurrence of these group types identifying position and place, together with the lack of much modification in the noun group, in the writing of first-year infants.

If we accept this particular view of grammatical development (and much of this approach to identifying writing stages appears to have only limited relevance for the teacher), we would be classifying Adrian as a writer 'immature' for his age. Even if this were the case, it seems that such descriptions of the structures of his writing would still leave the teacher with very little idea of how to act upon this information. For example, would it mean giving Adrian some of the exercises advocated in *Control and Create*? Such analysis of structural features (independent of context), I would argue, simply draws attention to 'what is not there' and never really identifies the actual problems that Adrian is having with writing.

Convey and Wilkinson, while noting such developmental features as increased use of subordination and variety of clause and group structure, also noted the dangers in assuming that all the children surveyed approached the task in exactly the same way. Any developmental framework for language, taking account of purpose, type of audience, and so on, must inevitably highlight individual–to–individual and class–to–class variation, and focus on the need to consider the uses of grammatical structure in relation to the context-bound nature of the writing task. For example, it is interesting to note that they identified as one of the most significant developmental features of the writing they examined a gradual increase, not of subordination features used, but of *variety* of structural types employed. Certainly, this evidence illustrates very much a view of children's writing development which regards the whole process as one that gradually involves each child in the acquisition and manipulation of a wide range of structural techniques to accommodate the ever-widening demands of the differing types and purpose of writing in the school curriculum. They also acknowledged that grammatical structure is as much influenced by how the teacher perceives, and actually introduces, the writing task, as it is to how a pupil responds. For instance, the second year junior class wrote about 'Me' making use not of a variety of grammatical structures, but of a simple listing device with repeated elements such as 'I have got . . .'; 'I like . . .'; 'I don't like . . .'; and '. . . are interesting for me'. These 'models', it subsequently emerged, were ones that their class teacher had listed on the board for the pupils to base their written work on. Accounts of syntactic patterning need, therefore, to be seen in relation to the situational constraints imposed upon them by the teacher, thereby providing a more accurate picture of the writing skills that the child is actually trying to employ. They can provide a useful starting-point for the investigation of the writing process and, if linked to the pupil's own 'learning about how to write', can often help the teacher to identify more accurately and precisely the effectiveness, or otherwise, of the writing and the *reasons* for such judgements. If language features are then more directly linked to the writing situation, such aspects of grammar might, indeed, 'provide teachers ... with the framework of knowledge that they need in order to be able, first to assess their pupils' grammatical abilities, and then to intervene appropriately to extend them' (Perera, 1984, p. 3).

(Margaret Berry, in the seminar discussion in Chapter 8, effectively employs such grammatical concepts as **transitivity** and **theme** to explore how the manipulation of such features in writing may be constructively considered both in relation to the organization of the text as a whole and in terms of the purpose and aim of the writing task.)

While the grammatical description of Adrian's writing at least highlights the need for some kind of uniformity and precision of approach in the syntactic analysis of texts, it also illustrates the need to consider such aspects in relation to use. This becomes particularly apparent when we consider the variety of writing tasks that children at primary and secondary level encounter. As they progress through the system, the demands increasingly require them to develop an ability to handle different structural patterns depending on purpose and audience-type. Identifying the likely problems of coping with such varieties (not, however, by pinpointing 'errors') requires us to consider language features such as vocabulary and grammar in terms of the *total* organization of a text − its patterning in relation to its communicative purpose. For this reason, a profitable extension to any grammatical description of writing would certainly include a consideration of **text organization**: using grammatical, phonological or graphological and semantic criteria, a description of the relationship between sentences in any text which contribute to the organization of that text into a coherent whole. In the case of Adrian's work this would focus on its *narrative* characteristics − an attempt to recount a series of 'events' in the order in which they occurred.

De Beaugrande (1980) argues that narratives are basically organized by the manipulation and identification of four primary concepts: **objects** (the introduction of characters and other specified items); **situations** (the 'environment' of any narrative in terms of the identification of place, time or circumstances); **events** (the introduction of specific states which identify a situation or a status quo); and **actions** (events that are intentionally brought about by some kind of agent).

Certainly, in Adrian's writing, there are objects ('a accident'; 'one of the cars'; 'the car'; 'a crash'; 'three crashes'; 'The car'; 'surt of a ambulance'; 'a black car') and there are situations ('around aroundabout'; 'down with him'; 'on the moterway'; 'not very good'). Indeed, some of them combine with events to produce the usual initial 'scene-setting' function of story-telling: 'One day there was a accident' and 'There was a crash around aroundabout'. There is also the hint of possible actions which form an account of what happened: 'Peter went walking down with him and collide'. The difficulty for the reader stems from interpreting the interplay between these four concepts to form a clausal coherence (from one object or situation to another: '*Peter* went walking down with him and *collide*'; '*the car* was a crash and *there* was three crashes on the moterway'); and to produce an understandable 'story shape' (events occur one after the other: 'was' occurs seven times; but actions only twice: 'went walking' and 'collide'). The total impression received is one where nothing actually happens. The reader moves from 'state' to 'state'; and the objects usually associated with determining actions are only implied ('there was a crash around aroundabout'), never explicitly identified (except in 'Peter went walking down with him'). The effect produced is strangely disorienting; we expect things to happen in stories and for people and objects to be related to these happenings.

Richard Brautigan (1963), in his short story, 'The Revenge of the Lawn', deliberately exploits this effect by telling his story primarily through event structures. Objects and situations are coherently organized but there are few actions; nothing happens. The narrative sequence is carried through using verb forms which describe events stretching indefinitely into the past and future: 'shines'; 'was'; 'had'; 'can imagine'; and so on. Although this form of narration produces a curious effect on the reader, nevertheless, in Brautigan's case, the organization of objects and situations is coherently enough applied for the reader to determine the text's *referential* and *evaluative* functions (see Labov and Waletsky, 1967; and Labov, 1972) – the point and purpose of the story is signalled sequentially as the narrative progresses. In Adrian's work, no such referential signalling occurs; his account becomes a list of almost unrelated objects and situations (except in terms of their lexical associations with the general 'accident' topic: 'accident'; 'crash'; 'collide'; 'moterway'; 'ambulance'; 'black car'). In fact, the lexical items, abstracted in this way, almost tell the story by implication. Overall organization is, therefore, indicated lexically but not really grammatically. There is very little, apart from 'went walking' and 'collide', to carry the story forward, and lack of explicit reference from one object to the next increases the discontinuity: 'there'; 'one of the cars'; 'Peter'; and 'it'.

The whole text would seem to be operating at a much more local level. It is likely, therefore, that Adrian in writing the story is functioning on a clause–to–clause basis. Although he knows what happened and the sequence in which the actions occurred (evidenced by the lexical organization of the text), the writing process only allows him to move from clause to clause, where 'and' functionally operates, not to make the text coherent, but as a convenient pause or stopping-place for the writer. Consequently, temporal and causal relationships between one clause and the next are lost. The repeated use of 'there was . . .' (frequently occurring initially in oral narratives relating personal experiences: Labov, 1972) means that Adrian begins his story, but his story remains a continuous beginning. Although the context is a different one, Luria's description of *The Man with a Shattered World* illustrates the problem Adrian has in assembling his text to form a coherent whole; as he moves from one linguistic unit to another 'the meaning of one word escaped him as soon as he proceeded to the next' (Luria, 1972, p. 122).

The process in Adrian's writing, therefore, cannot simply be 'corrected' by detecting 'errors' related solely to the written form of the language (that is, by inserting the appropriate full stops, commas, capital letters, and so on, in the appropriate places – an exercise frequently employed in schools but functionally ineffective). It is essentially, for Adrian, a question of coming to terms with the differences between the *written* and the *spoken* (Harris and Kay, 1981; Kress, 1982) *but* in relation to the representation of events and actions in a time sequence. Oral story-telling in a variety of ways (explored through pictures, comics, personal anecdotes, 'live' accounts of events, and so on) might well prove a useful activity to encourage; and the organization and sequencing of such narratives might be explicitly identified by both teacher and pupil (rather like the 'traditional' language teaching based on the specific identification of nouns, verbs, adjectives, and so on).

Using a systematic and principled basis for the analysis of text organization will provide the teacher, I believe, with the means of both identifying and developing those language features of writing (grammatical structure, cohesive ties, lexical reference, speech–writing differences, and so on) *within* a coherent whole, thereby enabling the writer to relate language form more effectively and purposefully to situation.

The work of such linguists as Grimes (1975) and de Beaugrande (1980) provides an effective, if complex, model for the teacher to use as a basis for describing texts. It is essentially a question of considering how different *parts* of any discourse can be seen to be communicating different *kinds* of information: events, actions, participants, circumstances, and so on. Such models can provide useful labels for investigating the organization of many different types of text (different in kind, purpose, audience, and so on). The relationship between the sequencing or ordering of events and actions in 'groups' and the identification and introduction of participants and circumstances can provide a useful insight into the problems a child has in organizing a text, and into the reasons for a text's 'effectiveness' or 'ineffectiveness'.

To illustrate the point further, consider the following exercise. You are presented (see Table 2.1) with a story written by ten-year-old Neil, which has been deliberately arranged so that you can respond to the text sentence by sentence. Cover the text up and reveal one sentence at a time, trying to predict what you might assume to be the next event or action in Neil's story. Your response to the possible nature of events, actions, participants and circumstances will, I think, reveal quite dramatically not only how stories are conventionally organized, but also how Neil has organized his story-line in relation to this convention. What usually emerges is that events and actions group themselves into a series of 'expected' (and sometimes 'unexpected') functional sets (such as setting the scene; developing the action; concluding events; reaching a climax; – Propp, 1958; Labov and Waletzky, 1967; Labov, 1972; Longacre, 1976) which identify and exemplify the ways in which stories are usually organized, and which, thereby, illustrate and clarify our response to them when such organization does not occur.

Several groups of student teachers, teachers (both primary and secondary school) and linguists have worked on the text in this way and some of their projections are tabulated in Table 2.2. The numbers

Table 2.1

S1	George and the Dragon
S2	Swiftly but silently a bloodthirsty creature moved through the forest.
S3	It was a tall burly creature and had eyes of flame with a tail ten feet long.
S4	He was covered with scales from top to bottom and could kill a man with a flick of his gigantic tail.
S5	That creature was a dragon the greatest dragon ever born, that dragon was Beowulf of the Dark Mountains.
S6	The villages around the Dark Mountains had long been ruined by the dragon and not a soul had ever won a battle with him.

Table 2.1 *(continued)*

S7   The king of the country where the Dark Mountains were had offered a reward of his princesses in marriage and half the kingdom to any gallant man who would slay the dragon.

S8   Beowulf was on the move heading towards the capital of Darhrania, Darhfran, to terroise the people.

S9   He was at the city gates and was chewing them up rapidly when the king walked out and said "If you keep away from here we will give you ten sheep every day and you can eat all the fruits in are orchards".

S10 The dragon agreed and so all went well until the city ran out of sheep.

S11 So the king gave the dragon cows, but soon there was not one living animal in Darhfran.

S12 So the king reluctantly put all the names of the citizens of Darhfran, including himself, into a big hat and every day pulled out two names to go to Beowulf for his dinner.

S13 Soon the kings turn came and he, being a fair king, agreed to go.

S14 So at the crack of dawn next morning, the king and a farmers lad called George, were put outside the city gates for the dragon to come and collect them.

S15 "Fear not" said George "I have some sleeping powder which I will throw on the dragon when he goes to pick me up and then I will give you the pleasure of cutting his head off"

S16 It was a very good plan but George didn't know that Beowulf never sleeps.

S17 The dragon came and took the king and George away to his lair.

S18 When George flung the potion at Beowulf, the dragon just sneezed and started crying.

S19 "Whats the matter?" asked George.

S20 "I feel very sorry" answered Beowolf "I've killed and ate a lot of people and I feel sorry, what would you say if I came and lived in your city."

S21 The king was taken aback but said yes

S22 so George, Beowolf and the king marched down the hill laughing.

S23 On the floor of the cave in which the dragon lived lay a packet in which was a powder.

S24 That powder was forgiveness powder,

S25 George had got the wrong one.

Table 2.2

GEORGE AND THE DRAGON	Projection one	Projection two	Projection three	Projection four	Projection five	Projection six
2	Once there was an *adj* dragon	Long ago there was a knight called George	A long time ago there was a chivalrous knight called George	George was a little boy who lived with his widowed mother OR old wizard who lived in mountains	Once upon a time there was a man called George	A long long time ago there was a man called George
3	Qualifying why he's moving through the forest	Its jaw gaped as it hungered for human flesh	He was a huge ferocious dragon	No-one knew he was there	It had a long scaly body and breathed fire	He caught the scent of an alien being
4	Ditto as 3	Ditto as 3	It was breathing fire	He was looking for food	As it moved through the forest it spied a human being	He left a trail of devastation in his wake
5	Fire breathing	Jets of steam issued from its dilating nostrils	People afraid	Suddenly he noticed movement nearby	Suddenly he was disturbed by a rustling in the bushes	With a fiery breath he ignited the forest
6	Reason for being there	Its reputation had spread far and wide/He went in quest of food	Ditto as 5	He had frightened local people for centuries	Everyone in the valley at the bottom of the Dark Mountains was afraid of Beowulf	History of dragon, i.e. maidens in distress
7	Fear and dread of villagers	The villagers lived in fear of the dragon's return	Ditto as 6	In the village lived a young boy whose dream had always been to kill the dragon	One day the villagers decided that someone must kill the dragon	Villagers looking for hero to solve problem
8	Many knights	Many had tried, but none had succeeded	Many had come and failed	Many came and many died but none won the princess's hand	A gallant young man named George was the only one brave enough to volunteer	Many princes tried in vain

9	EITHER People wondering whether knights will come OR the knights go out to meet him	News travels fast (something happened)	In Darhrania there lived a young peasant called George	Word soon reached the village and panic spread	The terrified people of Darhrania sent to the king for help	Messengers sent to find someone to help them – desperate
10	Accept/run out of sheep OR reject/if he demands to plot he demands human flesh	Dragon agrees	Beowulf replied: "Give me the princess and I will trouble you no more"	The dragon said he'd only accept the princess's hand	With a mighty roar the dragon said no and swallowed the king in one mouthful	Dragon does a deal
11	The dragon asks for more OR dragon's actual demands	Something else (cattle)	The people were terrified of what would happen now that they had no sheep	By this time the villagers had named their champion George	The people were terrified and did not know what to do next	Alternative – all the cows
12	What can we give him OR saying what they can give	Meeting – drew lots	Ditto as 11 – this time, no animals	Living in the village was a brave young man called George.	The people began to fear for their lives and begged the king to do something	King's despair and desperation felt by villagers
13	People's reactions	Daughter's name	It fell that the princess's name was drawn out of the hat	Many died but one day the name of George was pulled out of the hat	One day the name 'George' was pulled out of the hat	George's turn. Is the king George?
14	Somebody is going to appeal throughout land	You can't go – you're the king	But a peasant called George volunteered to take the king's place in return for princess's hand in marriage should he return	The name pulled out with the king was that of George	A gallant young man called George said he would go in his place	King eaten – princess sends out messengers OR king and princess together OR king makes plan
15	EITHER their feelings OR dragon approaching OR Beowulf's sword	The dragon approached	Soon the ground trembled as the hungry dragon approached	The king was amazed at the courage of George as he went to almost certain doom	As the dragon approached they trembled with fear	George not prepared to succumb so easily

Table continued |

Table 2.2 *(continued)*

GEORGE AND THE DRAGON	Projection one	Projection two	Projection three	Projection four	Projection five	Projection six
16	Dragon approaching – can we get away with it?	Ditto as 15	King pessimistic	But George stumbled and in the process spilled the sleeping powder upon the king who immediately fell asleep	As the dragon drew nearer George pulled the sleeping powder from his pocket	King will give daughter
17	Dragon approaching and throwing sleeping powder	EITHER however, George also had his trusty sword OR dragon advances	Dragon approaches	The dragon crept silently down the mountainside swishing his ten foot tail	As he threw the powder George found to his dismay that the powder had no effect	Dragon became more annoyed
18	Description of dragon's lair + binds them – thinking of another plan – sleeping powder	Just as the dragon prepared to eat them George threw the sleeping powder	George's attempts – sneezed	Just as the dragon was about to swallow them the king asked if he could contact his daughter	Whilst in the dragon's lair the king and George devised a plan	Lair description
19	Their reactions OR why he is crying	Dragon apologetic	George analyses dragon's problem	While the dragon was crying they heard the sound of laughter and music	"What's the matter with you?" George asked the dragon	Feel sorry for dragon – try to find a solution
20	Sob story	Sneezing puts dragon's fire out	Dragon repents – unloved – persecution complex	I'm a lonely dragon – I have no friends	"I'm lonely" replied the dragon	"Got no friends" said dragon
21	Conditions	Accept dragon's apology	Agree on condition	How can we trust you not to eat anyone else	"You can do that on one condition" said George	Agree on condition 1) central heating 2) not eat anyone else

22	George – conditions	Return to city	Return to city	So George, the king and the dragon set off for the village	The three returned to the village	They returned to the village – villagers surprised
23	Townspeople – reactions	Villagers frightened	People amazed	People in the city were surprised to see them all	All the people were amazed and rushed outside to greet them	Princess sees them – runs to creature and is eaten
24	Purpose of powder	Powder had caused reaction	Magic powder (transformation)	Out of the powder grew a wizard who brought everyone back to life	It was a magic powder	Mix up of powder
25	Mistake in powder	King and George had forgiven dragon	Forgiveness + happiness + joy abound – dragon becomes vegetarian	Everyone forgave the dragon and they all lived happily together	So the people forgave the dragon	Powder wears off as getting to village

relate to their produced sentences from those outlined in Table 2.1. Such projections do, if you come to look at them closely, reveal a great deal about the way we believe that narrative is organized and (perhaps more importantly) give us insight into how stories can be more effectively realized. The following observations offer a selection of such features for comment, but there are many more which you may wish to investigate yourself:

(1) Neil's title, *George and the Dragon*, conventionally predicts the introduction of participants ('dragon', 'George', 'a knight', 'a little boy'), circumstances ('A long long time ago', 'Once upon a time'), and events ('there was') to establish the initial setting. The actual start of Neil's story comes as much more of a surprise, for we are thrown immediately into what, conventionally, (and in oral narratives), would be a subsequent part of the story – the *actions* ('moved'). Even the explicitly-predicted *participants* ('a chivalrous knight called George', 'George was a little boy') are translated to one that is inexplicitly defined ('*a* bloodthirsty creature'). (Incidentally, it is, I think, important to note at this stage how, in relation to the linguistic organization of the whole text, both grammatical structure (for example, word-ordering: 'Swiftly but silently') and lexical choice ('bloodthirsty') also contribute to the effect produced.)

(2) The subsequent 'extended' description of objects and situations (physical features, name, place of origin of the dragon) consistently defies, at this point, the general projection of actions ('what happened next'): 'People afraid'; 'He was looking for food'; 'He caught the scent of an alien being'. The projected main action is delayed. Indeed, even when the description of the dragon is completed, Neil still does not return to the predicted 'what happened next'; 'He went in quest of food'; 'People afraid'; 'Suddenly he noticed movement nearby'. Instead, he backtracks in time to the situation prior to the action at the beginning of his story by means of the past perfect tense ('The villages *had long been ruined* by the dragon') and only returns to the initial action two sentences later, surprisingly (note the projections 'Many came and many died' and 'Many princes tried in vain') reverting to a past tense reflecting progressive action ('Beowulf was on the move') which is subsequently supported by 'He was at the city gates and was chewing them up rapidly'.

(3) In contrast, the bargaining sequence between the dragon and the king is set up by establishing a predictable pattern. The 'and so all went well until the city ran out of sheep' leads to projections which demand 'cows', then 'all living animals' and, finally, human beings – a development which progressively intensifies

the seriousness and desperate nature of the situation. This progression increases the projective demand for 'George' as a participant (incidentally, consistently expected to be introduced into the narrative much earlier on): 'But a peasant called George volunteered'; 'A gallant young man called George'; 'The name pulled out with the king was that of George'. But even such explicitly introduced versions of George's entrance are defied by his eventual low-key arrival: 'the king and a farmer's lad called George'.

(4) Even the conclusion of the story (typically, the point in story-writing where children, because of time or lack of interest, try to finish quickly) runs against convention. 'So George, Beowolf and the king marched down the hill laughing' traditionally predicts a 'conventional' ending: 'People amazed'; 'Villagers frightened'. The final twist in the story is effected (like many detective stories) by backtracking on objects and situations which have deliber- ately not been specifically identified previously for the reader (the reason why the dragon starts 'crying' is usually interpreted by many as Neil's attempt to move to a story-ending as quickly as possible). In spite of some confusion between 'forgiveness' and 'repentance', information ('That powder was forgiveness powder') is deliberately and effectively concealed to the very end: 'George had got the wrong one'.

These responses to the text do, I think, illustrate quite dramatically the importance of text organization in the writing process; and, as previously suggested when discussing Adrian's work, developing a conscious awareness amongst pupils of the way narratives are organ- ized will provide them with much insight into the potential for change and variation within a time-related form in relation to 'reader awareness'. Most readers argue that Neil is an effective story-teller primarily because of his selection and manipulation of narrative elements but always in relation to purpose, audience and overall effect. In fact, recent evidence of reader response to a variety of children's stories (Wilkinson, 1985) shows that coherence of structure and organization of narrative are major factors in determining the effectiveness of the product.

Experiments with the sequencing of time-related texts can, therefore, be both profitable and rewarding in developing an awareness of organization and of the nature of the communicative process between writer and reader. Indeed, such work can be usefully extended to consider non-narrative organization, where events tend not to be ordered in a time-related way. Many children have even greater problems with such texts, not only because they tend to be organized in different ways (see Chapter 4), but also because of the extremely influential role that oral and written narrative plays in a child's life within and outside school. Consider, from this viewpoint, the difficulties that ten-year-old Ian is experiencing in constructing the following text, which arose from a class project on Georgian England. Ian's task was to contribute some written work on press gangs. Using a textbook for reference (see Perera, 1980, for some indication of the problems of reading non-narrative texts), he copied out the title from the book, 'The Royal Navy, Ships and Sailors', and proceeded to try to take from it the relevant references to press gangs:

THE ROYAL NAVY, SHIPS AND SAILERS

The men of that time would hide themselves because they would be caught by the press gang to go to the Navy.
The Navy would get no volunteered men for the navy, the men wouldn't go because it was to dirty They would get to eat dried food like salted meat and many other salted things, they would get dirty water and get very ill and most of the time die. So thats why they didn't like the navy, the press gang would even go into pub and look for likely man to serve the navy. They would even have a man getting married in a church or somebody fishing.

Ian has, in fact, made a valiant attempt to impose some kind of organization by using the explicit signal 'So thats why they didn't like the navy', but as a conclusion, rather than as an introduction: 'the reasons why they didn't like the Navy were . . .'; and the unusual use of the present tense to indicate a meaning of a future event which is fulfilled in the past (Leech and Svartvik suggest that such forms are 'rare and rather literary in style', 1975, p. 73) creates a sequence very different from what Ian is probably more at home with (events happening in the order in which they occur). This gives Ian the task of organizing these verbal items in a 'timeless' form; hence, his particular attraction to the 'anecdotal' narrative: 'They would even have a man getting married in a church'. Further difficulties arise in coherently relating one element to the next; so, partly because Ian is using information from a book, the text contains many 'unattached' referential devices: 'The men *of that time*'; '*the men*'; '*They* would even have'. Here, Ian has yet to discover a suitable framework for presenting his ideas which, on the evidence of the way in which it is assembled, he does not at the moment have.

Such types of writing are inevitably complex and highly-structured, but they are varieties which the child will come into contact with increasingly as he moves from primary to secondary school. Emphasis on their description in terms of text organization would, therefore, provide a useful means both of identifying and appraising the range of writing skills needed across the curriculum and of developing the competence needed to acquire such skills by promoting manipulation and explicit awareness of their basic features. It is important not to become too absorbed exclusively with the grammatical structures of any text, simply because it is, at this level, easy to ignore context. Looking at the organizational features of a text not only allows you to consider grammar and coherence, it also focuses much more directly on the importance of situation and on the needs and responses of the reader. It is in this context that text evaluation becomes, for the child, not an assessment of 'worth' but a communication of 'effect'.

Suggested Further Reading

de Beaugrande, R. (1980), *Text, Discourse and Process* is a complex work, but one which offers a detailed investigation of the discourse structure of a wide variety of texts.

Grimes, J. (1975), *The Thread of Discourse* is an informative study of discourse structure, concentrating in particular on speech, but containing much of relevance to the investigation of both narrative and non-narrative texts.

Harpin, W. (1976), *The Second 'R'* is an important discussion of the nature of children's writing in terms of purpose, types and stages of development. In particular, the book concentrates on the linguistic investigation of the grammatical structure of texts.

Longacre, R. E. (1976), *An Anatomy of Speech Notions* offers a detailed analysis of the structure of spoken discourse and, like Grimes, provides many useful insights into the organization of different kinds of texts.

Perera, K. (1984), *Children's Writing and Reading* is one of the most detailed and comprehensive attempts so far to provide teachers with a grammatical framework for the investigation of children's writing. Its title is perhaps misleading in that the book concentrates on describing the main grammatical developments in children's writing through the primary and early secondary stages, and only peripherally considers reading.

3 Responding to Children's Narratives

PAM MORGAN

Text A: Edward
The metallic door opened electronically as the strange, hooded figure
entered the elaborately sophisticated control room. Turning to his
second in command, Egor gave the order. "Fire" he yelled.

At Sir Richerd Melonthock – (Minister of Defence)'s mansion Sir
Richerd's wife Eileen, was preparing his meal. Just as he was about to
switch on the video monitor to watch the news the Priority 1 Emergency Warning Tone, blared in a screaching row. As he leaped onto the
couch he stabbed the already flashing red button. Tipping backwards,
the couch desened as the floorboards slid back, revealing a massive,
cavenous, monorail station. The couch decended entering a large,
streamlined, red monorail train which speeded away into the distance.

At Central Control Tracking Station Cape Carnaveral 25 top officials
watch horrified as the tiny, flashing spot on the radar screen picked up
speed and shot towards the edge of the screen! Sir Richerd had not
been told that the Alian Attach, Persuit Craft was due for repairs, and
would explode when it got out the Earth's atmosphere.

When Eileen was told about her husband's death, all she could say
was, "And it was bacon and eggs for tea, his favourit."

Text B: Carmen
The creaky door opened noisily and I went into the house the door
Squeaked as I closed it. I went to investigate I went into the dining hall
and I heard footsteps behind me but no one was there. When I turned
back round again the cups had tea inside they was not any in before
I knew there was something suspisious going on. I couldn't find any
thing in there so I went up stairs. They creaked noisily I got a fright I
heard footsteps behind me I looked but their was nothing. I looked
carefully at the creaky stairs I saw footsteps they were very big. I
carried on going up the stairs When I came to a bedroom. I went in I
saw a picture I saw the eyes move. I ran straight out of the room I ran
down the creaky stairs I heard foot steps behind me I turned around
and I saw a old man he had one eye and no hair I said why are you
following me the old man just laughed. I started to run faster a man
closed the door I just sat on the stairs a cried The End

The Teacher's Response – a Suggested Approach

I have opened this chapter with these examples of children's writing because I wish to discuss the problems posed for the working teacher by such pieces of work. They are by no means extraordinary. They are the work of two first-year secondary school pupils in a mixed ability class and are typical of what any English teacher could expect to find in a set of first-year stories handed in for marking. The lesson which preceded the production of these stories was on 'describing words'. A teacher–class discussion was followed by the class being given the sentence:

The _____ door opened _____.

A range of appropriate adjectives and adverbs was elicited and the children were asked to fill in the blanks for themselves and use the sentence they had created as the beginning of a story.

I discuss these texts in detail below but first I wish to consider why these stories can be seen as presenting 'problems' to the teacher. They can be viewed as such because these texts are the kind of evidence on which the teacher must base a whole range of crucial decisions, including assessment of a child's level of ability, and including the content and organization of future lessons directed at the development of a range of writing skills. The teacher has to aim at helping the child improve the quality of work no matter what level the child is already working at. There is a need for the response to the writing presented by the child to be a continuation of the teaching process and more than minimal 'marking'. It is, therefore, important to use the child's attempts at writing as an element in a constructive process of development.

From a linguistic perspective there are, perhaps, three ways in which one can approach a text when marking and these three correspond to three aspects of the organization of language. One can concentrate on the use of individual words or lexis: this normally means a focus on spelling errors and misuse of words. Alternatively one can concentrate on the structural organization up to sentence level. Here we would expect a focus on grammatical and punctuation problems. The third option is to look at the organization of the text above sentence level. This entails, in the present context, consideration of narrative structure.

Although much attention has recently been focused on the first two options (Gannon and Czerniewska, 1980; Harpin, 1976; Kress, 1982; Perera, 1984; Shaughnessy, 1977; Trudgill, 1975), hitherto the third option has not been systematically explored, being touched on under such labels as style, rhetorical expression, plot or argument. Such vague labels indicate difficulties of definition which explain the neglect of overall organization in teaching strategies. However, returning to the texts at the beginning of the chapter, I want to argue that if one could respond to these pieces of writing in such a way as to give guidance about such things as discourse organization (pacing, intro-duction and development of character, suspense techniques, and so on), then it is possible that one could help all children including both the more and the less able writers. The child who is already fairly successful could be helped to develop skills already possessed; and it would also be possible to focus on problems that affect much less successful writers. Often the inability to organize stories at this higher level underlies many of the lower level problems children face and, if they could be helped with structure, the increased confidence and sense of direction that would follow would help them to confront other problems in their writing. For example, difficulties with complex grammatical constructions often arise only because the line of thought or organization of discourse is not clear. In addition, the 'and then . . . and then . . . and then . . .' sentence linkage found in many stories may reflect a lack of knowledge about the range of 'shapes' available for the construction of a story.

Unfortunately, while much has been written about narrative fiction and plot, making that a relatively accessible area of information (see, for example, Genette, 1980; Chatman, 1978), comparatively little has been written about discourse structure in terms of teaching. Many people are also unaware that it is possible to choose deliberately how to organize a discourse. There seems to be an assumption that once a pen is taken up then what is written just flows from the pen, out of the control of the writer. This is particularly so with schoolchildren and particularly so with stories.

If one's aim is to approach marking and remediation, to say nothing as yet of teaching, at discourse level, then the question arises of what basis there is to build on − what, in fact, do children know, consciously or unconsciously, about the structure of longer pieces of writing? It might be inferred from what I have just said that children lack conscious control but this is not so. Tell any eleven-year-old child a joke without a punch line and the omission will be commented on. The same child will protest if ordered to turn the television off, eat a meal or go to bed ten minutes before the end of a film, and not just to be awkward. Children can tell stories themselves with a tolerably well-formed structure and can frequently argue quite coherently. By the time they reach the first years of secondary school most of them can do these things (at least orally) fairly well. This seems to be at odds with the idea that writing 'flows' beyond their control.

Part of the problem is, of course, the transfer from oral to written language, that is, learning to use in a new medium skills they already possess in one medium. This is part of the process taking place as, in response to the language demands placed on them at this stage, they begin to develop the range of writing skills required. The teacher is faced with the problem of deciding on the most appropriate ways to encourage this development and so it becomes increasingly important to be aware of the nature and variety of the skills the children need to possess and to increase our knowledge of the stages in the process of their acquisition.

Narrative Structure

To investigate what children 'know' about narrative it is necessary first to establish a framework of story structure. Some linguists, often in pursuit of very different ends and despite differences in their approach, have devised models that demonstrate a basic consensus as to what constitutes simple narrative organization. All such models identify stories as consisting of several basic units which form themselves into a coherent whole, each unit contributing a specific and identifiable 'function' for the story in its entirety.

Labov, 1972 (for an earlier and more detailed exploration, see Labov and Waletzky, 1967), working from oral narrative data and concentrating in his analysis on identifying the role of the independent clause as it carries the temporal sequence of the story, identifies five such basic units or categories:

(1) **Orientation** – this serves to identify features of the situation in terms of person, place and time.
(2) **Complicating action** – this unit comprises a series of events which 'build up' the actions of the story.
(3) **Resolution** – this determines the result of the narrative (that is, what finally happened).
(4) **Coda** – this is usually presented as an optional element, and in oral narratives serves to return the listener from the recounting of past events to the present conversational situation.
(5) **Evaluation** – this is a problematic but crucial element. It is *problematic* in that it is usually identified as occurring sequentially, but, in terms of its function (particularly in written narrative) of determining the 'point' or 'purpose' of telling a story, it can be much more flexible, it would seem, in its occurrence. It is *crucial* in that it is seen as vital to the effective telling of any tale. As the narrator becomes increasingly 'sophisticated' in his art, this element becomes more implicitly embedded and integrated into the structure of the story as a whole.

Van Dijk (1977), looking essentially at the problem of summary and recall of narrative, has also suggested that narratives consist (like all texts) of **macrostructures** (large-scale units of text organized sequentially) and that, as a consequence, there are macrostructural rules which govern the construction of discourse. Like Labov, he identifies categories in the structure of narrative:

(1) **Setting** – this category contains elements which identify time, place, and other circumstances such as character.
(2) **Complication** and **resolution** – these two units are seen as together defining any basic story episode (that is, events which are finally resolved in some way).
(3) **Moral** – like Labov's evaluation, this element helps the 'audience' to identify the 'point' of the story.

Such categories, Van Dijk argues, will determine the organization of the whole structure of narrative discourse and, indeed, similar labels can be applied to the macrostructure of other text types.

Likewise, although approaching the area from a cross-cultural perspective, Longacre (1976) also considers narrative structure in terms of *plot* organization. Many of his categories are similar to those above, even if the description is somewhat more detailed:

(1) **Aperture** – what may be identified as the 'Once upon a time' type of opening.
(2) **Exposition** – this contains crucial information on time, place, 'local colour' and participants.
(3) **Inciting moment** – described as the 'get something going' moment, this is where the planned and predictable movement of the exposition is broken into in some way.
(4) **Developing conflict** – this is where the action intensifies.
(5) **Climax** – at this point, everything comes to a head and confrontation and 'final showdown' are inevitable.
(6) **Denouement** – here a crucial final event happens which makes a resolution possible.
(7) **Final suspense** – details of the resolution are finally worked out.
(8) **Conclusion** – the story here comes to some sort of satisfactory end.

Longacre also introduces the notion of **peak** which, like evaluation and moral, indicates the main point of the story.

Although these linguists have worked from very diverse angles with material taken from widely differing contexts (and it is important to note that the models which they have devised are specific to that material and that context), there is sufficient correlation between the categories devised to suggest a basic model of the macrostructure of narrative that is broadly applicable to both spoken and written stories. What is particularly useful, when analysing children's writing, is that the notion of what constitutes 'effectiveness' can be identified more readily by using such categories. It should be noted that although the elements tend to occur in a certain sequence it is the manipulation and organization of such features (together with the presence of evaluation, moral, or peak elements) which create a satisfactory and satisfying text.

Children's Understanding of Story Organization

As well as knowledge of story organization there is a second requirement and that is that the teacher needs to know what understanding of the organization of text children possess. In an attempt to gain some insight into the 'state of play' concerning the development of skills in organizing discourse in the early years of secondary school some school-based experiments were carried out focusing on the larger scale organization of discourse, that is, *above* rather than *below* sentence level. It was decided that presenting children with texts taken from their normal school reading scrambled at sentence level and requiring them to re-assemble the text might give some insight into the 'knowledge' they possessed of what was an appropriate discourse structure. The premise was that if the pupils did, in fact, possess some understanding of the larger, macrostructural organization of the texts presented to them, it might be possible to discern something of this from the patterns of choices, including errors, made in re-assembling the scrambled texts. One might have expected that the main strategy used by the children in the task would be that of identifying simple links between words in pairs of sentences without reference to the overall structure. This would be consistent with the notion of a 'flow' of ideas. It turned out that this, in fact, seemed to be a part of what was happening but was by no means the whole story.

The children who performed the tasks were first- and second-year secondary pupils of mixed ability and the texts were taken from the school books in use, one being a narrative, the other being a piece of non-narrative from a social studies book. The non-narrative text was included to provide a comparison. It was anticipated that the children would not have as much experience of non-narrative organization as of story structure (see Chapters 1 and 2). The texts were cut up at sentence level and each sentence presented on a separate slip. Here are the texts in their original state.

Text C: Narrative

FOLLOWING A FIRE ENGINE
(1) Joe had just found a small pool which was solid ice safe for skating on with the toe of one foot, when there was a great clanging of bells.
(2) A fire engine rushed past, covered with ladders, hoses and firemen

in helmets, the brass everywhere gleaming in the cold sunlight, the engine bright red and glossy as it flashed past.

(3) In case the fire was nearby Joe ran off in the direction the fire engine had taken.

(4) Joe ran a long way keeping a sharp look out for fires everywhere, but it was no good.

(5) The fire engine had disappeared.

(6) It's always the way with fires.

(7) You never see them, because they're tucked away somewhere you never dream could catch fire, like the one just round the corner that time when some curtains caught alight.

(8) Joe heard the bells and ran all over the place, but when he finally went round the corner, there was the engine with all the firemen standing about, and a lot of people watching, but of course the fire was out.

from 'A Kid for Two Farthings' by Wolf
Mankowitz reprinted in *Explore and Express (Book
1)* by Adams, Foster and Wilson (Macmillan
Education Ltd, 1971)

Text D: Non-narrative

FARMERS OF THE NEW STONE AGE

1 The change from hunting to farming was almost certainly due to women.

2 In the Old Stone Age they had spent their time looking after children and collecting seeds, herbs and berries for food.

3 As they did so some must have noticed how the seeds were blown by the wind, covered with dust and made to grow by the sun and rain.

4 What was to stop them scratching a hole with a stick and planting seeds themselves?

5 So farming started, probably in western Asia where wheat and barley grow wild.

6 Near Mount Carmel in Israel archaeologists have found skeletons lying beside horn sickles (curved for cutting ripe wheat).

7 Round their skulls were shell headbands.

8 Round their necks were rough strings of beads.

9 Here were some of the earliest farmers.

from *The Ancient World* by Cootes
and Snellgrove (Longman, 1970)

The sequencing exercise raises some interesting points about children's knowledge of text organization which are relevant to an assessment of the stories by Edward and Carmen which are discussed below.

With Text C, the narrative text, it was clear that the children had a definite sense of the beginning of a story. There was almost complete unanimity of choice of the first sentence of the original text. This is not surprising since this first sentence *Joe had just found a small pool which was solid ice safe for skating when* ... is the only sentence which provides an orientation giving the reader details of characters, of where the action is taking place and of what sort of thing is about to happen. It is also significant that in the non-narrative task where the original first sentence does not perform this orienting function that none of the children chose to put it first, preferring one of two other sentences that do perform this function. It was noticeable, too, that the children had few problems in their choice of a concluding sentence for the story. Even those who did not choose the original last sentence did, in fact, contrive to establish an appropriate conclusion.

The exercise, then, suggests that children have a concept of how a story should begin and end. However, the sequencing exercise was also interesting in relation to the organization of the middle of the story. While there were variations as to suggested structure for some parts of the middle, these too could be interpreted as significant. There were some sentences that were more 'mobile' than others. On investigation these sentences proved to be descriptive sentences with no markers of time and not at all concerned with furthering the action of the plot. On the other hand those sentences that did contain time markers were those which had a tendency to be placed consistently 'correctly'.

This suggests that children at least recognize (1) that description does not further the action and that there are a limited number of places where it can appear in a story and (2) that the timing elements and ordering of actions in a story are structurally important. The children, then, seem to have a perception of narrative which involves a fairly strict sense of the ordering of events and also accepts limits on the places in a story where a pause is allowed for description.

As far as the relationship of the choices made to the density of the direct links between words or phrases in pairs of sentences is concerned, there is not always a direct correlation. In those places where the density was greatest the number of 'correct' choices was also very high but there were places (in the narrative text) where the number of direct links between sentences was low and yet in the reassembled text these sentences were placed in the order in which they occurred in the original text. As noted above, the sentences which show a tendency to be placed 'correctly' in the majority of scripts are distinguished by the fact that they each have a temporal marker. It seems that the children are demonstrating a sensitivity to the temporal ground-plan of story structure and that this is the stronger process rather than the simple matching of links or the identification of cohesive ties between adjacent sentences.

In the non-narrative text it was very noticeable that the children had much greater difficulty in reproducing the original order. They could focus on items like orienting sentences such as *In the Old Stone Age*... and *Near Mount Carmel*... and also on simple organizing devices such as lists, for example, *Round their skulls*... *Round their necks*, but found difficulty in achieving a satisfactory overall shape. This suggests that story structure is much more familiar to children at this age and that they are only beginning to develop an understanding of simple kinds of discourse structure.

Even though there are a great number of other factors involved in such sequencing tasks (and one cannot draw conclusions too freely), it still seems safe to say that:

(1) children have a particularly strong sense of the macrostructural organization of a story;
(2) this is stronger than their sense of non-narrative, particularly at lower secondary stage;
(3) even though they 'know' about story structure and find little difficulty, using a variety of linguistic techniques, in reconstructing a story, when it comes to writing they face different problems. Translation of their knowledge from the one activity to the other is not an easy task, being greatly affected by the constraints of the writing process, as we shall see in the two stories to which we can now turn.

Commentary on the Stories by Edward and Carmen

The first and most immediately striking point is that the dictates of the writing task (Write a story beginning with 'The _____ door opened _____') distort what we might assume to be the children's natural narrative style at this stage of development. The *in medias res* opening entails the deployment of orientation detail subsequently. It needs, in effect, to be embedded. It is, then, worthwhile seeing how each child has coped with this problem.

An intuitive response suggests initially that Edward (Text A) is much more skilful in handling his narrative structure even if the story overall is uneven. He has successfully introduced a mysterious Egor and, complete with sufficient background information to establish them as characters, Sir Richard and his wife Eileen. His orientation element, then, appears sound thus far. If we accept that Edward is using his knowledge of story structure to withhold deliberately details of plot, then the elusive nature of the rest of the story is excellent, but can we in fact give him this credit? What about the mysterious Egor? Presumably he is either an 'Alian' or a saboteur. Was Sir Richard going to fight him or was Egor somehow connected with the explosion of the 'Persuit Craft'? We are not told what happens next either. What has Egor fired at? Is the arrival of a missile the next instalment?

What Edward has done is typical of many such narratives, in that he has spent a great deal of time and effort on introducing the characters and situation but has failed to follow through the rest of the story in the same amount of detail (for further examples of this sort of problem see Chapter 8). It is as if he has a firm grasp of narrative structure *in toto* but is unable to fill in details of information inside that structure (thereby failing to utilize the appropriate orientation and action *in relation to* evaluation).

Using the structural elements of narrative identified earlier we can 'chunk' Edward's story as follows:

(1) *First orientation* – the introduction of the mysterious Egor – a character who is, either deliberately or unintentionally, presented with minimal explanation.
(2) *First complicating action* – the detonation of a 'missile'.
(3) *Second orientation* – the introduction of Sir Richard, his wife Eileen, the mansion and their meal.
(4) *Second complicating action* – a parallel 'event' to the first complicating action – the 'Emergency Warning Tone'.
(5) *Further complicating actions* – Sir Richard's reactions are described.
(6) *Climax* – Longacre's term can here account for a subtle change of perspective. Events are now seen through other eyes (25 top officials) – and in what may be considered to be a sophistication of the narrative technique we learn by implication of the explosion of Sir Richard and his craft.
(7) *Resolution* – an effectively abrupt conclusion but faulty, I think, because although we have Eileen's reaction the rest of the elements remain unresolved. (For further discussion of 'reader trust' of children's stories, see Chapter 8)

Carmen, on the other hand, is working at a different level. She has a concept of story structure, but not as sophisticated as Edward's, and although she attempts to use a recognizable story structure she is not always successful. Essentially hers is a story with minimal orientation and several episodes each consisting of an action and a resolution, although the resolution elements are not always managed satisfactorily. She seems to have very little appreciation of the needs of her audience and so neglects to provide us with an orientation section. We don't know *who* (apart from the egocentric 'I'), *where* (apart from 'a house') or *what* anyone is doing (except 'investigating'). As the story progresses there is also little subtlety of movement or pacing. She uses the basic temporal linkage 'and then' but makes little attempt at timing events one against the other to create a sense of more than linear movement. It is noticeable that this kind of writing is expressed mostly in free clauses with the simplest kind of subordination. What we seem to have is an egocentric writer describing only what happens to herself and her perception of the events around her with little acknowledgement of the needs of an audience. This could be seen as skilfully creating an atmosphere of the self facing a hostile environment but even for a sophisticated writer this piece would be flawed in that it does not give us sufficient clues to enable us to supply the answers.

There is an attempt to build up the action of the story to a climax but, as little is done to introduce any form of suspense, this is not very successful. There is little differentiation between the events that make up the complicating action and the introduction of 'the man' is on exactly the same level as the cups that fill themselves, the footsteps and footprints, and the eyes that move in the picture – all unexplained. Thus, although we have the elements of a story structure, again we have a problem with the 'contents' of each of the different parts. This is particularly so at the end. Here there is an indication that Carmen herself was unsure that it was sufficient, since she feels a need to write 'The End' to make the conclusion emphatic. She seems to have been unable to think of a suitable resolution and so gave up the struggle much in the same way as her *alter ego* does in the story. This does not mean, however, that she has no concept of an ending but that on this occasion she was unable to devise one.

So here we have a writer who has problems with the orientation of a story, is very dependent on the simplest of time linkages to move the story onward and, although conscious of a need for an ending, finds herself unable to supply one. Here sequential non-projective organization is particularly noticeable, in comparison with Edward's 'simultaneous' recording of two separate but related events (Egor's actions and Sir Richard's reactions).

How, then, could a more conscious knowledge of story structure help a teacher with the task of developing these two children's story-writing abilities? In the first place, knowledge of story structure enables a precise identification to be made of structural weaknesses. This provides a necessary basis for development. To make possible a discussion of structural issues some basic metalanguage is needed. The elements of story structure identified by linguists, as discussed above, provide a principled framework for a metalanguage which does not need to be of a technical nature but must be precise. For example, **setting** may be a more readily accessible term than orientation. Increased awareness of how stories are organized will help children to identify in their writing those features which contribute to the success of the story – features such as the sequencing of events, appropriate orienting information (who, what, where) and the sustaining of evaluative elements throughout the text, thus providing the reader with a sense of the purpose of the story.

A Mixed Category Text

Before concluding I want to consider one further text in which there is apparent a move from non-narrative to narrative organization. Again this is a feature of children's writing that occurs commonly at the lower secondary stage and, of course, before. The piece was produced in an English lesson as an exercise in writing a different variety of English and was intended by the writer to be suitable for the first page of a history textbook.

Text E: Gillian
The Romans came to Britain after the Britons who they conquered when they came to Britain.
   Julius Caesar used to be a Dicator for the Romans when there wasn't a king but his friends killed him because he had big ideas about being a King. Augustus was a King and he did well for Rome.
   Claudius was a king too and he decided to conquer Britain because he wanted it for quite a few reasons. After a lot of trouble the Roman army went to Britain and fought a battle with Caractacus and Togodumnus at carmeldunum the Romans beat them and then went to Maiden Castle in Dorset on the way Hugh the Gaul saw 20 of them coming fired at them with a sling he knocked one out, hit the others ones arm he was with Di and Alwin and they all told the other Britons that Romans were coming. The next day Di and Hugh killed a lot of Romans but in the end the Romans killed them so the Romans defeated the Britons.

The text is obviously intended to be non-narrative and in terms of overall structure Gillian has successfully managed an introduction that includes the necessary time reference (even if it is a little vague), *The Romans came to Britain after the Britons...*, and introduces the topic. She then decides, quite reasonably, that she needs to give some background information and so describes the previous events in Rome. It takes her some time to get back to Claudius and his reasons for coming to Britain but she has employed a reasonable means of organization, not quite, however, achieving the right balance of quantity of information and relevance. She then returns to the main topic and, although omitting some important details (she was writing without the aid of a reference book), carries this on to the battle at Carmeldunum and then Maiden Castle. Here the discourse organization changes radically and with the introduction of a specific place and time, and to some extent a behavioural situation, we are into a short story. It is not a particularly well constructed story but the move into narrative is marked. We may surmise that narrative is used here as a means of concluding a non-narrative piece by a child who is making great efforts to cope with the demands of non-narrative writing but still finds them daunting.

What this brief review of the discourse structure of Text E suggests is that Gillian has a developing grasp of how to cope with a short non-narrative text but insufficient experience as a writer to produce an 'inner layer', that is, what should be contained within the larger scale organization; it suggests, also, that she (as did many of the children attempting this task) slipped into story as a means of filling in the inner layer, demonstrating the greater ease with which children at this stage use narrative rather than non-narrative structure.

Conclusions

Thus, in terms of a teacher's response to a child's writing, it may well be that comments and discussion aimed at overall structure will at least help the child to improve one element of the process of writing, that element being one where they already have some knowledge on which to build. Teaching can also be developed along the same lines, building on the notion of a story as possessing a discourse structure and giving the children the opportunity to practise the separate parts as well as the whole in their writing. It is important to emphasize at this point that I am not suggesting working with story elements out of context as this might well have the same limitations as doing grammar and punctuation exercises out of the context of language in use.

Lessons could be devised in two ways. First the pattern of the sequencing tasks could be followed, using whole stories and cutting them into different length sections. This enables attention to be focused both on the macrostructure or overall organization, and on the signalling devices used to link the separate parts together. As I have said before, the children show some ability at this and it could be a useful way of increasing awareness and helping the development of skills already possessed.

Secondly, one can use a variety of 'cloze' techniques selecting different levels for attention. For instance, the children could be presented with stories without beginnings and asked to establish the orientation of the story; alternatively one could focus on the complicating action/climax section, giving the children stories with a beginning and ending but no middle; obviously one can also ask for an ending to be provided consistent with a given orientation and complicating action. This is attempting to use the concept of macrostructure which the child already has and focusing attention explicitly on the contents of the units that make up the parts of the whole. I have, incidentally, found that the stories children write themselves provide good material for this sort of work; this has the added advantage of making the work immediately relevant to them.

Writers of fiction see writing as a craft: why should children be allowed to think of it as a process beyond their control?

Suggested Further Reading

Chatman, S. (1978), *Story and Discourse: Narrative Structure in Fiction and Film* is a useful and readable introduction to the discourse of narrative, concentrating in particular on literary texts.

Labov, W. and Waletzky, J. (1967), 'Narrative analysis: oral versions of personal experience' is an important investigation into the way in which people organize oral narratives when recounting personal experiences. This research has influenced much of the more recent work on children's story writing.

Labov, W. (1972),'The transformation of experience in narrative syntax' is a further discussion of Labov and Waletzky's original research with more detailed consideration given to how speakers structure narrative and convey story purpose.

4 Organization in Children's Writing (Non-fictional)

JOHN HARRIS

In this chapter I offer a description of some features of the organization of texts produced by children in the middle years of schooling. I shall consider different levels of organization from inter-sentence connection to larger discourse designs. I shall also make suggestions about development in writing related to organization, and suggest how an understanding of text organization can be useful in the diagnosis of children's writing difficulties. These points will be informed, additionally, by consideration of the nature of written text and the varieties of writing within the school context.

Organization is popularly understood to mean the way in which a text is put together. Thus we may find a teacher commenting on an essay that 'This is not well organized – there's no introduction and no 'real conclusion.' I am not concerned here, primarily, with organization in this overall structural sense – the architectonics of text, if you wish – but in a more limited and specific sense that is to do with the means by which sentences are linked together and sections of text are integrated with each other to achieve an overall coherence.

Two preliminaries are necessary, however, before elaborating the description of organization. We need to look at a range of differences between speech and writing that impinge on aspects of organization; we need, also, to take account of the types of writing that are commonly practised at junior and lower secondary levels.

Speech–Writing Differences

Possibly the most extreme statement of the relationship between the spoken and the written modes of language was that made by Bloomfield to the effect that 'writing is not language, but merely a way of recording language by means of visible marks' (1933, p. 21). Such a view is echoed popularly (in the folk-linguistic view) by comments such as 'If only these kids could speak properly then their writing would get better.' In diagram form this view of the speech-writing relationship can be represented thus:

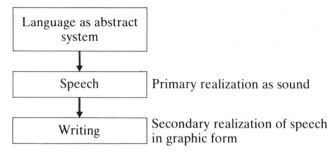

There are, however, many compelling pieces of linguistic data – a concise account can be found in Stubbs (1980, Chapter 2) – that suggest the speech–writing relationship is less direct; that both are, in effect, realizations in different media of the abstract system of language. In a simple form this suggests that the diagram needs to be reformulated in this way:

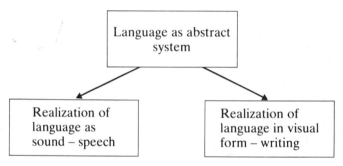

Although this is, admittedly, an oversimplification since there are many points of interference between the modes, it does provide an important basis for considering the problems that children have to confront in organizing writing. Let us consider two examples.

Modifying speech into writing
The first example is highly typical of the early writing activities of infant school children. If a child has drawn a picture of somebody kicking a ball he may well, when asked by his teacher to provide a sentence as a caption, produce an utterance such as *he's kicking the ball*. Indeed, a shy or not particularly articulate child may produce no more than *ball* or *kicking the ball*. It is common practice for teachers to expand and modify such utterances when writing them down for the child to copy and read back. A likely modification might read *A boy is kicking a ball*. When we isolate the utterance:

(A)   *he's kicking the ball*
      and the written sentence
(B)   *A boy is kicking a ball*

some crucial differences are apparent. In (A) the presence of the pronoun *he* forces us to refer to the picture to establish the identity of the person referred to, while in (B) we do not need to establish identity since the use of *a boy* is, from a linguistic point of view, self-defining. Similarly, the use in (A) of *the* (technically, a specific determiner) requires us to look elsewhere to establish identity – 'which ball?' we ask ourselves. The answer, of course, is the one in the picture. In (B), however, no such question is raised by the use of the non-specific *a*.

This example shows that speech is usually closely related to the context in which it occurs while writing strives to be free of any local context. Reference in speech is typically to the shared context, for instance to objects or people seen by both participants. In writing, reference is often to something already present in the text or to something that is to follow. In this sense a written text aspires to be a free-standing structure within a particular cultural context; a spoken text may be regarded as a lean-to built against a wall that is the context of its occurrence.

Planning in Speech and Writing

For my second example I am supposing that the boy, John, has advanced a little in years. Playing football in the school yard with his friends, Fred Smith and Kevin, he kicks the ball through a classroom window. Mr B. emerges.

Mr B.	So we've made our mark again, have we, Smith?
F. S.	No, sir. Not me, sir! Not this time, sir!
Mr B.	O, Yes! Who, then?
	(pause)
Mr B.	Come on. If you don't tell me, Smith, I'll have to assume it was you. Well?
	(pause. Boys exchange glances)
F. S.	John, sir.
Mr B.	You did?
John	Yes, sir. I did.

There are, of course, imperfections in this illustration – in particular, that I am representing speech in writing. This means that the important contribution to meaning made by intonation is 'read in'. The two occurrences of *yes*, for instance, have contrasting meanings. The first means something like 'I do not believe you'. The second is both affirmative and confirmatory. Such differentiations of meaning are not, of course, normally available to the writer unless he is writing dialogue to be read or performed and uses a gloss to indicate interpretation. Rather than say *John, sir* where emphatic stress is placed on *John* an author may need to write *It was John who kicked the ball through the window* in which the form itself of the sentence gives prominence to the item of information that is regarded as unexpected.

A second point in the dialogue is that several of the utterances are highly elliptical – whatever is not essential is omitted. In the structure of the exchanges and in the shared context utterances such as *Who, then?* or *You did?* are not only perfectly acceptable and intelligible, they are, in fact, more appropriate than fully expanded utterances such as *Who was it, then, who kicked the ball through the window?* or *Was it you who kicked the ball through the window?* These expanded, fully explicit utterances are more appropriate to writing. And the person in the real world who talks as if he were writing tends to be regarded with great suspicion.

It is, indeed, possible to push this idea further. It is normal in linguistic thinking to regard casual speech as elliptical (as noted above). This implies an idealized form – the written– from which certain easily recoverable items have been omitted. Another way of looking at it is to suggest that speech, particularly in casual contexts, tends towards minimum verbalization and that this is the normal (unmarked) form. Writing, however, tends towards highly elaborated verbalization because it has to be self-sufficient. In this it is the less usual (marked) form. From an ontological perspective this interpretation both fits the evidence more aptly and carries with it important implications for the learning of writing.

Another feature of the dialogue is that the exchanges have an almost ritual pattern to them. The contributions made by the two boys are cued in by the teacher's questions. In this sense – which is to do with linguistic planning – the boys do not have to think much about the *form* of their contributions. These have to be answers to the questions posed, unless there are compelling reasons for either to depart from this normal rule of conversational exchange. That is, of course, a different matter from saying that Fred Smith may have to think hard before revealing the culprit.

I recognize that not all speech has the same degree of mutuality in planning; nor is a child's experience of talk entirely that of responding to another person's initiatives in dialogue. But it seems to me important to bear in mind that much of it is and the contrast between speech and writing in terms of the planning required is crucial. A child's preschool experience of language will not be useful to him in this respect. Written language planning is essentially an ability that has to be learned at school and a child's development as a writer can be seen specifically in these terms.

I shall end this discussion of speech–writing differences on a controversial note. Until the recent upsurge of interest in discourse and text analysis, modern linguistics had been tied almost totally to the notion of the sentence. Yet, ironically, for all the assertions of the primacy of spoken language (as, for instance, by Bloomfield quoted above), the grammars developed were based on idealized written texts rather than actual spoken texts. Kress, however, suggests 'that the main organizing unit of the spoken text is not the sentence... it consists of clauses of equal or near equal syntactic status "chained" together in sequence' (1982, p. 31). He summarizes the difference between the grammatical structure of speech and writing in this way:

> Speech, typically, consists of chains of co-ordinated, weakly subordinated and adjoined clauses: writing by contrast is marked by full subordination and embedding.

This is not to suggest that there is any absolute distinction grammatically between speech and writing. What it does suggest is that the syntactic choices made by a speaker will normally differ considerably from those made by a writer. As I develop the discussion of linguistic organization the importance of this difference in syntactic choices will become apparent.

Even though I have dwelt at some length on the differences between speech and writing, the account is necessarily limited. I have not, for example, made any distinction between types of speaking and types of writing, except incidentally. There are, of course, many varieties of which account would need to be taken in a full discussion – a useful introduction can be found in Gregory and Carroll (1978, Chapter 4).

Types of Writing in School

In primary schools over the last twenty years two major categories of writing have become established in practice – the 'creative' and the 'factual'. Often, factual appears to mean everything that is not creative. Within the scope of creative we find such assorted varieties as poems, playscripts, stories and autobiographical writing. This simple two-fold distinction needs to be challenged. It is difficult, for instance, to maintain any real distinction between a report of a visit to a local museum and an account of the death of a pet rabbit. In practice, however, it is likely that the former task would be regarded as factual, the latter as creative. Both tasks, in fact, take the form of first person, past tense reporting and both are to do with the recall of actual experiences. If the factual–creative distinction has any validity it is frequently more to do with notional divisions within the primary curriculum than with the form and content of the writing. The distinction is based on a simplistic notion of writing that, at worst, sanctions the practice of only a narrow range of writing at primary level.

At secondary level a similar narrowness of range can be seen in the way that the term 'essay' is used. This term is so useful a catch-all definition that no refinement is attempted. Yet problems abound in practice. I have had experience, for instance, of pupils, who, when asked to write an essay based on source materials in history, produced a numbered set of points. What they wrote, in fact, was a set of notes, not an essay. There is a second way in which the term 'essay' lacks adequate definition. There is, for example, a crucial difference between an essay describing what happens in *Antony and Cleopatra* and one evaluating that play on a comparative basis with *Caesar and Cleopatra*. Both may be legitimately termed 'essay' but that provides no means of determining why most sixth-formers will find the first task much more accessible than the second. However, I suggest that when the organizational demand of different sorts of 'essay' is considered, it becomes possible to pinpoint why one is likely to prove more challenging than another. The notion of 'essay' can, in fact, be refined in a way that is directly useful to classroom practice. This refinement is based on different types of organization which are typically realized by a different range of linguistic devices.

Organization – a Preliminary Definition

The notion of a text being organized on a particular basis is not easy to grasp, nor is it an approach that is current in thinking about children's writing development. A useful way of thinking about it is by analogy with the party game of making up a story going round a circle with each person contributing in turn. For instance, the first person may offer an opening like this:

> One day two children called Janet and John went into the woods where they met a . . .

The next person to contribute already has strong constraints within which to make his offering. He knows that he has to say what happened next to Janet and John and, specifically, whom they met, and so on. Complications can, of course, arise when other characters are introduced. Generally speaking, the rule is that any other character introduced has to be seen to be relevant to the narrative so far developed. A witch, for example, would be seen as relevant; Julius Caesar not so.

Stories, and many other types of writing, are, like the party story-game, organized on a **time-related** basis. To make up, or determine upon, the next bit, the writer has to ask 'what happened next?' The principle of time-related organization is very powerful and holds good whether we are dealing with a story deriving from the imagination, an account of a visit, of a biological process (such as germination) or a history essay retelling, say, the events of a battle. In fact, much of the writing in the middle years of schooling will be found to be organized on a time-related basis. However, as children progress to top junior stage and beyond they will increasingly be required to tackle writing that is not organized in this way. Writing that involves making comparisons, presenting arguments or interpreting evidence is organized on different bases. This can be appreciated if we return to our party game.

Suppose that the first contributor, instead of the opening of a story, offers something like this:

Cooking is one of the great pleasures in life, if you do not have to do it every day . . .

It is likely that the second contributor will find it difficult to know what to say next. The question 'What happened next?' that elicited the next part of the story is quite inappropriate because nothing has happened. The only possible question is 'Can you say something more about cooking?' As an organizing principle, it is not very helpful. It might, for example, prompt the next person to say 'I like fish and chips, and you don't have to cook them.' This is a perfectly legitimate answer to the question, but, taken with the original proposition, there is no sense of coherence. The two statements appear to have no real connection.

When writing is not time-related some overall plan is required. Such a plan has to be determined from the outset and the end kept in mind from the beginning of the act of writing. If children are unable to create and hold in mind such a plan it will be difficult for them to construct a coherent piece of writing. In contrast, it is possible – even if it is not desirable – to create a coherent story or an account of a school trip proceeding bit by bit, and there is no absolute necessity of knowing how it is going to end before starting to write. Obviously in talking about 'story' in this way I am referring to narrative that is very simple in scope and sophistication. There is a world of difference between this and highly wrought artefacts of narrative art – Conrad's novels, for instance.

In Table 4.1 I suggest a classification of some of the more common forms of school writing. This is offered tentatively as a starting point for further discussion and refinement. It certainly does not purport to be a comprehensive taxonomy.

In this classification I am suggesting that the non-time-related categories will be inherently more difficult in terms of organization for the young writer. It can also be seen that a traditional term like 'essay' can now be sub-classified more precisely according to the organiza-

Table 4.1 *A Classification of Types of School Writing on an Organizational Basis*

Time-Related	Non-Time-Related
FICTION	
Stories	Poems that do not relate
Narrative poems	events but deal, for
Playscripts	example, with states of mind
NON-FICTION	
Personal narratives and	Cause–effect
autobiographical writing	Comparison–contrast
Reporting of –	Categorizing
visits	Descriptions involving
activities	spatial or locational
processes	dimensions
experiments	Argument and
events (literary &	hypothesizing
historical)	

tional basis – that, for instance, in the previously introduced example the essay giving an account of the events of *Antony and Cleopatra* is basically a time-related report, whereas the essay requiring a comparison of that play with *Caesar and Cleopatra* is, in general terms, organized on a **comparison–contrast** basis. Even to writers at sixth form level or in higher education this latter form of organization poses problems that are both conceptual and linguistic.

I recognize, incidentally, that **cause–effect** writing may be time-related, but, even where it is, the expression of causality often requires an inversion of the real-world ordering in terms of the sequencing of the clauses that realize those events in the text. In simple terms this means that mature, adult writers will tend to combine the following clauses

I was tired   (1)
I went to bed (2)

in this way:

I went to bed because I was tired

where the sequence is event (2) + reason + event (1). A young child (and an adult speaking) is much more likely to co-ordinate the clauses in a sequence that follows the real-world occurrence, as in:

I was tired so I went to bed.

In the remainder of this chapter I will add detail to the ideas so far advanced about organization and this will be done through text-based discussion. It may, therefore, be useful to establish the main stages of the argument in outline first. I am suggesting that the production of a written text involves several levels of planning and determining linguistic choices. The top level is the pre-planning of the content or propositions. The basis of organization at this top level carries with it implications at lower levels. The lower levels have to do with sentence connection, sentence structures and clausal relationships. The relationships between these levels are shown in Table 4.2. As can be seen the implications of organization at these various levels differ according to the basic configuration of the text, whether it is time-related or not.

Organization in Two Short Texts

I now turn to two short texts to develop the description of organization in more detail. Spellings and punctuation have not been altered.

Table 4.2

Time-Related		*Non-Time-Related*
desirable but not strictly necessary at minimum level.	Preplanning	necessary to overall coherence of text.
can be simple and is likely to be, typically, of the S–V–O (C) order that is most closely related to speech.	Sentence structure	likely to need to be varied and to include complex structures.
need be no more than simple time connectives.	Conjunction	will need to be varied. Connectives are usually essential to make explicit the semantic effect whether realizing causal or adversative relationships.
can be achieved by simple means such as pronominalization.	Sentence connection	likely to involve a wide range of devices, some of which require planning over two or more sentences.

Text 1: Kerry (J 1)

Yesterday we went to Heaton park. We went on the coach. It seemed a long way. When we got there the driver had to find a place to park. When we found a place to park, we went into the park. We walk up to the animals. This is what we saw. We saw some peacocks. One of the peacocks was shoing off its feathers then we saw some hens then we saw some baby sheep we saw some horses then we went to the play area me and Julie went to the sea-saw then we went on the roundabout. Helen fell off the roundabout and cut her knee then we went back to the coach for our lunch. I had a bag of crisps.

This is an interesting combination of typically time-related clauses and some more sophisticated features. Organizationally, the sequencing of the clauses and sentences parallels the real world occurrence. One imagines the writer saying to herself 'what did I do next (that I can remember)?' Although the sentence or clause connectors are normally simple *and*, *when*, *then*, the account does not lack coherence. The time-relatedness of the sequencing in itself provides an underlying coherence. Within this framework, and with this sort of subject matter, the selection of detail is not a major constraint for either writer or reader. It is, of course, a different matter when the subject matter is subject to more pressing external constraints as, for example, in the reporting of a scientific experiment or the describing of a historical event. Information in this latter type of text is constrained by criteria of relevance and completeness.

There is, however, a feature of organization in this text that is of considerable interest. The sentence *This is what we saw* stands out as different in kind and in function from the rest of the text. *This* here is a nominal used in a way that is usually described as cataphoric, that is 'forward looking' (see Halliday and Hasan, 1976, pp. 68 ff.). In my experience, instances of nominals *this* and *that* used in this forward looking way are invariably found in sentences that serve a **metastructuring** function (for a full discussion, see Harris, 1980, Chapter 8). By this I mean that the writer is concerned not so much with the content of the text as such but with his sense of the structuring of the text. It is as if the writer inserts a subheading 'Catalogue of animals' before going on to list those seen; or, to take a different analogy, says to the imagined audience 'Now I am going to list the animals I saw'. In this sense these types of metastructuring sentences in written text are like the focusing moves identified in classroom discourse by Sinclair and Coulthard (1975).

In developmental terms it is highly unusual to find a metastructuring sentence in writing by a lower junior child. In this particular text its presence is not essential to the coherence of the whole. However, as the writing demands made on pupils increase in complexity, the ability to employ such devices becomes increasingly necessary. It is a demand that many secondary pupils are unable to meet. Whether this is because they are not able to in an absolute sense or whether they have not been helped to and see no reason for utilizing such devices is another question.

Text 2 provides an interesting contrast. It is a piece of geography writing by a lower secondary pupil and is concerned with the interpretation of a weather map. The complete text is in three parts. Here I am reproducing only the last part. The text is set out in discrete sentences to facilitate analysis. It was written as a continuous paragraph. Spellings and punctuation have not been altered.

Text 2

S1   *Because* of the high pressure cool air must be pushing down trapping the fog *and because* there are only gentle breezes *because* there is not (a) huge gap between high and low pressure the winds are not strong enough to blow the fog away.

S2   The Sun will not have rose *because* it is only 6.00 a.m. in Winter the temperature is low.

S3   *This is also due to* the cold air pushing down causing high pressure.

Perhaps a useful starting point might be to suggest that there is an intuitive feeling that the pupil has understood the complex interrelationships of cause and effect. In the realization of these in the text, however, there are obvious problems. This is, incidentally, an important general distinction. Because learning in school is so habitually assessed by the evidence of pupils' written work, inadequacies in the writing can often blind us to the fact that learning has taken place. Recently in a discussion with me of his less able pupils' writing problems a craft, design and technology teacher said, 'They can all do the practical work; mostly they can explain to me what they've done but they can't write it down and that's what they have to do to get a respectable grade in CSE'. The suggestion, then, is of three levels:

(1)   Understanding and/or performing a practical task;
(2)   Recounting and/or explaining (in talk where the teacher's questions support the planning of the pupil);
(3)   Providing an account or an explanation in writing (in which, of course, the organization is entirely in the hands of the writer).

While talking it through may be helpful to the third stage, it is not in itself enough. This is evident in Text 2.

In terms of organization there are in sentence 1 several factors in a dependent relationship. The writer has expressed this dependency by *because* on each occasion which suggests that, although a high ability pupil, he does not possess a wide range of alternative means for expressing the causal relationship. Interestingly, other pupils in the same group displayed a similar characteristic but with different connectors. For instance:

> Another *factor for* the amount of fog is *the reason that* there is only a light breeze *because of* the small gap between high and low pressure. *The reason for* the low temperature is *the fact that* it is 6 o'clock and the sun has not yet risen and it is also Winter. *Another reason for* the low temperature is the cloud cover which is intercepting the radiation.

The second major point, while seeming obvious, is, nevertheless, fundamental to the whole argument. Whereas Text 1 deals with events that occurred in time, and this time relatedness provided the writer with the basis for organizing her text, Text 2 deals with factors at one point in time rather than with a series of events. The conditions for entry into the text do not, therefore, depend on any real-time constraints. To illustrate this I shall rewrite each text from 'bottom to top' as follows:

> *Text 1
> I had a packet of crisps for lunch.
> We went back to the coach.
> Helen cut her knee.
> Then she fell off the roundabout.
> Then we went on the roundabout . . .

> *Text 2
> There is cold air pushing down causing high pressure. This also keeps the temperature low.
> So also does the fact that the sun has not yet risen because it is only 6.00 a.m. and it is Winter.

The rewrite of Text 2 is acceptable, that of Text 1 clearly unacceptable. This suggests vividly that the young writer is likely to find the constraints of time-related organization a powerful support in the creation of coherent texts.

My last point concerns the amount of information in the first sentence. I suggested earlier that children at the lower junior stage tend to realize each event of a story or a report in a clausal structure or simple sentence and to chain these together by loosely co-ordinating connectors such as *and* or *then*. In Text 2 the concern is, of course, not with events but with factors and in the first sentence it is likely that the writer has included so much information because he sees it as forming a conceptual whole. He is, ironically, operating the popular notion of the sentence as a unit 'that expresses a complete thought'. Now, while the writer of Text 1 is operating a notion of a sentence as equalling an event, the older pupil (Text 2) is operating a notion of a sentence as equalling a complete thought. The fundamental problem is that a sentence is neither an *event* unit nor a *conceptual* unit but a *syntactic* unit. Part of the writer's planning and organization at a micro-level is, therefore, going to be concerned with the way in which he breaks up a complex set of interdepending factors into syntactic units and then deploys resources of connection to express the interdependency. It is necessary at this point to consider these resources of connection systematically.

Sentence Connection

It is not always appreciated how versatile English is in its resources for sentence connection. Winter (1977) points out that there are three broad categories of clause–sentence connectors – the subordinators, the sentence connectors (usually referred to as conjunctions) and a range of lexical items of connection. These he terms Vocabularies 1, 2 and 3 respectively. To these three I would add a fourth – the use of *this* or *that* as nominals with a subordinator to indicate the nature of the intersentential relationship. Each of these can be illustrated by reworking a section of Text 2.

(1) *Subordinators – Vocabulary 1*
    The sun will not have risen *because* it is only 6.00 a.m. in Winter.
(2) *Sentence connectors – Vocabulary 2*
    It is only 6.00 a.m. in Winter. *Consequently* the sun will not yet have risen.
(3) *Vocabulary 3 item*
    There are two *results* of its being 6.00 a.m. in Winter. The sun will not yet have risen. The temperature will also be low.

In this example *result* is incomplete in its semantic effect – it has only a partial meaning – and the next two sentences fulfil our expectation of the meaning. These two sentences, therefore, do not require any further means to indicate their relationship to the initial sentence. As sentence 1 is read the word *results* signals that more information is to follow. The reader processes sentences 2 and 3 in the light of that signal. Besides *result*, there are many Vocabulary 3 items that occur commonly in discursive writing – a full list can be found in Winter (1977). Here is a short selection:

action	event	reason
cause	expect	result
compare	fact	situation
conclude	kind	solution
condition	manner	specify
contrast	point	thing
differ	problem	way

(4) *Nominal and subordinator*
The sun will not yet have risen. *This is because* it is only 6.00 a.m. in Winter.

I have already pointed out in Text 1 *this* used as a nominal in a metastructuring sentence which, I suggested, operates on a different plane within the text. Here there is an example of it used again as a nominal but this time standing in, as it were, for the preceding sentence. Halliday and Hasan (1976) refer to such a usage as 'extended reference' where, they imply, the reader is forced by the presence of *this* to look back to clarify the location of the reference (just as looking forward is **cataphora**, so looking back is **anaphora**). I suggest, however, that readers and writers characteristically work forward in a text – while, of course, reflecting back now and then – and this leads me to prefer an explanation that a nominal (unless in a metastructuring sentence) replaces in a given sentence either a preceding clause or sentence or, sometimes, a longer portion of text. In the present example this means that the reader processes the second sentence as

(This   )
                                        is because . . .
(The sun will not have risen)

This example makes particularly clear the flexibility of sentence connection in English and the need for the writer to make appropriate decisions about the division of his propositions into the syntactic units that are sentences. There is, of course, nothing inevitable about such a process.

Implications for Writing in Schools

Although I shall add much more detail to the description of organization shortly, it is worth linking the discussion so far to classroom practice. There are two significant points for pupils–as–writers.

First of all, certain types of non-time-related writing require that the writer is able to make decisions about dividing content into syntactic units about which there is no inevitability and over which, as a consequence, the writer has sole control. The successful operation of this 'chunking' task requires, firstly, that the pupil can bring flexibility to his planning, a highly self-aware and reflective approach to his writing and that he has at his disposal a range of resources for sentence connection. In the second place, these types of writing require also, I believe, that the pupil is allowed 'mental space' – that is, time in which to experiment at a drafting stage – and, in addition, that he receives from the teacher positive and informed intervention on an individual basis. This second set of requirements is commonly ill-served both by the practice of writing in schools, as was shown in Chapter 1, and by the limited understanding of writing and the writing process possessed by many teachers.

The second point relates to development. I stressed in the discussion of Text 1 that many children at the junior stage appear to write stories and simple reports a clause or sentence at a time and to relate these clauses in a loosely co-ordinated manner, realized typically by *and* or *then*. It is clearly a major step forward from a diet of story and simple report writing to tasks that make demands for the expression of causality or, as I shall suggest, comparisons. It is in these forms of writing – to be found in the non-fictional and non-time-related section of our organizational categories – that the writer must, at a minimum, be able to project forward in his planning over two or three sentences at a time. He must also have acquired the habit of casting back when necessary to have an overall sense of how his text is developing. In developmental terms, then, the understanding of sentences as syntactic units and the ability to plan ahead over stretches of text are both important indicators of a pupil's progress as a writer.

A Systematic Description of Sentence Connection
A Note on the Descriptive Approach

Readers familiar with the exhaustive account of cohesion by Halliday and Hasan (1976) may be confused by the different terminology and categorization employed here. This is not a wilful variation but an attempt to focus on sentence connection and text structures from a process or productive point of view. Halliday and Hasan's perspective is that of the analyst – typically anaphoric or backward-looking. They refer, for instance, to reference items such as *he* or *it* as giving the analyst 'search instructions' to look back in the text to recover the referent. I do not accept this perspective. My classification is consistent with a process perspective. I should, however, point out that for the most part I am dealing with the same range of cohesive items as Halliday and Hasan. A full justification of my position can be found in Harris (1980).

So far in the discussion I have, perhaps, implied that **conjunction** in its various forms is the main means of sentence connection. In written English, however, sentences can be joined by many means. Here are the four main ways:

(1)   by replacing an element or elements in a first sentence (S1) with pro-forms when they recur in a second or subsequent sentence. The most common of the pro-forms are the third person pronouns. Here

is an example of this feature, which we call **replacement**, in operation.

S1   Henry V set out for France.
S2   When *he* got *there* he besieged Harfleur

The pronoun *he* (twice) replaces Henry V in S2 and the pro-form *there* replaces (*to*) *France*. We have already seen above the way that *replacement* can operate with longer bits of text being replaced by *this* or *that* as nominals.

(2)   A form of replacement is **deletion** where an element in S1 is replaced by zero ∅ in S2. This is a feature much more commonly found in speech than in writing as I suggested in my initial exploration of some differences between these modes. It is also referred to as **ellipsis**.

(3)   (a)   **Confirmatory identity signals** are used when an item in S1 recurs in S2 and it needs to be shown that it is the same. The most common identity signals are *the*, *this*, *these* and *those* used as pre-modifying determiners in the noun group. For example:

S1   When we prick our finger with a pin the stimulus of pain generates a nervous impulse.
S2   *This* impulse travels along the sensory neurone in the arm.

In this example the use of *this* in S2 identifies the impulse as the one already mentioned, not another one. We should note, however, that *the* is an extremely complex word and its occurrence is in no way an inevitable indication of sentence connection by identity signalling. Often *the* signals identity within the noun group cataphorically as in *the sensory neurone in the arm* where the identity of the neurone is '*the one in the arm*'. *The* is also used homophorically as in *the sun, the moon and the stars* where there is only one member of the class of objects to which reference is being made. We should also note that the type of discourse exerts a strong influence. In fiction, for instance, we feel no problem of identity if the opening sentence of a story reads

The cat uncurled itself before the blazing fire.

The identity is related to the imagined situation. In non-fiction the use of *The cat* initially in a text could only be generic as in

The cat is the largest family of mammals.

Despite these qualifications it is not uncommon to find in children's writing *the* used as an identity signal where there is no previous mention of the item that it is premodifying, which, therefore, creates a sense of context-bound writing. An example of this is found in S11 of Text 3a (see below) where *the line of stakes* requires a previous mention of 'stakes' but there is none. Obviously the characteristic of much school writing by which a pupil is writing for a teacher whom he knows already knows the facts under discussion positively encourages such context-bound features. In a fully self-sufficient text, of course, such features are not permissible.

(3)   (b)   **Comparative identity signals**
This is a complex feature of organization in certain types of text. I shall postpone discussion of it until looking at Comparison—Contrast writing in which comparative identity can play a crucial part.

(4)   **Conjunction** is the most immediately recognizable form of sentence connection which, as I have already suggested, includes not only conjunctions but units that are conjunctive in function. Comprehensive descriptions of the types of conjunction have been made by Halliday and Hasan (1976) and Quirk *et al.* (1972). For most analytical purposes I have found it useful to identify four main types:

   (i)   Temporal   e.g., then, previously, later.
  (ii)   Additive   e.g., moreover, and.
 (iii)   Causal   e.g., so, therefore, consequently.
 (iv)   Adversative e.g., but, however.

An Organizational Analysis of a History Essay

To fulfil the claim I made earlier that linguistic organization provided a diagnostic framework for looking at problems in pupils' writing I shall link the rest of the discussion of organization to an analysis of a piece of history writing by a second-year secondary pupil. It concerns the battle of Agincourt and falls into two sections. The first, section A, is an account of the main events leading up to and including the battle. In organizational terms the writing is clearly time-related. The second section – B – is subdivided into five parts and concerns particular aspects of the battle. This second part is not time-related in its organization. Both sections were based on classwork and on a textbook account. The classwork was a more dominant influence on section B, the textbook on section A. The pupil, incidentally, is regarded as of above-average ability.

Reproduced below is the whole of section A and three parts of B (1, 3 and 5). Each sentence is numbered and set out separately for ease of reference. The writer's original paragraph indentations are shown by horizontal rules. As before, spellings and punctuations have not been altered.

Text 3
Section A: THE BATTLE OF AGINCOURT
S1   Henry V claimed the throne of France.

S2 In August 1415 Henry V sailed to France and landed at the mouth of the river Seine.

S3 He captured Harfleur and on October 9th, he set off to Calais with a fairly small army.

———

S4 During this time it had rained heavily and the ground had become muddy and the rivers swollen.

S5 Henry found it difficult to cross the river Seine and so had to use fording places.

S6 But these were protected by french army who moved in parallel with the English army.

S7 But Henry reached a bend in the river and was able to cut across and beat the French to a fording place.

S8 But by the time the army had marched to Calais the soldiers were cold, wet and hungry and they found a large French army blocking their way in between Agincourt and Tramecourt.

———

S9 The French army was large with mounted knights and knights on foot.

S10 They thought they could easily win.

S11 First the French horsemen advanced but were met with arrows which caused them to beat a hasty retreat and few reached the line of stakes.

S12 The French knights on foot came next.

S13 Even though large in number the English were not perturbed and they continuously beat them back until they came no more.

S14 It had been difficult for the French to advance as the battle was fought between woodland and partly in ploughed fields.

S15 There had been a road across the battlefield.

———

S16 The English had won a great victory.

Section B: WHAT IT MUST HAVE BEEN LIKE TO FIGHT AT AGINCOURT
(1) *Waiting for the Battle*

S1 One of the most important factors in waiting for the battle was that the men were on their feet in cold wet weather from 7 to 11 am.

S2 The men were undoubtedly tired even when they started to fight.

S3 In contrast to the English the French were in a good mood before they started as they were certain from the size of their army that they could easily win.

S4 The men had been short of food for 9 days and so were hungry as well as wet as the temperature was between 40 and 50 F.

S5 Lots of the English were ill but only through minor things such as stomach upsets.

S6 All the archers carried sharpened stakes made of wood to defend the English from the French mounted knights.

S7 They were driven into the ground at an angle away from the English.

(3)   *Cavalry v. Infantry*
S13   The only result of cavalry v. infantry was that the better horses amongst the French jumped and cleared the long wooden stakes.
S14   But the horses landed on the English cavalry killing many of them.
S15   But several of the French were also killed on impact.
S16   This caused many casualties.

(5)   *The Wounded*
S26   The English soldiers had only surface cuts many of which healed overnight.
S27   But some had fractures.
S28   Not many English soldiers died.
S29   The French soldiers had however sustained many deep penetrating wounds several of which were fatal.
S30   They also had a tremendous amount of skull fractures.
S31   Lots of the French died overnight from exposure.
S32   In the morning the English soldiers went round the battlefield killing any live French soldiers.
S33   This action was perhaps not so terrible as most of the French would have died more painful deaths in the near future.
S34   Altogether there were some six thousand dead soldiers.

In relation to this text I want now to explore a range of organizational features in detail.

Pronominal Replacement and Sentence Segmentation

The normal (unmarked) operation of pronominal replacement of the subject in written English is simply described. Where there is only one person, a collective group or object as the constant subject focus this is introduced as a lexical item. Subsequently, in either a sentence or subordinate clause, it is replaced by a pronoun. In a co-ordinated clause it is replaced by zero $\emptyset$. Thus:

> *John* got up. When *he* had washed, *he* had his breakfast and $\emptyset$ left for work.

Bearing this in mind as the norm, there are some interesting aspects of replacement in Text 3, section A. In the first three sentences this is the pattern.

S1   Henry V ...
S2   Henry V ... and $\emptyset$ ...
S3   He ... and he ...

Clearly it departs from the norm. Why? There seem to be two possible interrelated answers. In the first place the two time phrases *In August 1415* and *on October 9th* appear to mark off in the mind of the writer separate phases of the expedition. If we accept that the writer sees each as a new start then we are less surprised to see the marked form of replacement by the reiteration of the lexical subject (Henry) rather than by pronominalization. It is also possible that the writer is composing each clause separately, much as I suggested younger children do in their writing. That, in itself, may account for the unusual repetitions of *Henry* and of *he* in S3.

Another example of the same phenomenon is found in the following version of the battle of Agincourt by another pupil in the same group as the writer of Text 3.

A S1   Henry V revived the claims to the French lands and Ø wanted to prove to the French that he could rule their country.

B { S2   In August 1415 *Henry* sailed for Normandy.
    { S3   He landed in the mouth of the Seine.

C S4   *Henry* then went to Harfleur with his army and Ø captured it.

D { S5   On October 9th Henry set off for Calais with a small army.
    { S6   He left the rest of his army to hold Harfleur.

This can be analysed as follows:

S1   Co-ordinated sentence regarded as a discrete unit (= a separate event) with repetition of the subject by deletion in the second clause.

S2-3   Second event unit marked off as discrete by initial prepositional time phrase as adjunct with repetition by reiteration of lexical name in S2 and by pronominal replacement across sentence boundary in S3 which is, of course, part of the same unit.

S4   Third discrete event again marked by temporal adjunct *then* with subject repetition by reiteration of lexical name in the first clause and by deletion in the second, co-ordinated, clause.

S5-6   Fourth discrete event unit with subject repetition operating exactly as in S2-3.

A, B, C, and D, therefore, I suggest, are seen by the writer as separate events and the text has been composed one event at a time. Hence, the unusual pattern of subject replacement. It might be argued that the pupils cannot operate pronominal replacement; but, in fact, elsewhere in their Agincourt texts they provide ample evidence that they can. There is, in fact, corroborative evidence from the work of Bereiter and his colleagues at the Ontario Institute for Studies in Education that children write or compose in discrete units: that, as they put it, 'Compositions are generated one sentence at a time, generally without any guiding framework.' I suggest that the unit at which children operate may not necessarily be the sentence, but that the comment is, in general purport, just. It points to an important generalization that text production is not a matter of creating isolated sentences but of creating interlinking structures. In these structures the girders are sentences, the corner pieces the various means of sentence connection and each has to be selected in accord with the overall design.

Replacement and Change of Subject Focus

If the process of replacement of single subject focus by pronominalization is, comparatively speaking, a simple operation, it can also be seen that the introduction of a second subject focus into the text creates a danger of ambiguity in pronominal replacement. For example:

> The French Knights on foot came next.
> Even though large in number the English were not perturbed and they continuously beat them back until they came no more.

It is, of course, the French who are 'large in number'. A similar problem is found at the beginning of Text 3 section B where the replacement is effected not by pronoun but by the general noun *men* which has no textually established antecedent. Here is an outline of the relevant part of the text:

S1 One of the most important factors . . . was that the men . . .
S2 The men . . .
S3 In contrast to the English the French . . .
S4 The men . . .

Each time *men* occurs it is understood to refer to the English, an item which is not introduced into the text until S3 and even then its position in the sentence does not enable it to be replaced by *the men* in S4 with its identity being clear. The point can be appreciated readily if the more common form of pronominal replacement *they* is used. This would give in outline:

S1 . . . they were on their feet . . .
S2 They were tired . . .
S3 In contrast to the English the French . . .
S4 They had been short of food . . .

Related to the problem of *men* introduced without an antecedent is the structure of the whole paragraph. This requires a comparison between the English and the French in respect of the situation they found themselves in prior to battle.

Part of the difficulty, from an organizational point of view, of handling comparisons is shown by the return to the English (the *men*) in S4 after the clear signal of the comparison in S3 *In contrast to the English the French*. Unless there is a second signal – here it would need to be an adversative conjunction (*but* or *however*) – and a restatement of the lexical subject, *The English*, we assume we are still in the same part of the comparison structure and, therefore, focusing on *the French*. The return of focus, then, in S4 to the English is not signalled, but, organizationally, needs to be. If, interestingly enough, S4 were placed before S3 this particular problem would be obviated. It is, moreover, generally true that in texts produced by mature writers it is impossible to re-order sentences without creating incoherence unless the text is substantially rewritten. In this text, however, as in many other school produced texts I have studied, not only is there a possibility of re-ordering, but even of enhancing coherence by so doing. That in itself highlights the difficulties of organization for the novice writer. I would add that it is my firm impression that such problems tend to occur with greater frequency in texts that are not time-related in their overall organization.

Place Mentions

Although it may not appear as an immediately significant point, the mention in S2 of Text 3A of the place at which Henry landed, the mouth of the Seine, is of interest. The reason for the mention is, of course, that that is where Harfleur is situated. The point is made clear in another Agincourt text:

S1 Henry V decided to claim the French throne.
S2 In Aug. 1415 he sailed to Normandy where he landed at the mouth of the river Seine.
S3 *There* he captured Harfleur

There in S3 replaces *at the mouth of the Seine* linking the mention of the Seine to that of Harfleur and so justifying the mention in the text of the place of landing. In the whole group of Agincourt texts, 20 in all, this is the only example of such a place mention. Along with other evidence it suggests that locational concepts cause particular problems possibly because our preferred mental set is temporal rather than spatial. There is, however, a wider issue here.

Relevance and Relationships in a Text

Just as the mention of Henry's place of landing appears to lack justification unless it is linked to Harfleur, so, in general terms, I would suggest that the justifying of particular items of information in a text is an organizational problem widely experienced in school writing at the top junior and lower secondary stage. Text 3A offers two additional examples. S4 provides a piece of background information – *it had rained heavily* – and two consequences – *muddy ground* and *swollen rivers*. Both these consequences were, of course, important to the outcome of the actual battle. However, the question in text organizational terms is more precise. How are these mentions subsequently justified? The *swollen rivers* mention establishes the setting for the immediately ensuing piece of text that describes Henry's problems with crossing the Seine and his eventual solution of the problem. What is not demonstrated in the text is that there is such a relationship. To achieve this some form of explicit link is needed between S4 and S5 such as *therefore* or *for this reason*. There is, incidentally, a factual error in the text. The river that Henry had to cross on his journey to Calais was, in fact, the Somme.

The other consequence of the heavy rain was the muddy ground. The actual effect of this was crucial to the battle since the French were hindered in their advance and, later, in their retreat by the condition of the ground. This point is not made clear in the text. It is, perhaps, implied in S14 but the relationship between the rain, the muddy ground and the French difficulties in fighting is not established textually. This gives the feeling that the mention of the muddy ground is redundant. Similarly, the mention of the road across the battlefield in S15 has no textual justification. Probably it is included simply because it had been mentioned in the lesson or textbook. This indicates, I believe, that there is a much greater dislocation than is often appreciated between the writing up of notes as an essay which is common practice in schools and the creation of a fully integrated and coherent text.

Comparison and Contrast

At a basic level comparison—contrast can be defined as the expression of a relationship between two elements or objects in respect of a quality or quantity, thus:

$$x \text{ is} \begin{cases} \text{like} \\ \text{unlike} \end{cases} y \text{ in respect of } z$$

Contrast is, of course, comparison + negative. In practice, the identification of the elements x, y and z is not always easy to make and it may often be that they represent multiple factors. From a cognitive point of view, it is widely recognized, making comparisons of any complexity is an advanced skill. What is not so commonly recognized is that the realization of the mechanics of comparison in writing makes specific and exacting demands. These demands are such that most pupils in their middle years of school are likely to find them beyond their text organizing abilities if they are not given appropriate support when required to tackle them.

It may be useful to list the typical linguistic demands of comparisons:

(1) Alternating subject focus
(2) Comparative identity signals
(3) Adversative conjunction

Since I have already discussed the first point at some length I shall devote the rest of the chapter to the last two features on the list, pausing only to point out that in Text 3B each section has an alternating subject focus.

Section 1: The English – The French
Section 3: The French cavalry – The English infantry
Section 5: The English wounded – The French wounded.

Comparative Identity Signals

Quirk *et al.* (1972) group together a range of cohesive items under the general heading of **comparison**. The group includes *more, most, less, least* and there are other items. Although I recognize that there are problems of classification in this area limitations in the scope of the present discussion will have to be accepted. More relevant to the present purpose is that they see these intersentential links as operating anaphorically, suggesting that 'we must often look at the previous context for the basis of similarity or difference.' However, within the perspective of organization with which I am here concerned I view identity signals as operating in a different way.

I have already described the operation of the specific determiners (*this*, and so on) which *confirm* the identity of an item already entered into the text. Here, I am concerned with the means by which a comparative, rather than an absolute, identity is signalled. Just as the absolute identity has to be established within the text (that is, endophorically rather than exophorically) so, too, does the comparative identity.

I suggest that from an organizational perspective all forms of comparative identity involve the notion of a set within which the comparison operates and that the set has to be present in the text for the organization to be coherent. For example, in

S15 Knights and archers were the two parts of the French army.
S16 The first to move were French mounted Knights armed with lances.
S17
S18 Very few reached the line of stakes.
S19 The others were shot or cut down.
S20 Next came French Knights on foot.

the others (S19) is understood in the light of the set of French mounted Knights minus the 'very few (who) reached the line of stakes.' The force of *the others* is, in effect, 'The French mounted Knights who did not reach the line of stakes'. Organizationally, the writer (and reader) proceeds by establishing

(1) Whole set   = French mounted Knights.
(2) Sub-set (a) = the few who reached the line of stakes.
(3) Sub-set (b) = (1) − (2) = the others.

As reproduced above, the short extract is a coherent example of comparative identity. With it can be compared another version:

S9   The English were said to had put up sticks in a horizontal fashion so that the horses wouldn't be able to get up over.
S10 The horses swerved to avoid the sticks and collide with each other −
S11 also the infantry was crushed by the French horses.
S12 The others crashed back into their own side.

Here, a distinction has to be made between *each other* in S10 which is non-cohesive and not comparative and *the others* in S12 which is both cohesive and comparative. But how can the identity of *the others* be determined? The first problem is that there is no certainty which set (textually established) *the others* belongs to. There is no certainty whether it is part of the set of French cavalry realized by *the horses* in the text, or part of *the infantry* also mentioned. In fact − but this is not established textually − the infantry is the English infantry. In neither case is there the possibility of discovering who *the others* is in relation to the whole set (whether cavalry or infantry) because both sets are treated indivisibly. That is, *the horses swerved* means 'all the horses swerved' and *the infantry was crushed* means 'all the infantry was crushed'. This leaves no possible group which can be realized by *the others*.

It would seem likely that what the writer had in mind but could not clarify either to himself or in the linguistic organization of the text was a threefold division of the set of French cavalry/horses:

(1) *The many* who swerved to avoid the stakes with which the English had defended their position and in the process collided with each other.
(2) *The few* who jumped the stakes and crushed some of the English infantry.
(3) *The others* who turned back and crashed into their own advancing infantry.

Here we can see that *the others* is clearly identifiable as the set of French cavalry minus (1) *the many* and minus (2) *the few*. This example illustrates the problems of handling two or more participants as subject focus in a text and in establishing a comparative relationship even between subdivisions of one of the participant groups.

The same problem is, in fact, also present in the previous example from which, it will have been noted, S17 was omitted. This sentence reads 'The English fired a shower of arrows.' Thus, in the complete extract we can see that the change of focus in S17 from the French to the English creates ambiguity for the antecedent of *very few* and *the others*. In outline, the structure as originally written reads:

S15   Knights and archers . . . two parts of the French army.
S16   The first to move were the French mounted Knights.
S17   The English fired a shower of arrows.
S18   Very few reached . . .
S19   The others . . .
S20   Next came French Knights on foot.

The final example of comparative identity also involves a striking instance of aberrant sentence order which, as I suggested earlier, is highly indicative of organizational problems. Here is the relevant portion of text.

S16   The French began to lose their man-to-man fights and the others fell over their dead comrades.
S17   Some French fell and suffocated in the mud.
S18   Then the French retrieved [retreated?] and ran away.

Here, *the others* cannot be interpreted comparatively (as it needs to be) because, while the set is established as 'the French' the comparative item means 'the French minus x'. Since we do not know what 'x' is, we cannot determine who *the others* is. However, if we interpose S17 between the co-ordinated clauses of S16, 'x' is then identifiable as the 'some [who] fell and suffocated in the mud.'

It is possible that the writer had in mind to include in S16 a statement such as 'some were killed . . .' but, having not done so, entered it as S17 without appreciating the violence that it would do to the organizational coherence of the text. This illustrates the necessity in the realization of comparative identity for the writer to hold in mind the set and its subdivisions before embarking on the realization of the ideas in the linguistic surface of the text.

The same problem is also present in the main illustrative text (Text 3B) where section 3 is incoherent probably because S16 needs to be transposed between S13 and 14, and S14 rewritten to realize a causal relationship. The section would then read something like this:

S13   The only result of cavalry v. infantry was that the better horses jumped the stakes.

S16   This, however, caused many casualties *because*
S14   the horses landed on the English . . .
S15   *But* several of the French were also killed.

This rewrite shows the need for the explicit realization of the causal relationship between S16 and S14 (*because*) and the adversative between S13 and S16 and between S14 and S15 (*However, But*).

Conjunction

At a minimal level it is possible for a writer to create a text that is both coherent and cohesive without the use of conjunctive items; it is unlikely, however, that such a text will be entirely satisfactory to the reader. Milic (1967) suggests that connectives provide the reader with 'the author's own key to the relations of the materials and throw the entire composition into focus.' As a prior requirement to the use of conjunctive items there must be a basic, underlying continuity in the meaning of the text – a semantic continuity.

Semantic continuity is more readily established in a text in which the basic organization is time-related. Where, however, a text has inherent in its structure, or in part of it, causal or adversative relations, the need for explicit realization will be greater, if not obligatory.

In Text 3B section 5, *The Wounded*, the power of the adversative conjunction *however* in S29 can be seen. Its presence is crucial to the underlying semantics of contrast. Alongside this can be set some examples of the same section of the Agincourt texts where there is no realization of the contrast. I shall cite only the relevant parts of the texts and indicate the missing adversative conjunction by [∧].

(a)   Most of the wounds for the English healed up quickly. [∧] The French suffered arrow attacks.
(b)   The English had more chance of survival because they hadn't had arrows fired at them and most of their cuts weren't deep. Fractures were put in splints. 'Unserious' deep cuts were bound up and healed quickly. [∧] The French had been attacked by arrows and there were many deep cuts.
(c)   The English's men had just slit wounds. [∧] The French had fractured skulls or overnight had died of shock of exposure.

In (b) and (c) an element of comparison is introduced by *more* and *just* respectively. A conjunction would complete the job.

Conclusion

My main aim in this chapter has been to describe some of the main features of written text organization set in a context that, on the one hand, differentiates the written mode from the spoken and, on the other, relates to the types of writing commonly required in school. The emphasis on cause–effect and comparison–contrast is, in this sense, entirely consistent with the high frequency with which such types of writing are called for in O and A level and CSE essay questions.

I have endeavoured to show that text organization operates at successive levels and that it is possible in reasonably precise terms to relate organizational problems to particular writing tasks. Thus a teacher should be able to anticipate the inherent demands of writing tasks – that, for instance, to ask pupils to describe the stages of a scientific experiment is a different – and usually less demanding task organizationally – than to require them to compare two sets of results or to account for specific reactions. Further implications for classroom practice are discussed in the last chapter.

Suggested Further Reading

Brown, G., and Yule, G. (1983), *Discourse Analysis* offers an excellent introduction to the subject.

Dillon, G. L. (1981), *Constructing Texts* is an interesting attempt to discuss writing from an organizational perspective. It is not a systematic study but is most approachable and full of useful insights.

Halliday, M. A. K., and Hasan, R. (1976), *Cohesion in English* is the standard reference work on intersentential cohesion.

Kress, G. (1982), *Learning to Write* is a pioneering work, particularly valuable for a discussion of speech–writing differences and of children's developing concept of 'sentence'.

Quirk, R. *et al.* (1972), *A Grammar of Contemporary English* is an indispensable reference work. Section 10 offers a succinct statement of types of intersentential linkage.

5 Undeveloped Discourse: Some Factors Affecting the Adequacy of Children's Non-fictional Written Discourses

MICHAEL HOEY

In a previous book, I make explicit a number of claims about the nature of **written discourse**, a phrase I use in much the same way as other contributors to this book use the word **text**. My justification for this choice of terminology is given in Hoey (1983b). These claims have always been present in unstated form in the work of Eugene Winter and his associates (see, in particular, Winter 1974, 1976, 1977 and 1979, Jordan 1980 and 1984). I claim that

> on the basis of (1) cultural and linguistic expectations about the type of discourse encountered, and (2) what the writer/speaker has already said . . . a reader/listener hazards guesses as to the content to come and its relationship to what has preceded. In so far as they guess correctly, they have a smooth ride; in so far as they guess wrongly, their comprehension is slowed down to some extent. If they consistently guess wrongly, it can be doubted whether they properly comprehend at all, though the fault may lie with either encoder or decoder. (Hoey, 1983a, p. 170)

I suggest that the reader's guesses can be represented as questions asked of the discourse, and note that

> the three possible results of a reader's scanning of a sentence – recognition of the sentence as answering the reader's question, recognition of the sentence as answering another, unanticipated, question, and non-recognition of the sentence as answering any question, anticipated or otherwise – are all the offspring of expectation and signalling. In the first place the reader interprets the sentence as an answer to one of his or her questions by using signals within the sentence as clues to how it relates to its predecessor. (ibid., p. 171)

The signals presuppose a competent writer:

When a relation is signalled, a message is being communicated about
the way in which the discourse should be interpreted; the writer is telling his or her reader to interpret the juxtaposition of the parts of his or
her discourse in a particular way. (ibid., p.178)

What I want to do in this chapter is consider the writing of children
at the stage when they are acquiring their competence as writers, when
they are learning to signal to their readers the relations between the
parts of their discourse, that is, in their first year at secondary school.

I use **relations** in the way first proposed in 1968 by Winter. He says,
'A clause relation is the cognitive process whereby we interpret the
meaning of a sentence or group of sentences in the light of its adjoin-
ing sentence or group of sentences' (Winter, 1971). In other words,
clause relations are concerned with the meanings we assign to· the
juxtaposition of pieces of information. For example: When we read
the pair (from E. Blyton's *Bertie's New Braces*):

Peter went red. He knew he'd been silly.

we read the second as providing a **reason** for the first. This relation
could have been made explicit for the reader by the insertion of
because or *so* (if the sentences are reversed) or *the reason*, that is, the
reason Peter went red was that he knew he'd been silly. Winter
discusses the ways in which relations may be signalled (1974, 1977 and
1979); see also Hoey (1979a).

Winter also divides clause relations into two broad classes – the
Logical Sequence relations and the Matching relations (1974).
Examples of the first class are **time sequence** and **cause–consequence**;
examples of the second include **contrast** and **general–particular**. He
further discusses clause relations in Winter (1977, 1979, 1982). Others
who have also made use of the same or a closely related concept are
Ballard *et al*. (1971), Beekman and Callow (1974) and Graustein and
Thiele (1980).

The samples I am using as my data were derived from the Open
University's post-experience course unit and can be divided into three
main groups:

eight pieces of work on an experiment with soup temperature
eight pieces of work on an experiment with vacuum
eight pieces of criticism or discussion of a poem of the child's choice.

The first group can be found in Appendix I to this chapter; the second
and third groups of pieces were written by the same children and a
selection can be found in Appendix II. The questions I want to consider are:

(a) to what extent do the children show their awareness of the reader in terms of their signalling? Coupled with this is an alternative question: to what extent do the children reflect their understanding of the material in terms of their signalling? Although these questions are very different, I know of no way at the moment of separating them.

(b) to what extent do the children show awareness of the reader in any other way?

We begin with the former of these questions.

In adult life the task of writing up a science experiment requires the ability to encode time sequence, to show the relationships holding between events, and to organize the whole so as to show how each part fits into the whole. All the children in the materials under review show themselves to be able to do the first. All those writing up the temperature experiment describe the experiment in terms of time sequence. Where they differ is in how they signal time sequence. By far the most common is *then*, as in this extract from Sara's report (spelling clarified).

> When we got in the class room we sat down the teacher was talking to us and the children were answering the question <u>then</u> the teacher told us to get something like a bunsen burner, tripod, glass beaker containing some water, soup powder, glass rod, asbestos mat, wire gauze. <u>Then</u> we lit the bunsen burner turned it on the yellow flame until the water boiled <u>then</u> we put the thermometer in the boiling hot water and see what it was, it was 100% hot. <u>Then</u> we tip the soup powder in the water. We turned the bunsen burner off . . .

Compare this with the following piece of Joanna's, in which a whole range of devices is used to signal time sequence:

> <u>First of all</u> we placed the equipment as shown in diagram. We <u>then</u> put 3cm of water in the beaker. <u>After this</u> we turned Bunsens air hold to close and <u>then</u> lit it. We left this to boil <u>when it boiled</u> we took the temperature of the water. <u>It was then</u> we added the powder tomato soup. We stirred it in <u>then</u> divided it into two cups one cup had a lid over it the other didn't. We <u>then</u> left this for approximately 10 to 11 minutes. <u>After that</u> we took the temperature of each one we did this to find the difference between the two temperatures.

In this discourse, *after this*, *when it boiled* and *after that* explicitly place events in the context of what precedes them, which *then* only does implicitly. Furthermore, two of the uses of *then* are to connect events encoded in the same sentence and a third is focused on as of special importance (*It was then*). Joanna has, in short, used all the tricks of the trade to disguise the fact that her sentences are only linked by simple time sequence. It is important to notice that the difference between the two girls' work is, in this respect, cosmetic only. Both have conceived of the experiment in the same way, and while variation in signalling of sequence is to be encouraged (within reason) it is no substitute for the more considered connection evidenced by more specific clause relations.

There is, however, a further difference between the work of the two girls which is of greater significance. Time sequence in language is not, as it may seem, a completely natural phenomenon. Events do not occur as discrete units in succession; the truth is, rather, that time is experienced as a continuous flow in which events have no clear-cut identity. **Events**, in other words, are activities in time deemed by the writer to be significant and therefore worthy to be reported. In part Sara's piece of work differs from Joanna's in the type of event she has considered worthy of reporting. Sara's time-sequenced events include talking in class, lighting the bunsen burner, and people testing the soup. Joanna's, on the other hand, are restricted to stages of the experiment. The events have been selected as worth reporting because they each contribute to answering the question 'Can you tell me how you set about testing whether soup stays hotter in an enclosed cup?'; they are, in other words, relevant to writing up the experiment. Sara's events, on the other hand, have been selected on the basis of their answering the question 'Can you tell me what you did in class today?'; as such they are often irrelevant to the experiment. The difference between the two can be highlighted by paraphrasing the relationship between the sentences of Joanna's piece as follows:

> The first step in the experiment was that we placed the equipment as shown in diagram. The next step was that we put 3cm of water in the beaker. The next step was that we turned Bunsens air hold to close. . . .

No such tight paraphrase connection can be added to Sara's text. Here only a much more general connection such as 'The first thing we did' is possible.

Consider now the following piece by Andrew:

> First we got an asbestos mat incase we spilt the boiling water, an asbestos dosn't burn. Then we got a tripod to hold to glass beaker above the bunser burner. Under the beaker is a wire gauze. We put the soup powder in after the water had boiled, then we put one lid on one container and the other without. Then after about 3 minutes after we took the temperature of the lided one and it was 63 degree centigrade and the one without the lid 57 degrees centigrade.
>
> And before we lit the busen burner we took the temperature of the water and it was 27½ degrees centigrade. When we took the temperature of the water when it was boiled it was 97 degrees centigrade.

Andrew's piece of work is another where the writer has selected his events for placing in time sequence on the basis of too general a question. The first four sentences of Andrew's answer do not really answer the question 'How did you set about testing whether soup stays hotter in an enclosed container?' but rather the question 'What did you do in connection with the experiment?' As evidence of this, notice that we cannot say:

> The first step in the experiment was that we got an asbestos mat, in case we spilt the boiling water.

In short, time sequence may be used to connect events which have been selected for reporting on the basis of one of a number of questions of differing generality. Relevance can be defined in terms of the question being answered. If the question is slightly too general, as in the case of Andrew's piece of work, the effect is one of lack of focus. We are left doubtful as to whether he fully sees the point of the experiment he has done. (An alternative explanation for Andrew's emphasis will be given below.) If the question is *much* too general, as in Sara's case, then we can be fairly confident that the writer either has not understood the purpose of the experiment or has not understood the relationship of the writing act to the experiment. Either way the consequences are more serious.

Although Joanna's work is relevant, it is not altogether well formed. We noted earlier that an adult's account of an experiment would normally be held together by time sequence, more specific clause relations, and a sense of overall organization. Joanna's text shows little evidence of clauses being brought together in relationships more precise than that of time sequence and no evidence of structuring at all. In this respect she is fairly typical of the sample.

On the whole, the majority of the science texts here cannot be analysed in terms of clause relations other than time sequence. A number of types of considered connection might have been predicted between clauses or sentences if the children had fully understood the experiment they were reporting:

(a)   **instrument-purpose** relations, answering the question 'Why did you do that?' or 'What was that for?'
(b)   **matching comparison** or **contrast** relations, answering the question 'What was the difference between the two cups' temperature?'
(c)   **basis-conclusion** relations, answering the question 'What did you conclude from this?' Connected with this, some evidence of **generalization** might have been expected.

It will be noticed that Joanna's work, though relevant, at no point answers the question 'Why did you do that?' until the very last sentence, and then the answer is not complete. Nor is there any evidence of comparison or deduction/generalization. This is worrying since a comparison of temperatures is at the heart of the experiment. Moreover, the questions 'Why are you doing something?' and 'What conclusions do you draw from what you have done?' are central to the learning process. It follows that we have to reserve judgement on whether Joanna shows evidence of learning; at very least we must say that she has not learnt to signal to her reader the relations she perceives.

An example of a piece of work that does show evidence of considered connection is Lara's. She shows the ability to use matching comparison, for example in the following:

> We lit the bunsen burner and took the temperature. It was 39° centigrade. Then we waited for it to boil. When it had boiled we again took the temperature. This time it was 100° centigrade.

The signals of the comparison are the repetition of the pattern *it was x° centigrade again* which shows that we have two comparable instances and *this time* which shows that we have a difference between the two instances. Likewise, she shows in her last two sentences the ability to use the **basis–conclusion** relation, though she does not use **generalization**. She also shows in her first sentence an awareness of purpose; which we shall return to below. From this evidence we can reasonably infer that Lara understands both the experiment and the writing process.

Lara also shows evidence of being able to structure her writing – the third factor in making discourses hold together. She is, however, almost alone in this. This is not because of any deficiencies in the preparation of the writing task by the teacher in question. In her worksheet, the teacher sets out the experiment in a clear **problem–solution** pattern (see Winter, 1976; Hoey, 1979b, 1983a; Jordan, 1980, 1984), with the second sentence 'You are going to check whether the advert is true' answering the question 'What method of solution is available?' Furthermore, in her oral instructions she makes the point that 'When you're actually writing up your experiment, can you make sure that you try and write it up as if the person you're writing the work for wasn't there at all?' Nevertheless only two of the eight answers can be said to be intelligible without prior knowledge of the experiment being described and, of these, one (Paul's) radically mistakes in another way the nature of the writing task being demanded of him. Lara's, then, is alone in being structured and self-contained.

Why is this, particularly as the teacher had taken pains to avoid the children's writing being flawed in this way? The answer is two-fold.

First, some of the children have failed to recognize the nature of the writing task and the concomitant requirements of the 'reader'. Secondly, in addition, some of the children appear to have not fully understood the purpose of the experiment they are describing.

To deal with the second factor first, three of the children in the sample, including Andrew and Sara, have not fully understood the purpose of the experiment. Sara, as we have already seen, has no sense of which events are significant and which are trivial. Andrew is better in this respect but makes no mention of the purpose of the experiment. He has striven to meet the teacher's requirements; he begins with detailed description of the equipment used but his account, like Sara's, is unstructured and without a statement of purpose.

Failure to recognize the special requirements of the writing task, the other factor involved in children's failure to produce intelligible accounts, is very understandable. When we talk, the person we are talking to is normally standing in front of us or is on the telephone. Every remark we make, therefore, has a clear audience and we can often tell by the reaction we get whether we have been understood or not. Moreover, our remarks in conversation are able to take into account both what has been said earlier and any shared knowledge between us and our listeners. As such, much will be taken as read and left unsaid. All of this, of course, is self-evident; what is not evident, however, to the child is that the same is not true of writing. Children do not always recognize that what they know is not necessarily knowledge shared by their readers. This requires a certain degree of imaginative sympathy with the intended reader that can only come with a good deal of practice.

Joanna shows signs of having understood the purpose of the experiment but not the relationship of the writing act to the experiment. She ends with a statement of purpose:

We did this to find the difference between the two temperatures

which, though by no means an adequate statement of the experiment's purpose, does indicate that the operations she has described are not merely mechanical. Another child, Ollie, is more to the point:

. . . the one with the highest recording was with the lid on. *So the shop was right.*

He has, alone of all the children, correctly identified the purpose of the experiment as being to evaluate the truth of the shop's claim. Even Lara, whose work is in most other respects better formed, only states her results in specific terms.

Both Ollie and Joanna have, however, failed to appreciate the difference between writing up an experiment for a reader who was not present when it was done and talking to someone who was. Ollie starts *We first heated up the water* ... which presupposes that the reader knows both what water is being referred to and why it is being heated up; this of course goes flatly against the teacher's (spoken) request 'You don't just say you started boiling the water, you'd have to say what apparatus you were using' and so on. Joanna launches straight into her account with *First of all we placed the equipment as shown in diagram* which does at least meet the teacher's requirement but fails to give any indication again of why the experiment was being done.

If we turn now to the two sets of work done by the other group of children, we will see in a magnified form the features of difference in signalling skill and lack of self-containedness of the writing. The second writing task, concerned with vacuum measurement, appears to have been a more daunting task. Of the eight pieces of work under consideration at this point, four appear to be partly or wholly copied. This suggests that factual reportage is a more frightening prospect for some children than writing of a more personal nature. (There is no evidence of copying with the 'poem' pieces from the same group of children.) This is presumably in part because reportage can be checked for accuracy and in part because it makes demands on the child's versatility in making clear the relations that hold between stated events.

There are major differences in the degree of skill with which the children handle the relations within each section of their answer. Tammy, for example, signals clearly the relationships between the clauses in her answer. For example:

When you hold your hands round the flask little bubles come out. The <u>reason why</u> the bubbles come out is <u>because</u> the heat of your hand.

Here she has signalled that the second sentence gives the reason for what is stated in the first in three ways. Likewise she has two signals of **result:**

The energy makes the little particle[s] move from each other, <u>so therefore</u> the metal bar is bigger.

Interestingly, Justine, who shares much of her wording, does not share these signals of clause relation. She omits the **reason** sentence and dilutes *so therefore* to *and theirfore*:

When you hold your hand over the flask bubbles come out of the bottom of the tube, the air comes out and we're making vacume.

and

The energy makes the little particles move apart from each other and theirfore the metal bar is bigger.

This dilution seems to reflect less certainly in the use of signals of relations. Again, Tammy writes:

We put the metal bar into the gauge and it fitted, but when we heated the bar, the bar with the busen flame exspand, so the bar wouldn't fit in the guage any more, it was to big;

which, when allowances are made for spelling and punctuation, conveys quite successfully a complex network of relations, thus:

CONTRAST
(... but)

CIRCUMSTANCE/CAUSE
(when we heated the bar)
↕
EFFECT
(the bar with the busen flame exspand)
↓
CAUSE
↕
EFFECT
(so the bar wouldn't fit in the guage any more)
↑
REASON
(it was to big)

Justine on the other hand presents the same material without the syntactic complexity and without the clause relators *but* and *when*. These are replaced by *and*.

The metal bar fitted into the gauge and we heated it the bar and the heat made the bar exspand so the bar wouldn't fit into the gauge anymore it was to big.

Likewise, Tammy's *The air has come out but the vacuum is left* becomes for Justine *The air has come out and Vacume is left* (though it is possible taking the sentence out of context to argue that this reflects a greater understanding of a vacuum by Justine). More significantly, where Tammy writes *The water has rised up to the tube and it over flows in the flask at the top. The beaker at the bottom will soon be empty and the flask will be fall*, Justine writes:

> The water rises up the tube up and down. The water travels up and comes out of the tube at the top. All the water from the beaker travels up the tube and ends up filling full the flask at the top.

The most striking feature of this is its gradual accumulation of detail through repetition. This has been described as a means of connection in a number of languages (Grimes, 1972), but it is not normal in English. If, on the other hand, the explanation is that the first two sentences are false starts and should have been crossed out, then some indication of the difficulty the child faced in this writing task is gained, since three attempts at expressing the same idea are more than one would expect in, for example, a piece of creative writing.

Justine is reasonably typical of the standard sample; she uses *when* clauses successfully and can signal simple relations. What she and most others in the sample show is that connection within sentences comes easier than connection across sentences. Apart from Tammy, only two show skill at connecting sentences, for example:

1 When we heated the bar the bar expanded and the bar couldn't fit the gauge as before. *This shows* that heating and putting energy into a metal makes it expand.
2 When the flame of a bunsen is passed over the flask the air goes out. *This causes* a vacuum and sucks the water up.

Again we find that others, sharing these children's material for the most part, have not got these connective signals.

As with the first group of children, we find that the writing often betrays a misunderstanding of the self-containedness of the writing process. Consider, for example, Tammy's piece (the numbering is the child's own):

1 When you hold your hands round the flask little bubles come out. The reason why the bubbles come out is because the heat of your hand.
2 When the bunsen burner flame is held over the flask the flame makes lots of little bubbles. The air has come out but the vacum is left.
3 The water has rised up to the tube and it over flows in the flask at the top. The beaker at the bottom will soon be empty and the flask will be fall.

There is very little connection between the three sections of this discourse, despite the fact that within each section the connections are clear. On the face of it, the discourse looks as if it suffers from the fault we have already discussed: inadequate signalling of connections.

For it could be argued that the first section is connected to the second in a matching compatibility relation which should be made clearer by the insertion of *again* after *the flame* in section 2; some degree of parallel repetition supports such as argument. Likewise, it could be argued that the last sentence of section 2 is connected to the first of section 3 in a cause–consequence relation, which needs to be made explicit by the addition of *so* or *therefore*; a causal connection certainly exists in the real world. Though plausible, however, such arguments would be mistaken. The real reason for the lack of connection between the parts lies in the child's view of the writing process as an extension of conversation. This can be shown by examining the teacher's written instructions to the children on how to go about the experiments she has prepared. They are as follows:

1   Put your hands around the flask. What happens?
2   Now warm the flask more with the flame of a bunsen burner.
3   Now let the flask cool while the glass tube is still below the surface of the water – what happens now?

It should perhaps be emphasized that these are instructions on how to go about the experiments, *not* on how to write them up. Nevertheless Tammy has clearly replied to them *as if they were still common ground*. So, if we interleave the teacher's instructions and the child's answer together, we arrive at an (almost) perfect conversation:

1   *T (experiment)*: Put your hands around the flask. What happens?

   Tammy: When you hold your hands round the flask little bubles come out. The reason why the bubbles come out is because the heat of your hand.

2   *T (experiment)*: Now warm the flask more with the flame of a bunsen burner.

   Tammy: When the bunsen burner flame is held over the flask the flame makes lots of little bubbles. The air has come out but the vacum is left.

3   *T (experiment)*: Now let the flask cool while the glass tube is still below the surface of the water – what happens now?

   Tammy: The water has rised up to the tube and it over flows in the flask at the top. The beaker at the bottom will soon be empty and the flask will be fall.

Interestingly, the two questions that the teacher asks as part of the *writing* instructions (that is, 'Why do you think there was space for the water to go into the flask? What had happened to the air?') are not answered directly. The child has structured her answer according to the experiment instructions she was given; she has not seen her answer as a self-contained piece of writing. It is important to realize that the child has in one sense made no mistake. After all, she knows that the teacher's questions are the ones she has to answer. She knows also that in normal circumstances no one else apart from the teacher will read her work. Her reaction then is thoroughly natural; why bore her teacher by repeating what they both already know? The trouble is that this judgement is often carried into adult life, where the needs of the readership may be less well defined or where records have to be kept for reference long after the time when they were written or where the person being addressed may have many communications on many topics to deal with at any one time. In such circumstances spelling out the situation becomes an important part of any communication. Five of the other discourses show whole or partial dependence on the teacher's experiment instructions. Consider Natalie's, for example. She deviates in her last sentence because she also answers the questions posed as part of the instructions on how to write up the experiment. Her text can be interwoven with the teacher's as follows:

1 *T (experiment)*: Put your hands around the flask. What happens?

   Natalie: The water in the beaker bubbles when you put your hands around the flask because the heat of your hands make the air pass down the tube and makes the water in the flask bubble when we heated the flask.

2 *T (experiment)*: Now warm the flask more with the flame of a bunsen burner.

   Natalie: The heat made the air expand till the air passed down the tube and made the water rise into the flask.

3 *(T (experiment)*: 3rd question not directly answered)
   T (writing): Why do you think there was space for the water to go into the flask — what had happened to the air?

   Natalie: I think there was space in the flask because the bubbles had the air from the flask so thir was room.

Notice that, with both Tammy and Natalie, repetition between teacher's question and child's answer is often quite high, for example:

(from Tammy's piece)

T: Put your hands around the flask. What happens?

Tammy: When you hold your hands round the flask little
         bubles come out.

(from Natalie's piece)

T: Why do you think there was space for the water to go
         into the flask — what had happened to the air?

Natalie: I think there was space in the flask because the
         bubbles had the air from the flask so thir was room.

To sum up the position here stated, the children's science texts at times show evidence of more cohesion with the teacher's instructions than they have internally.

Another type of dependence on something outside the child's own text is manifested in the discussion of the poems. The children are not tempted to echo too closely the teacher's instructions in this case because her instructions are couched as a number of fairly general alternatives, but they are tempted to mould their answers to the poems rather than allow them to stand as complete pieces of writing on their own. Consequently we get several examples of apparent vagueness or absence of connection. An example is Tammy's (I have numbered the sentences for convenience of reference):

S1   The first paragraph is sort of describing that everything is bigger than the fly, S2 the poet is sort of saying this is the way the fly sees everything. S3 One of the quotation I like is

> 'How large unto the tiny fly
> Must little things appear!'

S4   When he says a rosebud like a feather bed, Its prickle like a spear, he sort of mean that a rosebud is so soft, and its prickle is sharp. Just like a spear. S5 Another quotation I like is

> 'A dewdrop like a looking-glass,
> A hair like golden wire.'

S6   He means a drop of rain on the grass, and on the second line he means a piece of hair is like a golden wire.

In many respects this is one of the better answers (as was the same child's science answer). Nevertheless, several of the sentences seem either unconnected or weakly connected to the sentences that surround them. For example, S3 seems unconnected to both S1 and S2, there being connection neither by repetition nor by an implicit question being answered. Likewise, S4 is only weakly connected to S2 and not at all to S1 and S3. S5, too, is not connected to S4, though it is strongly connected to S3 and S6. Some of these 'faults', however, disappear if we read the answer alongside the poem which it is interpreting/evaluating:

	S1 The first paragraph is sort of describing that everything is bigger than the fly,
How large unto the tiny fly Must little things appear!	**S2** The poet is sort of saying this is the way the fly sees everything.
	S3 One of the quotation I like is 'How large unto the tiny fly Must little things appear!'
A rosebud like a feather bed, Its prickle like a spear;	**S4** When he says a rosebud like a feather bed, Its prickle like a spear, he sort of mean that a rosebud is so soft, and its prickle is sharp. Just like a spear.
A dewdrop like a looking-glass A hair like golden wire;	**S5** Another quotation I like is 'A dewdrop like a looking-glass, A hair like golden wire.'
	S6 He means a drop of rain on the grass, and on the second line he means a piece of hair is like a golden wire.

If read across from left to right, it is nearly completely coherent, and a reversal of S2 and S3 makes it still closer to being completely so. In other words, S4 and S5 connect not to their predecessors in the text but to the next pair of lines in the poem. Indeed, it can now be argued that even S2 is only fortuitously connected to the generalization in S1; S1 is a summary of what the whole poem is about. It happens that the first two lines are themselves a summary of the poem. Four of the other pupils, incidentally, use the poem to organize the answer to varying extents.

We have looked in the latter part of this chapter at several ways in which a child can make his or her own text dependent upon a previous text in a way that has for the most part to be avoided in adult writing.

It must be emphasized that though this is a potential writing hazard it may go hand in hand with careful thinking. So Tammy, for example, shows some insight into the poem she is examining and some understanding of what poetry study can involve. Some of the others whose pieces of work are more self-contained are perhaps somewhat less capable of commenting pertinently. To some extent, the same is true of the science pieces. Those who have concentrated on answering the teacher's questions at the expense of internal coherence have in some cases succeeded in being more relevant than several of those whose work is more self-contained. It follows that any guidance must be sensitive to the fact that the need to develop writing skills and the need to develop skills appropriate to a particular discipline may at times be in conflict.

Appendix I

WORKSHEET: MAKING SOUP
This advert was seen in a shop.

'TAKE HOME OUR SOUP – IT STAYS HOT FOR HOURS IN OUR SOUPER CONTAINERS!'

You are going to check whether the advert is really true.

Equipment:
(1) Bunsen burner
(2) Tripod
(3) Asbestos mat
(4) Wire gauze
(5) Glass beaker containing a depth of 3cm of water
(6) Soup powder
(7) Glass rod

Instructions
(1) Place the beaker of water on the tripod, light the bunsen burner and bring the water to the boil.
(2) Put in two spatula measures of soup powder and stir with the glass rod.
(3) Turn off the bunsen burner.

The Experiment
Carefully lift the beaker off the tripod.
Pour half of the soup into each of the containers. Use a thermometer to measure the temperature of the soup in each container.
What is the temperature of each container?
_____

Put a lid on one container.
Leave the containers for about 30 minutes and then measure the temperature of each container.

MAKING SOUP SARA

When we got in the class room we sat down the teacher was tooking to us and the children were answering the question then the teacher told us to get something like a bunsen burner, tripod, glass beaker containing some water, soup powder, glass rod, asbestos mat, wire gauze. Then we lit the bunsen burner trend in on the yellow flame in tell the water bobed then we put the thermometer in the boiling hot water and see what it was, it was 100% hot. Then we tip the soup powder in the water – we tound the bunsen burner off, and we see if the soup all right and we see the temperature of the soup if it was quit hot. We was wrighting down what it was and at the end we called try the soup and it was tomto soup, but I did not try it, it did not smell very nice but over people tryed it. We was film by the camers. There wore three cammers and we had to stop in some parts when the teacher was speaking to us and we had to repeat it again.

[diagram omitted]

MAKING SOUP JOANNA

A list of apparatus	Tripod
Bunsen burner	Asbestos mat
Beaker	Wire gauze

First of all we placed the equipment as shown in diagram. We then put 3cm of water in the beaker. After this we turned Bunsens air hold to close and then lit it. We left this to boil when it boiled we took the temperature of the water. It was then we added the powder tomato soup. We stirred it in then divided it into two cups one cup had a lid over it the other didn't. We then left this for approximately 10 to 11 minutes. After that we took the temperature of each one we did this to find the difference between the two temperatures.

[diagram omitted]

ANDREW

[diagram omitted]

This is apparatus I used (above).

First we got an asbestos mat incase we spilt the boiling water, an asbestos dosn't burn. Then we got a tripod to hold to glass beaker above the bunser burner. Under the beaker is a wire gauze. We put the soup powder in after the water had boiled, then we put one lid on one container and the other without.

Then after about 3 minutes after we took the temperature of the lided one and it was 63 degree centigrade and the one without the lid 57 degrees centigrade.

And before we lit the busen burner we took the temperature of the water and it was 27½ degrees centigrade. When we took the temperature of the water when it was boiled it was 97 degrees centigrade.

HOT SOUP EXPERIMENT   LARA
Equipment

Bunson Burner	Soup powder
Tripod	Mixing Rod
Asbestos Mat	Water
Wire Gauze	Thermometer
Glass Beaker	

Experiment
To see if soup is hotter in a container with a lid on or off.

What we did
First of all we set up our equipment as in the diagram i.e. Asbestos mat on the table, tripod on the mat, metal grid on the tripod, beaker on the grid. Water in the beaker. Underneath the tripod is a bunsen burner which is attached to a gas tap.
We lit the bunsen burner and took the temperature. It was 39° centigrade. Then we waited for it to boil. When it had boiled we again took the temperature. This time it was 100° centigrade. Then we poured the soup powder into the water and using the mixing rod we stirred it until all the lumps had gone. Then we poured in into two containers putting a lid on one and leaving the other one open. We waited for fifteen minutes.

Result
The soup in the container with a lid was hotter than the other one. It was 70° centigrade whilst the other one was $63\frac{1}{2}^\circ$ centigrade.

MAKING SOUP   OLLIE
We first heated up the water and measured the tempreture. We poured in the tomatoe soup and put the soup and put a lid on one of them and waited for aboute seven minnits and then took the tempreture and the one with the highest recording was with the lid on. So the shop was right.

Appendix II

WORKSHEET: HEATING A GAS
On this table you will see what happens when a gas is heated
Set up the apparatus below

[illustration omitted]   glass flask containing air
                            glass tube
                            beaker containing water

(1)   Put your hands around the flask.
      What happens?
(2)   Now warm the flask more with the flame of a bunsen burner.
(3)   Now let the flask cool while the glass tube is still below the sur-
      face of the water — what happens now?

Write up the experiment in your own words — why do you think there was space for the water to go into flask — what had happened to the air?

You may like to use these words:

heat, energy, vacuum, movement.

HEATING A GAS   TAMMY

(1)   When you hold your hands round the flask little bubles come out. The reason why the bubbles come out is because the heat of your hand.

(2)   When the bunsen burner flame is held over the flask the flame makes lots of little bubbles. The air has come out but the vacum is left.

(3)   The water has rised up to the tube and it over flows in the flask at the top. The beaker at the bottom will soon be empty and the flask will be fall.

Heating the Bar

(1)   We put the metal bar into the gauge and it fitted, but when we heated the bar, the bar with the busen flame exspand, so the bar wouldn't fit in the guage any more, it was to big. The energy makes the little particle move from each other, so therefore the metal bar is bigger.

Third experiment Heating a liquid

[not finished]

HEATING A GAS   JUSTINE

(1)   When you hold your hand over the flask bubbles come out of the bottom of the tube, the air comes out and we're making Vacume.

(2)   When the bunsen burner flame is held over the flask the flame makes lots of bubbles.

The air has come out and Vacume is left.

(3)   The water rises up the tube up and down. The water travels up and comes out of the tube at the top. All the water from the beaker travels up the tube and ends up filling full the flask at the top.

Second Experiment   Heating the bar

(1)   The metal bar fitted into the gauge and we heated it the bar and the heat made the bar exspand so the bar wouldn't fit into the gauge anymore it was to big.

The energy makes the little particles move apart from each other the theirfore the metal bar is bigger.

Third Experiment   Heating a Liquid

[not finished]

HEATING A GAS   NATALIE

The water in the beaker bubbles when you put your hands around the flask because the heat of your hands make the air pass down the tube and makes the water in the flask bubble when we heated the flask. This heat make the air expand till the air passed down the tube and made the water rise into the flask. I think there was space in the flask because the bubbles had the air from the flask so thir was room.

Heating a Iron and Brass bar
After heating the iron and brass bar was heated it started to bend.

[not finished]

THE FLY by Walter De La Mare   TAMMY

The first paragraph is sort of describing that everything is bigger than the fly, the poet is sort of saying this is the way the fly sees everything. One of the quotation I like is

> 'How large unto the tiny fly
> Must little things appear!'

When he says a rosebud like a feather bed, Its prickle like a spear, he sort of mean that a rosebud is so soft, and its prickle is sharp. Just like a spear. Another quotation I like is

> 'A dewdrop like a looking-glass,
> A hair like golden wire.'

He means a drop of rain on the grass, and on the second line he means a piece of hair is like a golden wire.

Suggested Further Reading

Hoey, M. (1983a), *On the Surface of Discourse* provides an ideal introduction to methods of analysing text types through features such as clause relations and signalling.

Jordan, M. (1984), *Rhetoric of Everyday English Texts* has a similar perspective and illustrates its applicability to a varied range of short texts.

Winter, E. (1977), 'A clause-relational approach to English texts – a study of some predictive lexical items in written discourse' is a special issue of *Instructional Science* devoted to an aspect of intersentential linkage not previously described systematically. It is a seminal paper.

6 Good Word! Vocabulary, Style and Coherence in Children's Writing

RONALD CARTER

1 Introduction

Vocabulary is a relatively neglected area of writing development. The focus for much recent work within the framework of 'language in education' has been on either syntax, cohesion or situational context in different writing activities. Vocabulary, or lexis, as some linguists prefer to call it, has similarly been a relatively neglected area in linguistics. Again the focus has been largely on syntax and, more recently, on discourse. Yet, for most teachers, vocabulary is important. For better or worse, 'he has a good vocabulary' is a distinct sign of praise. 'Good word' is regularly written by teachers in the margins of pupils' writing. Pupils are often exhorted to make greater use of a dictionary or thesaurus. Socially-responsible linguists, therefore, have a duty to make accessible to teachers what findings there are regarding the structure of vocabulary in English. The more that is known about lexis, as with other levels of language organization, the better equipped teachers will be to effect a systematic and principled development and assessment of vocabulary use.

In this chapter I shall concentrate on vocabulary in children's writing with particular reference to its role in the overall coherence of a text. I shall provide some hypotheses regarding vocabulary development and try to show how different aspects of lexical organization can operate according to the nature of the writing task. This chapter is, therefore, both speculative and investigative. The speculation comes with the original hypotheses which are then investigated. As with all hypotheses, certain features are corroborated, others not attested and still others left requiring further investigation, and the chapter should, therefore, be seen in the light of such inevitable constraints. In keeping with several other chapters in this book, examples are drawn from the work of eleven-year-old pupils at the point of transition from junior to secondary school.

2 What's in a Word

This is not the place for a detailed definition of a word. Such a definition directly involves linguistic, philosophical and semiotic criteria –
to mention but three areas of concern. Within linguistics, it can involve syntactic, morphological and phonological (including supra-
segmental) criteria. Reviews of the literature on the definition of a
word are plentiful. Among the most helpful and clear are Lyons
(1977; 1981).

My intention here is to make clear only those characteristics of
words which I consider it most helpful and enabling for us to operate
with for the purposes outlined above. To do this, some basic
metalanguage will need to be introduced. The concepts and
characteristics described by the metalanguage are necessary. Short
cuts and simplifications can be provided but serious analysis of
children's language is not usually helped by such routes. I take this
path recognizing that many who use this book will be busy people but
give an assurance herewith that the terms introduced do provide a
basis for subsequent analysis of children's writing.

2.1 Closed-Class v. Open-Class Lexical Items

For a start, the term **lexical items** or **lexemes** will be preferred to word.
This allows us to see phrasal lexemes like 'kick the bucket' (to die) or
'it's raining *cats and dogs'* as single lexical items, even if they are made
up of separate orthographic words, that is, sequences of letters bound
on either side by a space as in 'kick-the-bucket'. **Closed-class** lexical
items comprise the limited and finite range of words which occur
regularly and play an indispensible part in the creation of the
coherence of a piece of discourse (which, incidentally, suggests that
teachers should ensure that children learn how to spell them correctly
before too much emphasis is put on spelling open-class words).
Closed-class items are words such as *a, an, the, must, because, with,
we, them,* and so on. That is, mostly pronouns, articles, auxiliary
verbs, conjunctions. Linguists have used a variety of terms for such
closed-class items, for example, grammatical words, empty words,
structural words, function words, functors, and so on. **Open-class**
items include nouns, adjectives, verbs, adverbs, and so on. The range
of open-class items is theoretically non-finite. Their role in discourse
is not as limited to syntactic functions as closed-class items. They
usually carry more information and are less predictable. Linguists also
know them by the terms full words, content words, lexical words.

Much work has been undertaken on the role of closed-class words
in intersentential relations; that is, study of their role in syntax has
been extended to an exploration of how such words operate between
and across sentences and thus contribute to the cohesion of a text (see,

for example, Halliday and Hasan, 1976; Winter, 1977; Nash, 1980). For example, the following three sentences, taken from the beginning of a piece of children's writing which we shall examine in section 6, lack cohesion:

S1   The giant ant is very, very big.
S2   All the children run away and the dogs grumble.
S3   And we stare at t.v.

(Passage A)

Here it is not clear whether the 'we' refers to the children in sentence 2; nor is there any preceding referent for '*the* children' and '*the* dogs'. There is thus no explicitly signalled relation between the sentences. Devices of simple repetition and the use of grammatical words could be deployed to secure greater cohesion. For example: 'The giant ant is very, very big. Our children run away from it and our dogs grumble very loud. We are afraid of the ant and stare at t.v.'

But the presence of cohesive devices alone cannot ensure the organization of a text. Take the following example (again from a piece of children's writing to be discussed in greater detail subsequently):

S1   Then we found our way outside from the cloak room.
S2   Next we went outside into the pleasents and we practest the fire drill makeing sure we were quick to line up in the pleasent.
S3   Then we went back through the cloak room.
S4   Then we had break and Jill dropped the crisps.
S5   We could go into the dining room or go out-side and eat our food.

(Passage B)

This piece of writing is cohesive in so far as several devices (for example *we*, *then*, *next*, and so on) underline a connectedness between the sentences but it is not consistently coherent. Part of the problem is the lack of variation in the devices used but, even if changes were made or more cohesive items added, it is unlikely that they would contribute significantly to the underlying organization of the text or remedy the general 'flatness' of the vocabulary used. When teachers write 'good word' and put a tick in the margin it is my claim that they are responding not merely to a word in isolation but signalling their perception that it contributes to the coherence and impact of the text as a whole.

Finally, in this brief discussion of 'what's in a word', we should try to locate more precisely what in vocabulary might underly our use of terms such as impact or flatness. It has to be recognized that judgement here may be more variable from one individual to another but it is certainly an impression among teachers to whom I have shown the two passages above that passage A contains unusual but expressive lexical choices not to be found in passage B. Examples pointed to are 'dogs grumble' and 'stare at t.v.'. Further exploration of 'expressivity' is offered below but we should note here that expressive words alone – however many and varied they might be – do not make for a well-organized coherent text, that relations *between* words are as important as what is *in* the word and that our judgements of effectiveness may also be relative to the category of writing undertaken. Here, for example, we might expect more expressive words in descriptive writing about a giant ant than in a report on a sequence of actions performed in a day at school.

To summarize, then, we may say that the number and range of grammatical words which contribute to the cohesion of a text are of significance in effective writing. But counting cohesive devices will not explain why some pieces of writing can be perceived to be better organized than others (for further discussion, see Hasan, 1980; Morgan and Sellner, 1980). Similarly, density and variability of open-class lexical words should be encouraged in children's writing but a relation of types to token – that is, the number of different words in a text (**types**) expressed as a relation of the total number of words (**tokens**) – is not of itself an effective measure of expressivity and cannot of itself either ensure that a text is coherent or account for why one text might be marked higher or lower than another for its use of vocabulary. (See Harpin, 1976 for discussion of type–token ratios as well as research critical of this measure by North, 1982.) Before proceeding to further investigation it is necessary, therefore, to give consideration to the kinds of relations in words – expressive and otherwise – which exist *between* and *across* different items in the structure of the lexicon. Such investigation begins with what is appropriately termed **structural semantics**.

2.2 Structural Semantics

The development of structural semantics owes much to work by John Lyons on sense relations in vocabulary. **Referential meaning** is the term used to describe the direct relation between a word and the object, notion or entity to which it refers; **sense relations** are the patterns of meanings contracted by one word with other words. The most significant of sense relations are **synonymy**, **antonymy** and **hyponymy**. (For a fuller review and definition of other terms such as converseness, incompatibility and opposition, see Lyons, 1981.)

Synonyms and antonyms are generally well understood but the term **hyponym** may require some explanation. As we shall see, it is also a concept which may be of some value in a model for vocabulary organization and writing development. Hyponymy may be loosely described as asymmetrical synonymy. *Tulips* and *roses* are hyponyms, for example, and are linked by their common inclusion under a

superordinate (or hyponym) *flower* in whose class they belong. The following diagram illustrates the principle of the relationship:

BUILDING
factory
hospital
HOUSE cottage, bungalow, villa, mansion
museum
theatre
school

Here house is a hyponym of building but also serves as a superordinate of another set of hyponyms. Hyponymy is usually, but not necessarily, confined to the syntactic class of noun.

2.3 Collocations

The **collocation** of a word can be generally defined by the statement that 'words are known by the company they keep'. That is, the construction in which the word is to occur, the partners it can have, may be a determinant of choice. Lexical items are required to 'fit' their collocates; they must harmonize with their verbal neighbours. For example, *lean* is a collocate of *meat*. We can speak of 'lean meat' but not usually of 'skinny meat'. Where unusual collocations are employed the writer may be intending to produce a particular stylistic effect but it is not conventionally permissible. Some words have a very wide span of collocates, for instance, 'nice', 'pretty'; others have a very restricted range. Sometimes the collocational relationship can be stereotypical and the formation of clichés results.

Another important aspect of collocation concerns the construction of **lexical sets**. Certain lexical items share collocational ranges. For example, it is predictable that 'water', 'liquid', 'milk' will share many collocates such as 'glass', 'refresh', 'pour'. Lexical items that overlap in their ranges or collocational 'span' are called a lexical set. Other items such as, for example, 'stag', 'geometry' and 'innocence' would, conversely, be unlikely to form a lexical set.

Psycholinguistic tests demonstrate that recall of words along a stretch of text is more accessible than finding synonymic, antonymic or hyponymic substitutes or alternatives. In other words, it is usually easier to provide a collocate than a synonym, particularly a synonym of the same syntactic class. (See Anglin, 1970 reported in Appendix 1. Research of this kind can be of significance for work in classroom vocabulary development.)

2.4 Expressive v. Non-expressive: The Notion of Core Vocabulary

Very approximately, the non-expressive meaning of a word is its denotative or referential properties. It is the basic meaning of a word.

Cat, for example, is the non-expressive meaning of the object to which the word 'cat' conventionally points. Expressive lexemes associated with cat would be 'pussy' or 'kitty'. Such words carry connotative or stylistic meanings which express an attitude or emotion or effect on the part of the user of the word and/or is produced in the recipient of the word by what can be generally termed the **association** it carries. (Languages vary greatly in the ways in which they can convey expressive meaning. English does not usually grammaticalize such meaning but relies instead on vocabulary and (especially in spoken English) intonation to produce such effects.) It should be noted, however, that 'cat' can be used expressively. For example, 'the big cats' (big game) or 'he's like a cat' (agile). But here the word is displaced slightly from its referent and the qualities associated with the object are invoked. The associations produced by a word work externally, so to speak, invoking the familiar contexts of use or situation in which the word is found or echoing and reinforcing the associations of the other words with which it combines.

Non-expressive meaning is thus more neutral or, as linguists prefer to term it, **unmarked**. Expressive meaning in vocabulary will usually be marked in some way to produce an effect. A more intuitive label for such kinds of vocabulary might be **core** vocabulary (non-expressive) or **non-core** vocabulary (expressive). From now on these will be the main labels or categories of expressivity to which I will refer.

To conclude this section on expressive meaning, in which a large number of synonymous or interchangeable terms have been introduced, it will be as well to reassemble the main points outlined under the collective heads of core and non-core vocabulary. This is a necessary process because core and non-core lexis may occur to differing degrees in different kinds of writing and needs to be recognized accordingly. It will be seen, too, that an account of core and non-core vocabulary overlaps with some of the points made above about sense and meaning relations and the processes will thus also serve as a partial summary of this whole section. My ultimate purpose is to get round to offering a framework within which comments on pupils' writing in the form of: 'Very expressive'; 'you need to extend your vocabulary'; 'use more varied words'; 'you can't use this word here'; 'inappropriate choice of words'; 'use simpler words'; 'use bigger words'; 'you express yourself in words very clearly and well'; 'not coherent'; 'bad style'; 'does not make sense here'; and so on, can be more systematically tied to formal features in the organization of lexis in English.

2.5   Core Vocabulary: Summary
(1)   Core vocabulary is characterized by collocational frequency. Core

words have a wide span of collocation. *Fat* is a core word: fat salary, fat cheque, fat man; *corpulent* is non-core.

(2) Core vocabulary will be basically neutral or unmarked in meaning. For example, snigger, grin, smirk, grimace, beam, smile: of these *smile* is the core word. Its neutrality can be gauged by the fact that the other words can be or tend to be defined as core word plus adverb, for example, beam = smile happily; smirk = smile knowingly or complacently. Conversely, smile cannot be described in terms of the other words plus adverb. It requires a definition of its basic semantic components.

(3) Superordinates are often core words.

(4) Core words often have clear antonyms; hot − cold; walk − run; laugh − cry. Antonyms for 'corpulent' or 'emaciated' are more difficult to find.

2.6 Non-core Vocabulary: Summary

(1) Non-core vocabulary has a restricted collocation with other words.

(2) Non-core lexis is usually marked by operating along different scales of affect from the core vocabulary which will usually occupy a central position. Non-core vocabulary can be marked for **intensity**: mutilate (non-core) − damage (core); **formality**: associate, mate (non-core) − friend (core); **evaluation**: radiant, gaudy (non-core) − bright (core), and so on.

(3) Non-core items will only rarely be superordinate.

(4) It is more difficult to find antonyms for non-core items. See (2): friend − enemy but mate −? bright − dull, but gaudy −?

The notion of core and non-core lexical items is a useful one which I hope will be seen to have some practical applications. It is naive, of course, not to recognize that further analytical refinement is needed in this area of lexical meaning. It is also necessary to admit to problems in precise definition; there is not space to cover these difficulties here but interested readers are referred to Carter (1982a, 1984) and Stubbs (forthcoming) for a fuller account with particular reference to the notion of core vocabulary. But a linguistically-principled working basis for description and assessment of children's vocabulary use needs to be laid if further advances are to be made both for the pupil and for the teacher developing the pupil's language. And a notion of coreness in vocabulary should be an important component of this basis.

3 Lexis and Coherence

Few appropriate analytical models exist which enable vocabulary to be examined for its role in the coherence of a text. Danes̆'s work on thematic progression has considerable potential for development and has been successfully applied to the analysis of coherence in writing (see Dillon, 1981; Morgan and Sellner, 1980; North, 1982). It is, however, focused largely on syntactic relations and does not, as developed so far, allow for particularly rich description of lexical patterning.

The model I shall adopt here is one outlined by Hasan (1980). Hasan's model is based on analysis of semantic relations in a text and does not accept any easy division or formal distinction between grammatical and lexical levels of analysis. Hasan proposes a lexical rendering of texts which focuses not simply on those lexical items which can be cohesively interpreted but on those which interrelate and **interact** recurrently across a text. Take the following example cited by Hasan:

1   Once upon a time there was a little girl
2   and she went out for a walk
3   and she saw a lovely little teddybear
4   and so she took it home
5   and when she got home she washed it
6   and when she took it to bed she cuddled it
                                    (Passage C)

Here there is **interaction** between clauses 2 and 5 because 'she' is engaged as a 'doer' in a related process of doing in both clauses. Similarly, the transitive process in clause 3, '*she saw a teddybear*', and related to clause 6, '*she took it* to bed' and '*she cuddled it*', embraces the same doer—doing relations across the text. More importantly the relation between words and here the actions denoted is multiple not singular. It is not a case of just a single connection between lexical items. In the following examples (also from Hasan) items can be cohesively interpreted but no deeper textual relation established:

1   The sailor goes on the ship
2   and he's coming home with the dog
3   and the dog wants the boy and the girl
4   and they don't know the bear's in the chair
5   and the bear's coming to go to sleep in it
                                    (Passage D)

Here there is cohesion between particular items and there is lexical repetition but there is no deeper semantic relation between the 'coming' in clause 5 and the 'coming' in clause 2 because a different 'actor' is involved in each case. The relation is thus singular and no interaction takes place. Hasan divides the items involved in such relations in the following terms:

relevant token   = those lexical items in a text which exist in some singular semantic relation to each other.

central token = that subset of relevant tokens which enter into direct and multiple interaction with each other.

peripheral token = the difference between the total number of tokens in a text and the relevant ones. Peripheral tokens would thus not need to be used in any summary or paraphrases of content and in a normally coherent text could be expected to be in a low ratio to the *total* number of tokens.

Of these tokens Hasan argues that it is the number of central tokens, expressed as a proportion of the relevant tokens, which contributes most to the **coherence** of the text. As she puts it, in simple terms, this enables us to account for our intuition that in the first passage the writer is discoursing on much the same kind of thing and stays with the topic long enough for some coherent progression/development to take place. This is not the case with passage D, even though there are a number of grammatical and lexical words which contribute to cohesion (see section 2 above for further discussion). In other words: passage C is cohesive and coherent; passage D is cohesive but not particularly coherent. In both cases, lexical or structural—semantic relations play a notable part in the respective textual organization.

4 Vocabulary, Coherence and Styles of Writing: Some Hypotheses

In this section some hypotheses are set up concerning the relationship between lexis and its use in different styles or **genres** of children's writing. In keeping with the analysis and discussion so far, the aim is not to examine vocabulary in isolation but in so far as it contributes to the coherent organization of a text. We have discussed the role of central tokens across a text and a further step must now be taken in the direction of the nature of the text itself *as a text*. It is at this point that we return to the notion of 'coreness' in vocabulary and explore ways in which core vocabulary and central tokens might interrelate in particular styles of writing. It is at this point, too, that examples of children's writing are examined in detail. This will be a relief to those who have patiently followed the preamble so far but it will also soon be obvious that it is only now by applying some hypotheses to actual data that the nature of these interrelations can be productively explored and further understanding in this complex area advanced. The hypotheses that follow are thus broad ones. They embrace individual words in the organization of text. They are also provisional. In the absence of existing models of analysis the basis for the hypotheses is provided by a combination of intuition, a limited number of notions and facts about lexical organization (notably section 2 above) and some preliminary research into the frequency with which teachers set particular kinds of writing for pupils to produce (see Appendix II).

4.1 Hypotheses

It is hypothesized here that by the age of transition from junior to secondary school children might be expected to demonstrate in their writing evidence of growing mastery of the following features of lexical organization:

I   that varied function or closed-class words will be used to promote cohesive intersentential relations.
II that there will be 'expressive' variation in lexical choices and evidence of structural and associative links between words.
III that in relation to (I) and (II) vocabulary will be structured in such a way as to achieve *coherence*. There will be a high proportion of central tokens and few peripheral tokens relative to the relevant tokens in the text.
IV that in relation to (I) and (II) vocabulary will be deployed with recognition of the 'genre' of the writing task. That, given writing tasks of summary/recounting and description, children would use more core lexical items in the former and more non-core items in the latter.

I shall now proceed to tests of these hypotheses by applying frameworks for the analysis of core vocabulary and (after Hasan) lexical coherence to two examples from two different genres of writing: recounting and description. (It should be noted that hypothesis IV will be seen to be more speculative than I to III.)

5   Vocabulary and Recounting

5.1   The Texts

Phillipa
 1   *My First Day at Belton Girls' School.* In
 2   the morning I woke up at seven o'clock. Everyone
 3   was hurrying down to breakfast. I had to put on
 4   my summer uniform and sandals and have everything
 5   ready by the time my friend's father come to fetch
 6   me. My friend's father is called Mr. Troutbeck
 7   and he let the telephone ring three times to let
 8   us known that he was on his way. When we arrived
 9   at Belton Girls' School my two friends had to
10   go a different way in so Mr. Troutbeck introduced
11   me to a Sixth Former and asked if she could take
12   me to where I was meant to go. The girl took me

13 into the dining room where all the newcomers were
14 and we were sorted out into forms. A teacher
15 talked to us about the school until our Form
16 Mistress came to collect us. Our group was
17 lead through a maze of passages until we come to
18 our room. The Form Mistress, whom was to be our
19 main teacher, was called Miss Greene. We were
20 put in our seats in alphabetical order then we
21 were given a piece of paper each and told to
22 divide it into five sections. This piece of paper
23 was to be our time table which took quite a time
24 to complete. Then we were given two other pieces
25 of paper to fill in. The lesson finished when
26 we were about halfway through the sheets. Another
27 teacher had a quick chat with us about gymnastics
28 then the dinner bell rang. I hardly ate anything
29 for lunch but I was not hungry.

Elaine
1 *My first day at Belton Girl's School.*
2   I reached Belton girls school and an older girl
3 took me to the dining room where our forms were
4 sorted out. Then Miss Greene came in.
5   Miss Greene then showed us to our class rooms.
6 We sat in our desks which were chosen by our names
7 in alphabetical order. Then we wrote out our timetables.
8 Next Miss Greene showed us around the school. She
9 then showed us the Dolphin block and the Anix. Next
10 Miss Greene showed us the cloak room where we hung
11 our blazers and changed into our inside shoes.
12   Then we found our way outside from the cloak room.
13 Next we went outside into the pleasents and we
14 practest the fire drill makeing sure we were quick
15 to line up in the pleasent. Then we went back
16 through the cloak room. Then we had break and Jill
17 dropped the crisps. We could go into the dining room
18 or go out-side and eat our food.
19   Then the bell went and we all went back to class
20 where our books were handed out to the class. Then
21 Miss Hackett took us for Gym. She talked about
22 swimming Gym and games. Then the dinner bell rang
23 so we went to our room. The an older girl came in
24 and took us down to lunch. After lunch we went
25 outside but when we went in the rong door we got lost,
26 but we soon found class.
27   Next we did a bit of English with Miss Greene.
28 We did a spelling test and we started to mark them,
29 but we did not finish marking. Then it was time for
30 Religious studys with Miss Ramsey we did not do

31   religious studys, but Miss Ramsey asked us questions
32   about our-selves, such as hobbies pets favourite
33   colour favourite food and weather. Then we had silent
34   studies we were allowed to read, sleep or write or
35   study. The at five minutes to four we were aloud
36   to go home. We lined up to go down to the cloak room
37   changed into our out door shoes and went home.

5.2 Commentary

(i)   Phillipa's writing illustrates a range of connected word choices. She is not given to repetition. Instead, she uses a number of apposite synonyms grouped around general lexical sets of *division* and *order* which seem to represent a dominant impression for her of her day. For example:

$$\left\{ \begin{array}{l} \text{put in alphabetical } order \\ sorted\ out \text{ into forms} \end{array} \right. \qquad \left\{ \begin{array}{l} \text{divide} \\ \text{order} \\ \text{sections} \end{array} \right.$$

$$\left\{ \begin{array}{l} \text{complete} \\ \text{fill in} \end{array} \right. \qquad \left\{ \begin{array}{l} \text{pieces of paper} \\ \text{sheets} \end{array} \right.$$

Other synonyms she employs are *fetch/collect*; *talk/chat* (though the latter may be judged too informal for the tenor of the overall passage). Elaine, too, records a clear sense of the order and regimentation of the day. She, too, employs a number of words from a related lexical set:

$$\left\{ \begin{array}{l} \text{line up} \\[4pt] \text{sort out} \\[4pt] \text{alphabetical order} \\[4pt] \text{drill} \end{array} \right.$$

But there is not quite the same degree of synonymic variation and in her final paragraph the verb 'do' is repeated three times within five lines of writing.

(ii) With reference to hypothesis II Phillipa exerts greater control and variation in the area of closed-class word cohesive linkage. Whereas Elaine is reliant on the temporal conjunctive 'Then', which is repeated six times, Phillipa uses devices of anaphoric reference, for example, 'Another teacher' (refers back to 'our main teacher'); 'the lesson' (which refers back collectively to the activities described in the previous three sentences). There are also temporal clauses which link clauses without recourse to conjunction. Thus, instead of 'A teacher talked to us about the school. Then our Form Mistress came to collect us' we have: 'A teacher talked to us about the school *until* our Form Mistress came to collect us.'

(iii) In Phillipa's essay there is one example of hyponymy. The word 'newcomers' is employed to include all the referents denoted by 'the children arriving at the school for the first time that day'. In Elaine's text there are more hyponyms (such as hobbies, pets). This may account, in part, for the feeling recorded among a number of teacher readers of her essay that it contains more *information.*

(iv) Phillipa also uses a metaphoric expression: 'A maze of passages'. This is not predicted as a common occurrence in recounting or summarizing. It might as a result be said to confer some distinctiveness to the writing here. The phrase does show an ability to exploit expressive, rather more abstract, relations in the lexicon (see study by Anglin, Appendix I). However, some teachers who have discussed this piece of writing consider this particular phrase to be clichéd. This demonstrates the difficulties of objectivity in assessment of performance in this context of language use. We might further note in this connection, as per hypothesis IV above, that neither girl uses particularly marked non-core lexis. For example, 'we were divided into forms' would be core and appropriate to this style or genre of writing. 'We were split up' would be non-core and not particularly appropriate stylistically to such a genre.

(v) Sample detailed analysis of lexical coherence is reserved for discussion of the other two passages in section 6.2. One problem for the busy teacher which is, however, highlighted by the two passages here is that Hasan's model is best suited to analysis of short passages of writing. Starting points for the teacher's analysis and for subsequent remediation or discussion with pupils might usefully be our intuitions (and/or those of our colleagues) as to which *parts* of a longer text appear most coherent or incoherent. A common observation by teachers I have worked with on these passages is that 'Elaine switches about a little too much in places'. Lines 12 to 33 are pointed to as a place where this results in potential confusion or incoherence. This can be attested informally by pointing out that interaction between lexical items tends to be cohesive but more 'singular' in the case of Elaine's essay. In other words, the processes and relations enacted between lexical items in the writing of Phillipa are more consistently developed and frequently involve, as we have seen, more than mere reiteration of lexical items. Elaine tends to write in such a way that often no more than two clauses are used to describe a process or set of actions before a new topic is introduced. In the lines referred to above, for example, there is little interaction between the relevant tokens in the last three sentences:

```
1   We went cloakroom
2   We had    break
3                           Jill dropped crisps
4   We could go dining room
5           go outside
6           eat food
```

While the subject 'we' remains constant and the actions depicted involve 'we' in actions which can be cohesively related, there is no real development of relations between the objects of the actions or places referred to in conjunction with those actions. Also the introduction of clause 3 lacks any clear relation to other relevant tokens. In this sequence at least there is no significant proportion of central to relevant tokens, though it is worth pointing out, prior to formal analysis, that this does not appear to be the case across the whole of Elaine's text. In the case of Phillipa, it is clear that interaction takes place between more lexical items resulting in a higher ratio of central to relevant tokens. For example:

```
1   Friend's father called Mr Troutbeck
2   Mr Troutbeck   let telephone ring
3   Mr Troutbeck   let know
4   We arrived school
5   Friends go different way
6   Mr Troutbeck introduced sixth-former
7   Mr Troutbeck asked       sixth-former
8   The girl took dining room
```

There are clearly related actions here. 'Mr Troutbeck' is engaged in a number of transitive processes (let ring, let know, introduce, ask) which ensures not merely subject continuity but interaction between the objects of the actions, too. There is similar interaction between 'friends', 'sixth-former'/'girl', and the pronominal 'we' has unambiguous reference. There is still no really sustained interaction of the sort evidenced in the short example cited in section 3 but this may be connected with an intended effect of rapidly changing locations and impressions; in fact, lines 19 to 26 offer, as we have seen, a fuller cross-sentential relatedness in the presence of items from the same lexical sets.

5.3 Summary

It must, of course, be remembered that the focus here is almost exclusively on the girls' use of lexical items. Our assessment of the passages must include reference to syntax, spelling, punctuation as well as to non-linguistic criteria such as content, selection of material, and so on. But it is my contention that evaluation of vocabulary has tended to be unsystematic and may not have received equivalent weighting against uses of language at other linguistic levels.

To conclude, it can fairly be said that Phillipa demonstrates more developed capacities in her handling of words and, in particular, the relations between words than Elaine does. A particular strength of hers would seem to be a control of synonymic variation and of more abstract lexical relations. Her ability to handle intersentential relations and variation in patterns of clause linkage is also apparent. Yet Elaine's writing may not be quite as loose as her punctuation, spelling and general presentation might indicate. Her last three paragraphs are not consistently well-organized but, intuitively at least, her other paragraphs seem better and she does include a lot of information about her day, with a range of hyponyms contributing to this.

Both girls seem to appreciate the lexical restraints of a summary/recounting writing task and, on this basis, the hypothesis does not seem unduly unreasonable. It must still be recognized, however, that constraints of space mean that some features of the hypothesis have necessarily not been tested in relation to these samples of writing and that, in any case, two pieces of writing represent very minimal data.

6 Vocabulary and Description

The procedure of text with commentary is again adopted here. In this instance two pieces of writing devoted to description will be examined. Both were produced by pupils, Mark and Richard, who were in the first six months of their secondary school career. The writing instructions given by the teacher were to describe a monster in such a way as to try to frighten the reader. The writing task emanated from reading and discussing examples of 'monster descriptions' in books and comics, on television and film. Once again, not all features of the hypothesis can be examined. A process of selection is undertaken and this may, of course, not accord with the features of the hypothesis considered significant in relation to the two texts by others reading or assessing them. And it goes without saying that the whole wider 'context' of knowledge of the pupils, previous lessons, preparatory activities, and so on, passes unexamined here but would not in any more general view of their language development.

6.1   The Texts
Mark

```
 1   The creature is called Dahimeod. It is
 2   pronounced DA-HE-ME-OD. He is big like
 3   a block of flats. His body is like a
 4   dragon's and his ears are hairy with sharp
 5   points. Dahimeod has two heads. He has
 6   three eyes and two enormous mouths on each
 7   head. His long neck is curling in plait
 8   shapes like a snake and he has poisonous
 9   knife claws which poison your blood. When
10   he walks, the ground rumbles and hisses.
```

Richard

```
 1   The giant ant is very, very big. All the
 2   children run away and the dogs grumble.
 3   And we stare at t.v. all the houses fall
 4   down. Its eyes are large and beamey.
 5   Paul and I get on our bikes and ride fast,
 6   the blue and cream buses colaps with the
 7   big ant.
```

6.2   Commentary

(1) The vocabulary used by Richard to describe the giant ant contains both core and non-core vocabulary although we should note that description is confined mostly to the movements of the ant. For example, *big* (twice), *run*, *fall down*, *large*, *ride*. Less usual, more expressive/associative effects are brought about by: 'we stare at t.v.' (a more core word would be 'watch'?); 'the dogs grumble' (a more core word would be 'bark'?; *beamey* (an invented word (?) which on the original script the teacher had crossed out and replaced with 'beaming'?); *colaps* ('collide with' might be the intended word here though 'collapse' could be seen as expressive of the way the buses are crushed by the giant ant and might thus link associatively with *fall down*). The notion of dogs that grumble and buses that collapse also indicates signs of exploitation of contrasting semantic features. Such mixing of lexical sets gives a basis for contextually appropriate imaginative/ metaphoric effects.

(ii) Mark's vocabulary usage is not noticeably more core than that of Richard. Core words would be *big, small, long, sharp, walk*. Basically non-core words would be *rumbles, hisses*. In this respect, both Mark and Richard appear to use vocabulary appropriate to the descriptive writing genre and thus operate in keeping with hypothesis IV.

(iii) In terms of hypothesis II, however, there is evidence in the text by Mark of more 'expressive variation' and greater signs of 'structural and associative links between words'. In particular, such effects are brought about here by invented words such as *plait shapes* and *knife claws* which in themselves are notable also for associative connections with *curling, hairy, snake* and *sharp* respectively. Also, 'The ground *rumbles* and *hisses*' links associatively with *snake* and *dragon's*. The word *poisonous* is also an unusual collocation but might be seen to link across clauses with *snake*. Mark also contrasts different semantic features more pervasively than Richard and produces in consequence some striking effects. (In this respect both writers are following the prescription of trying to frighten the reader and do so in a non-clichéd, non-stereotyped manner. We should note, however, the inevitably subjective element in assessment of 'effects' in writing like this:

His *body* is like a *dragon's*.
His *ears* are *hairy* with *sharp points*.
Three eyes and two enormous *mouths* on each *head*.
Poisonous knife claws.

(iv) With respect to hypothesis I, however, some differences between the two pieces of writing can be noted. In general, Mark uses more closed-class lexical items which ensure cohesive links between the different sentences/clauses of his text. In particular, the pronominals *It, he, his* in every sentence but the first ensure smooth transition and impart a consistency and completeness to the description. This is also underscored by lexical repetition (*poison, heads, big, DA-HE-ME-OD*). In the case of Richard, it is not always clear what the point of reference is for the pronominals and anaphoric items which are used (for example, *we, all the, its*). It should be noted though, in keeping with observations in section 2.2, that Richard's text does not *lack* cohesive devices (or at least a significant number of closed-class words which can contribute to this). The presence of potentially cohesive items is observable in both descriptions. Teachers who have been asked to evaluate the two pieces of writing unanimously assess Mark's writing higher than that of Richard and point to the fact that Richard's does not 'hang together' as a main factor in their assessment. (It can be noted again that coherence is clearly not dependent on the *number* of cohesive devices employed.) This points again in the direction of hypothesis III and requires further, more detailed, investigation. The analysis should also be seen as a procedural complement to the informal discussion of coherence in the summary/recounting writing of Phillipa and Elaine above.

(v)   It can be seen from Figure 6.1 that Mark's writing is much more consistently and coherently patterned. The mostly relational processes which describe the monster Dahimeod enact a series of statements which relate consistently to the subject (hence the fact that the left-most column can be blocked); and the same processes are also described using lexical items which interrelate or interact with each other. These interrelations are brought about by items from the same lexical set, such as mouth, eyes, head, hair, body, ears, neck (hence the fact that interaction between these items can be arrowed) or by a process of associative linking which has been described in (iii). Thus, for example, *plait*, linking with *curling, hairy, snake, poison*, and so on. These relations are marked by broken arrowed lines partly to suggest that the interaction between items cannot be stated independently of a reader's recognition of implicit links and thus their own intuitive or subjective colouring. It is of interest to note, too, that as Mark's writing develops he begins literally to branch out. There is a greater density of expressive–associative linking as well as a syntactic development from relational to action clauses (for example, It *is*/he *has* → *poison* your blood, *walks, rumbles, curling*, and so on). This works to counteract an impression of lexico-syntactic structural repetitiveness.

In the case of Richard, however, there is only minimal interaction between lexical items. Too many separate processes and relations are triggered by the separate and constantly changing themes/subjects that any 'development' is at best notional (*is* there a connection between 'we' and 'Paul and I' and 'the children'?) and exists only across a gap of four or five clauses (for example, giant ant ↔ big ant) or requires too great a degree of inference on the part of the reader *without*, it should be added, any support by means of associative cross-linkage. (To indicate the implicit relations dotted lines are used.) Note particularly the absence of blocking in the diagrammatic lexical rendering of Richard's text as well as the number of separate blocks. In Richard's text there are twenty-two relevant tokens but only five of these tokens (that is, under 25 per cent) could be said to be central tokens. In the case of Mark there are forty-six relevant tokens of which thirty (or over 66 per cent) could be said to be central tokens.

I am using the term 'could be said' to express some caution in the face of an analytical system which still requires refinement and which teachers may not always wish to use for such extensive application (see below, section 7.1). It is important, however, for enough mastery of the system to be acquired for its principles to be understood and for an analysis of relative degrees of

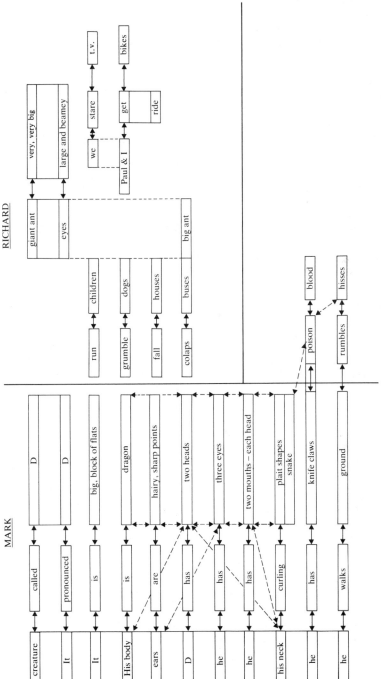

Figure 6.1 Lexical rendering: relevant and central token analysis (after Hasan, 1980).

coherence in writing by children to be undertaken by their teachers.

6.3 Summary

As far as use of vocabulary in the context of an appropriate style is concerned it would appear that Mark has produced the more effective piece of descriptive writing overall. His deployment of lexical items reveals a richer overall patterning and mastery of organization. But we cannot dismiss Richard's piece. It is not particularly coherent and may require readers to retrieve too much of what is implicit but it is inventive in places, is appropriate generically as descriptive writing and shows potential for further development. Our 'judgement', though, is to some extent dependent on the nature of the hypotheses advanced and, inevitably, on the kind of subjective colouring which attends evaluation of effects in writing. The hypotheses require further discussion and development but they have allowed us to analyse some relevant linguistic components of vocabulary use relative to genres of descriptive and summary/reporting writing.

Before proceeding in the next section to review these hypotheses and to suggest related teaching procedures it is necessary for us to recognize the limited nature of the discussion of these four pieces of writing. The limitations can be noted under three main headings.

First, as far as language analysis goes, there has been almost exclusive reference to *one* level of language. Little has been said about such important aspects of language development as syntax, spelling, graphology, reference to audience, and so on. It is dangerous to focus too exclusively or to attempt assessment of writing without due recognition of other factors of language organization. Secondly, there is a wider context of knowledge which will and should affect how we 'mark' such essays. Knowledge of the individual child's previous performance, recognition of his/her emotional, psychological and social development, awareness of the social, racial or cultural background the child comes from (with its attendant linguistic environments) will all be relevant factors which have been necessarily excluded from full consideration here (see Wilkinson *et al.*, 1980 – but also review by Carter, 1982c). Thirdly, different writing tasks under different conditions by the same children may result in reversal of roles and relative successes. Much more evidence would need to be gathered before any really helpful profile of these children could be constructed. It would be interesting and useful, for example, to consider the ways in which these children or children like them performed in the more common school writing task of narrative (see Appendix II).

7 Suggestions and Developments: Applied Linguistics and Linguistics Applied

Discussion of linguistic models of analysis and their application to classroom teaching and language development inevitably centres on questions of relevance and usefulness. Teachers understandably want to feel an immediate pay-off from the precious time they invest in linguistic analysis and they are right to point out, as we have already recognized, that there is much more to language development than linguistic analysis of texts produced by children. The applied linguist has to work in a way which gives due credence and recognition to such concerns.

A further concern, and one which can be perceived as particularly frustrating, even unsettling, to the practising classroom teacher, is the inevitably provisional nature of the models of analysis which are proposed. Related to this, therefore, is the need for hypotheses to be tested and refinement to be worked into the models but in a manner which is also sufficiently rigorous to satisfy the linguistic demands of linguists. Once again some of the details and procedures involved will be perceived by some teachers to be beyond their more immediate concerns. The applied linguist is, therefore, perpetually strung between the exigencies of linguistics applied (improving the linguistic basis of analytical procedures) and applied linguistics (assessing what is relevant to contexts of application), particularly since any dividing line between linguistics applied and applied linguistics is never distinct and unambiguous (see Brumfit, 1981; Widdowson, 1981).

It is for these reasons that I propose to divide discussion of further development into two parts: one particularly targeted at language researchers and those with specifically linguistic interests and the other targeted at the teacher seeking further principled application to teaching of what has been learned from the discussion so far. Such a demarcation does not, of course, prohibit readers from reading both parts as they wish and inevitable overlaps will become apparent if they do.

7.1 Working with the Hypotheses: Linguistic Perspectives

(i)   Further work in the definition of core vocabulary is required. The notion is an intuitively attractive one but needs to be tested in relation to a wider range of language uses and genres to ensure that criteria are not being proposed for qualitatively different kinds of core vocabulary. Collocational frequency appears still to be a main criterion and this might be investigated in relation to computer-based text corpora. It should be noted here, however, that different school subjects may have their own subject—intrinsic core vocabulary (see below and Perera, 1982) and that the relation of core vocabulary to expressivity is also a relative one. For example, is the idea of 'varied' lexical items itself a relative one and merely a matter for introspective analysis? Also it has to be remembered that there are contexts in writing where core lexical items can be expressive and achieve stylistic impact by relational contrast with surrounding expressive non-core words. Use of informants to explore the existence of inter-subjective assessment of lexical effects could also extend work in an area which, in the examples of writing summary/ recount and *description* above, does appear to have received a measure of confirmation. (For further development of the notion and proposals for further criterial tests see Stubbs, forthcoming.) It would furthermore be revealing to examine whether text-specific connections hold between core lexical items and Hasan's notion of central tokens.

(ii) The relations between Hasan's lexical interaction and theme/rheme analysis could be examined further. The ways in which different kinds of text are formed by lexical as opposed to syntactic cohesion between preceding rheme and subject theme need to be investigated. Is there, for example, any notably *lexical* patterning in the stylistic effects explored by Dillon (1981) in relation to 'simple linear' or 'constant theme' progession? This would also lead to more detailed specification of the nature of the **interaction** between lexical items as well as fuller analysis of the relationship between such interaction and the syntactic processes in which the lexical items are situated. For example, does a different kind of lexical patterning accompany relational processes as opposed to, say, mental or action processes? Would non-core vocabulary be better foregrounded in descriptive writing if the verbs are relational and non-transitive?

Other questions which seem pressing are: (1) Is there a broader semantic connection between lexical interaction and the kinds of lexical signalling in texts investigated by Hoey and Winter (compare Winter, 1977; Hoey, 1983a)? Winter's notion of Vocabulary I, II and III may be of special significance in this connection (see also Chapter 4 above); (2) Is there a minimum 'distance' beyond which interaction will be seen *not* to function irrespective of what might be connected retrospectively? Is such a distance related to clause length, sentence units, number of words? An example here would be the kinds of **coherence** which obtain between reference to the 'giant ant' in Richard's descriptive piece in lines 1 and 7 or the classification by lexical set of 'dragon' 1.4 and 'snake' 1.8; or 'sharp' 1.4 and 'knife' 1.9 in Mark's piece. What kind of processing of text accompanies immediate and retrospective recognition of such textual relations and how do we evaluate their contribution to successful writing?

A further topic with particular relevance to coherence in genres, styles or 'categories' of writing is the important research of Martin and Rotherey. Martin and Rotherey (1981) have explored the syntactic–structural properties of different genres of children's writing and examined relative proficiencies across genres. It would be interesting to collate their findings concerning the dominant syntactic and discoursal features of 'narrative', 'observation/comment', 'report', 'discussion' genres with the hypotheses investigated here concerning the specifically lexical features of different genres. For example, their category of 'recount' which seems to bear the closest relation to the summary/recounting category explored here in examples from Phillipa and Elaine was found to include: (1) nearly 50 per cent material process clauses; (2) dominance of focus on events; (3) absence of attitudinal strings; (4) exophoric reference to the writer and his/her class (thematic); (5) successive temporal conjunctives. These findings are, for example, not dissimilar to aspects of the discussion in section 5.2 above. (For a related study of text typologies see Werlich, 1976. See also Appendix II.)

(iii) Finally, the nature of the data and its context needs to be reviewed in relation to the hypotheses. The data used in this essay is static in more ways than one. Not only should fuller contextualization be provided concerning social, cultural and personal environments (see above) but a longitudinal study may introduce greater 'dynamism' into the examination of *processes* of lexical development. Testing of the hypotheses in relation to children between 7 and 11 or 11 and 13 would enable us to *place* more effectively such examples as those above. Studies could also be undertaken in relation to initial hypotheses concerning age, sex, social class, first and second language learners, intellectual ability, written v. spoken language use and so on. For an initial study see Rutter and Raban, 1982.

7.2   Extending the Hypotheses: Classroom Perspectives

7.2.1   TESTING LEXICAL COMPETENCE

Vocabulary is a level of language organization which is peculiarly unamenable to formal testing if only because the answer to the question: 'What do we mean by knowing a word?' is bound to be an unsatisfactory and problematic one. In particular, we must recognize with Donaldson (1978) that it is 'naive to assume that a child's understanding of a word is a once-and-for-all affair' and with Andersen (1975) that for children (as for adults) boundaries between word meanings are vague and constantly shifting according to new contexts and functions. 'Learning how to mean is more than just increasing the number of words in your vocabulary; it is to do with learning how meanings overlap and interact with one another' (Halliday, 1975). A test presumes that word meaning is stable. It may be possible to test knowledge of core words in a restricted sense but it is, paradoxically, often core words which have some of the widest range of meanings (for instance, consider the meanings of core words such as fat, happy, car, and so on). Certainly, any formal test which removed words from their internal and external relations to lexical, situational and generic contexts would be to test vocabulary in potentially dangerous isolation. It should be pointed out, however, that tests of this kind *do* exist and are in use in primary schools, notably: *The Picture Language Scale* (5 to 7 years); *The English Picture Vocabulary Test* (pre-school to 11 years); *The Crichton Vocabulary Test* (4½ to 11 years). It might be more productive if teachers were to devise some kind of marking scale according to which children might be rewarded for 'variation' in open- and closed-class usage, for lexical cohesion, use of attitudinal words/metaphor specific to genre, number of relevant tokens in a text, and so on.

7.2.2   SCHOOL SUBJECT VOCABULARY

Attention is drawn here to research by Katharine Perera (Perera, 1982) into the different language demands put on pupils by different school subjects and the kind of learning difficulties created by subject-special language organization. Her concerns are largely with syntax but observations on vocabulary are offered and these can make a most useful starting point for further examination by teachers. Such work is of particular relevance to children in transition from junior to secondary schools where academic subjects are encountered in greater isolation from each other and are usually taught by different teachers. Among the kind of observations made by Perera with reference to vocabulary are (a) the pervasive presence of technical vocabulary such as the following from a secondary school geography textbook: stratum, scarp, humus, tsunamis, sawah, carboniferous, levees; (b) familiar words with special meanings, for example, *body* (scientific bodies), *nap* (pile on cloth), *mean* (average), *relief* (height of land), *battery* (shed for hens). Here the very familiarity of the basic or core meaning of these words can be disadvantageous because the child has to cope with it in an unfamiliar and unexpected sense. Teachers will doubtless be able to collect their own examples.

7.2.3   APPLIED LINGUISTICS AND TEACHING STRATEGIES: EFL + EMT

There has been some growth recently in the application of lexico-semantic theory to vocabulary teaching, though the emphasis has been on the second or foreign language learner. There is space here to examine no more than one representative example but see Wallace (1982); Meara (1980); Nation (1982); McCarthy (1984) for detailed reviews and an introduction to associated teaching techniques. It is symptomatic that all the work in this connection proceeds in the more linguistically sophisticated and principled field of Teaching English as Foreign Language (TEFL) and not in Teaching English as a Mother Tongue (TEMT).

The Words You Need by Rudzka *et al.* is a book that could be used equally well with native as with non-native students of advanced English. The authors make particular use of the theory of semantic fields which postulates that the vocabulary of a language is, as noted above (see 2.3 and elsewhere) a network of overlapping and inter-relating lexical sets. For example, walk, run, stroll, amble, trot, jog, are all verbs of motion; stroll also belongs to another set which includes wander, ramble, saunter, roam, where the 'components of meaning' are more centrally to do with movement which is leisurely. Using this basis of semantic theory, the authors devise semantic grids by which students can check their own intuitions or work out – often more precisely than a dictionary definition – the components of meaning relative to a particular semantic field/lexical set. Channell (1981) describes this procedure with the following diagram:

Being surprised

	affect with wonder	because unexpected	because difficult to believe	so as to cause confusion	so as to leave one helpless to act or think
surprise	+	+			
astonish	+		+		
amaze	+			+	
astound	+				+
flabbergast	+				+

The authors of *The Words You Need* also attempt to face the problem of teaching collocation. Knowing a word is in many senses knowing with which other words it can collocate and the learning problems are certainly more acute in this area in the case of foreign language learners. Various exercises are developed to provide practice in finding appropriate partners for words. An example is again taken from Channell (1981):

	woman	man	child	dog	bird	flower	weather	landscape	view	house	furniture	bed	picture	dress	present	voice
handsome		+									+				+	
pretty	+		+	+	+			+	+	+		+	+	+		
charming	+	+								+				+		+
lovely	+		+	+	+	+	+	+	+	+	+	+	+	+	+	+

Such grids cannot, of course, explain a word's meaning (the authors recognize that learning a word involves several procedures); neither can it wholly account for everything which a competent user of the language 'knows' about that word. What can be encouraged, particularly but by no means exclusively, in native speakers is the ability to produce different degrees of expressive meaning (humour, irony, stylistic impact, and so on) by a variation of collocational partners or by partnering words from non-related semantic fields. This whole area of vocabulary development can be augmented by the use of standard cloze procedures in the classroom, particularly with attention to substituting, guessing, exploring words which play a key role in the cohesion and coherence of the text.

8 Conclusion

The main conclusion here must be that much remains to be done in this whole area before yet more refined and systematic procedures can be developed, instituted and evaluated fully in the classroom. It is, however, an area of both linguistic theory and language development which repays further investigation. Choice of words and use of words, though never isolable from the other processes of discourse, remain a powerful signal of learning — in at least two senses of the word learning. It is hoped that some of the ideas and reports outlined here will play a part in establishing a linguistically principled basis for current assistance and future investigation for teachers, student teachers and educational researchers. Linguistic analysis and linguistics-based hypotheses must be used cautiously and with due concern for their relevance. And we are only talking of a *basis* for vocabulary development. It is difficult, however, for 'good words' to be systematically encouraged or assessed without such a basis.

Appendix I

One of the most interesting studies of vocabulary development in children and adults is by Jeremy Anglin. Anglin's work, summarized in *The Growth of Word Meaning*, is characterized by an overt concern to chart development over a large span of years and to draw general conclusions concerning the main landmarks of that development. His work also makes different use of informants from different age groups who are subjected directly to tests designed to measure the growth of what Anglin terms a 'subjective lexicon'. Anglin's main findings can be summarized as follows:

(1) **The Syntagmatic–Paradigmatic.** This refers to the finding that in tests of free association young children will link words from different parts of speech, whereas older subjects respond by providing words which are predominantly of the same part of speech. Thus for children 'eat' is associated with a stimulus word *table*. For adults the most common response to the word is 'chair'. Other tests which involve asking informants to *cluster* a list of twenty words into semantically related sets reveal that younger subjects work on a syntagmatic principle of ordering according to thematic groupings. The groupings of the older subjects are reported to be less idiosyncratic, to contain words which are paradigmatically related (that is, they can be substituted syntactically) – and this includes words which are antonyms – and/or which regularly belong to the same conceptual category (that is, are hyponyms). One aspect of lexical development, then, is the increasing perception of syntactic and conceptual *relations* between words.

(2) **Concrete–abstract progression.** Related to (1) is a growth in awareness of the more abstract relations which hold between words. The awareness of these relations manifests itself more in the way in which lexical items can be collocated than in distinctly measurable sets of hierarchically organized or nested features relating words. For example, adults show much wider tolerance of the possible predicates a noun might share than children who, for example, generally operate with tight categories (for example, plus animate). For example, according to Anglin, children up to a certain age would consider 'the cauliflower sneezed' as not admissible within any context. Having appropriately demarcated such relations 'adults' can develop to greater degrees of abstraction in their use of lexical items and have a stronger basis, too, for the use of metaphoric expressions and for greater expressivity in general. For example, research by Asch and Nerlove (1967) confirms that a child at three years of age categorically denies that adjectives such as bright, hard, and so on, can be used to describe people, whereas by twelve increasing comprehension has led to fascination with more extended meanings of these terms.

(3) **Generalizations**.   Although this should not be taken as evidence for powers of abstraction, the growth of lexical meaning can also be measured on another level as the ability to distinguish broad classes to which words belong. Such development is from the ground up (Anglin, p. 59). In other words, he or she might first see that roses and petunias are *flowers* and that ashes and oaks are *trees*; then that flowers and trees are *plants*; then that plants are *living things*, and so on. This will greatly facilitate the increasing ability to relate categories of features reported in (1) and (2).

Anglin's study is one worth consulting. His data is limited but the empirical nature of his research works to substantiate hypotheses about lexical development grounded in a sharply linguistic awareness of the organization of words. It will be seen that speculations and assumptions, from which the hypotheses in section 4.1 (especially I and II) were formed, owe something to Anglin's general conclusions.

Appendix II

In order to determine the frequency with which different categories of writing were required of pupils aged between nine and thirteen, a brief pilot survey was undertaken among teachers in middle and secondary schools in Nottinghamshire. Teachers of English responded to a questionnaire in which they were invited to rank five categories of writing in order of frequency. Eighty-seven teachers returned the questionnaire and the following preliminary results were obtained:

(1)   Narrative
(2)   Summary/recounting
(3)   Description
(4)   Discussion
(5)   Report

Clearly such a survey needs to be extended in the following ways before any meaningful results emerge:

(1)   Not only teachers of English should be involved. Science teachers may, for example, place report in first place. Teachers were only asked to record their judgement of writing tasks set in their own classes.
(2)   Results concerning relative distributions need to be obtained.
(3)   A checking procedure needs to be developed to ensure that the same writing task is understood by the same category. Summary, for example, may mean different things to different teachers.

These very preliminary results do, however, validate a claim that summary/recounting and description are genres worthy of investigation.

Acknowledgements

I am grateful to Margaret Berry, Mike McCarthy, Mike Stubbs, Michael Toolan and to the volume editors for many helpful comments on an earlier draft of this paper. Responsibility for what remains is, of course, my own.

Suggested Further Reading

Anglin, J. (1970), *The Growth of Word Meaning* is a useful study of vocabulary development in both children and adults which seeks to identify main 'stages'.

Carter, R. A. (ed.) (1982b), *Linguistics and the Teacher* is a collection of essays on many aspects of the relationship between linguistics and education. Very readable, the chapters by Katharine Perera are particularly valuable.

Lyons, J. (1981), *Language, Meaning and Context* is an interesting introduction to the area of word meaning and semantic theory.

Meara, P. (1980), 'Vocabulary acquisition: a neglected aspect of language learning' is an article on language teaching to be found in *Linguistics and Language Teaching Abstracts* which links semantic theory to the teaching of vocabulary.

7 Evaluating Teachers' Responses to Children's Writing

NICOLA COUPE

> The alienation of so many pupils from the writing process may largely stem from a sense of frustration with teachers who ride roughshod over the gaps in learning that mistakes signify. (Dunsbee and Ford, 1980, p. 18)

The issues involved in considering teachers' responses to pupils' work are many and varied. This is, perhaps, initially reflected in the many different words used for identifying the nature of such a response: marking, correcting, evaluating, assessing, grading, and so on. Factors such as awareness of reader, type of audience, nature of task, and the process of writing are all bound to influence and, to some extent, determine the teacher's reaction. Writing will inevitably have different aims on different occasions, and responses can therefore range over many aspects of both *content* (what is being conveyed) and *presentation* (how it is being conveyed).

In their discussion of the mistakes that young writers typically make, Dunsbee and Ford (1980) outline three main types; those which arise from the technicalities and conventions of the written language; those related to the use of register in a specific subject area; and those concerning the pupils' grasp of subject content. They note that teachers usually confine their attention to one or two of these areas, and, indeed, question the feasibility for *all* teachers to consider a broader focus when responding to texts – presentation, understanding of content, *and* linguistic competence. It would also seem pertinent to question whether even the English specialist has the competence (or the time) to do this.

Since the subject of teachers' responses to children's writing is such a vast area, I propose to limit my discussion to those written comments that typically appear on returned scripts. By reference to a sample of such comments, I shall argue that many are in fact linguistically and/or pedagogically ill-founded, and that what is needed is to establish initially a more principled and specifically identifiable framework for describing language, from which basis responses to a text may more effectively be made.

The data which forms the basis of this chapter was collected in the course of a research project (based at Westminster College, Oxford) into the narrative writing of first year secondary school children. One school in the sample provided the research team with 156 previously marked scripts, representing the compositions of six classes of first year comprehensive school children, and the responses of five teachers. Although my own research was concerned with certain linguistic aspects of the texts, I became increasingly diverted by the teachers' comments, which in many respects I found linguistically and pedagogically more interesting. Whilst they are the responses of a small group of teachers from one school, they are the kind of comments with which all teachers, and generations of learner–writers, will be familiar. Working without reference to any existing model for the assessment of children's writing (see, for instance, Britton *et al.*, 1975; Wilkinson *et al.*, 1980; Assessment of Performance Unit (APU) 1981, 1982a, 1982b, and 1983), I listed every remark written in the teachers' handwriting, and attempted to classify them simply on the basis of 'what they were about'.

In order of frequency of occurrence the following headings emerged:

(1) General evaluation
(2) Content
(3) Punctuation/sentence
(4) Spelling
(5) Personal response
(6) Instruction for child action/reflection
(7) Paragraph/new line
(8) Grammar
(9) Presentation
(10) Length
(11) Unspecified error

1 *General Evaluation*
This category accounts for almost 25 per cent of all comments, and includes remarks such as: 'Good'; 'Well written'; 'An excellent piece of work'; 'Merit'; 'This isn't your best work'; 'You could do better'. There is no attempt made to indicate what features of the texts in particular suggest a creditable or below par performance, and, whilst there is a valiant attempt at elegant variation made from one script to another by one teacher in the sample, 'Good effort' accounts for thirteen of the nineteen comments made by another. One imagines that such a remark would quickly lose whatever power it has to encourage. As this is by far the largest category, most responses can be interpreted as 'I have read this piece of work and I am pleased or disappointed in it'.

2 *Content*

The remarks in this category still tend to be very general, but there is some attempt to indicate specific features of the text. These seem to be related to the teachers' own understanding of what makes a good story, which is typically defined in terms of the separate elements of the text, and the way in which these are put together to form a coherent whole. 'Detail', 'description', 'ideas', and 'interest' are words which occur frequently, and there is occasionally reference to particular events in the narrative, as in 'Rather a complicated story. I don't understand the bit about the comedian.'

3 *Punctuation/Sentence*

This comes considerably lower down the list in terms of frequency, but has almost twice as many references as 'Spelling' below it. The oblique, which appears in many of the actual comments, serves a useful purpose for the teacher; it suggests she knows there is a relationship between the items on either side, but is not quite sure what it is. We will return to this category later.

4 *Spelling*

This category will be explored in detail below. For now it should be noted that the comments on the scripts reflect a wide variety of different approaches and techniques employed by teachers to deal with spelling mistakes.

5 *Personal Response*

This includes those comments which generally give the impression that the teacher has enjoyed reading the child's work. There is usually reference to the first person, suggesting that the teacher is acting as 'partner in communication' rather than assessor (Britton *et al.*, 1975). Examples from this category are: 'I enjoyed reading this, D, a lovely idea – I hope it's not true though!'; 'I like the idea of a robot rebelling . . .'; 'I especially liked your description of the thoughts that passed through your mind when the alarm rang. Very realistic!'; 'A tragic story – I feel quite depressed'.

6 *Instruction for Child Action/Reflection*

These responses call for the child either to act on or reflect upon aspects of the text. Comments characteristically point out a mistake or problem but rarely offer help to the pupil to rectify the mistake or solve the problem. Examples are: 'Divide your story into sentences please and return it to me'; 'Count the number of times you use 'now' on this page'; 'How could Bobby have a gun in his pocket?'; 'Look at the errors I have underlined'.

7 *Paragraph/New Line*

These terms are used interchangeably, and there is also some confusion over the rules governing their use. 'Use a new line when someone else speaks' appears on one script, followed by 'new paragraph' where the same speaker continues to speak after an intervening narrative sentence. Another teacher advises: 'Paragraphs esp. when somebody speaks'. There is no distinction made between paragraphs as units of discourse, and new lines indented to mark a change of speaker.

8 *Grammar*

Although a precise, technical term, this seems to be interpreted in a wide variety of ways, usually lacking precision. 'There's something wrong here, but I can't quite put my finger on it' would often seem an appropriate gloss here, and I shall consider the reasons for this later in the chapter.

9 *Presentation*

Comments here are largely restricted to neatness: 'Try and keep your work tidy'.

10 *Length*

Comments in this category often appear to reflect some criteria private to the teacher: 'I would like to have read more'; 'A very long account of an eventful weekend'; but 'You might try to write a shorter piece next time, so that you can check for mistakes' provides an interesting insight into one teacher's perception of the purpose of story writing.

11 *Unspecified Error*

'A lot of careless errors' is typical of the comments in this category; they are of doubtful value, and there are few of them in the data. However, if the various squiggles, crosses, question marks and brackets had not been excluded, this category would have appeared much higher on the list. It should be noted, however, that such *ad hoc* categories, by their very nature, overlap and, therefore, several remarks are entered in more than one category; for example, 'Divide your story into sentences' appears under both Instruction for Child Action and Punctuation/Sentence.

It is not possible to discuss all of the categories at length, and I propose to restrict a more detailed consideration to four areas: content, punctuation/sentence, spelling and grammar. I have selected these as being particularly problematic, not only for the learner writer, but for the teacher, whose comments on these features more than any other reveal the lack of a means for identifying the writer's problem with any degree of precision.

Content   (2)

Although many teachers might admit to a lack of confidence in their approach to the linguistic aspects of a text, most seem less daunted by the task of assessing content. It seems reasonable that the assessment of the content of expository writing should be to some extent less problematic than the assessment of the content of narrative, and yet the comments teachers write about *what* children have to say in their stories, rather than *how* they say it (accepting that the two are not completely separable), reveal them to be less tentative in their judgements than one might expect. And the writers themselves are at a double disadvantage where the teacher not only holds certain expectations that they are required to meet but neglects to let them know these. 'You'd never have guessed what I was really looking for' would be an appropriate heading for a very large sub-category of the comments relating to content. Consider, for example, the following piece of writing which earned the comment: 'Well told, though you could have put in a lot more detail and description.' The task was an 'essay test' and, from a list of titles, Richard chose this:

The Balloon Race

It was a cold, but sunny September morning as I drove into a large field on the outskirts of Plymouth. I was flying balloon No 182 in the 500 strong first ever Daily Mirror European balloon race. We were under starter's orders at approximately 09.00 hours. We all knew the route we had to take, over 6 European countries. By 3.00 pm I was flying over Brest in France and had one of the one-hundred leading places, I was doing well.

For the next five or six days it grew quite cold as we flew over towns and cities such as Bilbao, Zaragoza, Montauben, Clermont Ferrand, and Dijon. By the time we flew over Luxembourg City there were only 50 of us still in the race!

Flying over Koln in Germany was very dangerous, as we had a very nasty storm, with thunder and lightning, which didn't clear until we reached Essen.

About 100 feet below us as we flew over Amsterdam I could see many windmills in action.

Hull City's football ground was to be our finish, and as we flew over the North Sea I steadily climbed into first place. As soon as Boothferry Park, Hull's ground came into sight, I knew I had done it, I'd won! But then disaster! I was flying too low and hit one of the stands!

For the next ten days I was in a coma at Hull Infirmary. Now nearly two years later I am totally paralysed apart from my arms and hands. But I will never forget the balloon race I won!

In linguistic terms, however, it is difficult to account for the teacher's comment here because Richard's story is full of detail and description.

There is much detailing of times, places and competitors throughout, and the degree of modification in the noun phrases of the opening sentences could hardly be further developed:

> a *cold but sunny September* morning
> a *large* field *on the outskirts of Plymouth*
> balloon *No 182*
> the *500 strong first ever Daily Mirror European balloon* race

However, when we read in the margin 'You could have put in a lot more description here', with an arrow pointing to the word *storm*, we are perhaps given a clue to what 'detail and description' mean to this teacher: something more poetic, possibly, with a good spattering of similes. But this would be inconsistent with the overall style of the piece; it is a well documented quasi-factual account of an event, not an emotional response. What the teacher seems to have been looking for here is not *more* detail and description, but detail and description *of a different kind*.

For the same essay test, Martin chose 'A Day at the Football Match' for his title. Too long to reproduce in full here, the story tells of how the writer dreams that he is chosen to play for Liverpool, and how by magic the dream comes true:

> I was sitting on the gate for about 5 minutes when something funny started to happen my eyes went all funny all my head felt as if it was going round and round . . .

At this point, the teacher notes 'this isn't really what the question asks for'. Martin goes on to describe his involvement in the training programme, and finally the big match itself. At the end of the story, we read: 'The story really wanted you to describe going to a match – the crowds, noise etc.' For *story*, read *teacher*.

There are several comments in the sample suggesting that it is the title rather than the teacher that imposes constraints on content, for example: 'it fits in with the title you chose'; 'Not really a ghost story'; 'only the first part fits in with the title of Journey by Night'; 'This isn't what the title means'. (If this is, indeed, the case, what do teachers make of an established author who writes a story about a dying miner, and calls it 'Odour of Chrysanthemums' – or of any of the vast number of published works bearing titles of less than obvious significance? It seems, perhaps, that 'real writing' is something different, and not to be judged by the same criteria.) This is not to suggest that teachers should never prescribe what children write about, or the style in which they write, but that they should make their expectations explicit. This is not, of course, possible where the teacher herself is not fully aware of what she is looking for.

Many other comments related to content are those of the 'dead end' variety: 'Rather a complicated story. I don't understand the bit about the comedian.' Where there is no suggestion that the writer should respond in some way, as here, it is difficult to imagine how, if at all, she might respond. Perhaps with another twenty-five books still to mark, the teacher hopes vaguely that the child will go back to her story to discover the cause of her reader's problem. And what would an eleven-year-old make of this remark: 'An exciting story with a good ending. But it's a bit predictable – there are lots of stories like this on television.' Can a story be both exciting and predictable? Isn't the influence of television itself predictable – and does it matter? If this writer's story is a good example of the genre, perhaps the teacher might do well to encourage her, rather than suggest, albeit obliquely, that its commercial potential is its flaw. But this is a teacher who searches doggedly for something to praise, and is almost painfully tentative in her criticism 'Possibly try and use paragraphs'. Under-pinning all her comments is a respect for the child's work, and a sensitive awareness of their likely effect on the child's own evaluation of her efforts. These are perhaps the most important elements in any teacher's response, and no amount of expertise in her subject will compensate for the teacher who does not – perhaps intuitively – recognize this. But whilst an appreciative and encouraging attitude is necessary, it may not be sufficient. Sound teaching strategy must be coupled with a sound understanding of the nature of what is being taught, and this is as true of the writing process as it is of any other aspect of the curriculum. Indeed, in view of its importance across the curriculum, it is perhaps especially true of writing.

Punctuation/Sentence   (3)

Where teachers are specific rather than general in their observations, it is the writer's failure to construct 'proper sentences' that is most likely to elicit a comment, and this is almost invariably related to the conventions for marking their beginnings and ends. A vagueness over the relationship between punctuation and sentence is evident in many of the comments: 'There is no punctuation which makes it difficult to read [sic]'; 'Write in sentences'; 'Check sentences and full stops'. It is a common belief that sentences are defined in terms of punctuation, but as it is possible to identify the sentence boundaries in a text from which the punctuation has been omitted, it must therefore be possible to define sentences in other terms (for further discussion of the sentence as a grammatical unit, see Lyons, 1968; Kress, 1982). Such misconceptions are well illustrated by the comment 'Your sentences are far too long', referring to a text in which the average sentence length is in fact two words shorter than that which has been claimed as the average for writers of this age (Hunt, 1970). The problem here is simply one of omitted full stops. Two of the stories are said to be difficult to read because they 'need to be divided into sentences'. In one, the problem is again a lack of punctuation, and the story is grammatically well-formed and coherent. In the other, the readability of the text is not so much hampered by a lack of punctuation, as by other factors. Here is Sharron's story, 'divided into sentences', employing Lyons' definition of the sentence as a grammatical unit.

A Robot in the House
[1] I am the robot[2]/ my name is metal micky and I don't know any one. [3]/I have only got one friend called hi-hi. [4]/ he doesn't know any one as well[5]/If I did now any one I would like to introduce my very nice friend who I have only just met[6]/ what is your name[7]/ShaRRon[8]/ I have meany more friends but that is my bisniss to sort out[9]/have you any friends hi-hi[10]/I have only you and Sharron[11]/are you telling the truth hi-hi[12]/yes[13]/you would not believe that I have not got any other friends. [14]/If I did I would be playing with them myself. [15]/well shall I go and make some more friends[16]/yes[17]/could I make friends with some Astronouts[18]/yes[19]/but how can I get to meet them[20]/well that aud pense[21]/can you get through to them by control to make them come and get me and go into space with them[22]/can I please metal micky[23]/why do I have to stay behind and play with ShaRRon[24]/you can play with ShaRRon if you realy insist. [25]/but you better not be to late Hi-Hi[26]/If you are you mynt want some thunder busters[27]/If you do you can by some in altor space and when you do you must not loose any money[28]/keep the money safe so no one can get it please[29]/If you don't you wont get any dinner[30]/'Oh well[31]/It is a Disgrace because you are only small[32]/you won't be able to fit into your bed at night(/) if you Dont eat all your Dinner up.(/) I will punish you for a week[33]/but one of the Astronnorts said Dont go home[34]./I said I better[35]/if I dont come home I will get a hard smack from my mummy[36]/Dad said that if I am not home when he gets home I will get a hard smack. [37]/I will not be able to play with my friend ever again[38]/If you don't believe me go to my house and ask if I can go out[39]/I bet I wont be able to come out[40]/ow is that right[41]/yes it is right[42]/If I don't come home when I am told to then I wont get a hard smack. [43]/If you don't come with me then I would not be Able to do it.

With the exceptions bracketed in the text, the sentences are unambiguously identifiable, and whilst the omission of many full stops does hinder a fluent reading to a certain extent, this does not seem to be the chief cause of the reader's difficulty. The main problem has more to do with the coherence of the text, which breaks down largely because the writer assumes that her reader shares her own viewpoint.

She fails to recognize the need to identify who is speaking at any particular point. Thus she sees no contradiction in telling her audience in S3 that she only has one friend, whilst going on in S5 to say that if she did know anyone else, she would like to introduce them to a second friend. But it is only as the writer makes her first conversational gambit that we become aware that both she and we are making this character's acquaintance for the first time. The story is located in the present, but it is a present locked within the writer's mind, and we are not given access to it.

There are other problems too, such as the apparently nonsensical exchange *why do I have to stay behind and play with ShaRRon/you can play with ShaRRon if you realy insist.* Whoever is speaking, it is difficult to see how this could make sense. Has the writer lost the thread of the story, or is she engineering a sudden volte-face on the part of one of her characters, in order to pursue another line of development? It may be that she does not know the meaning of 'insist', and interprets 'if you really insist' – which she has probably heard from adults – as a threat rather than a concession. Only the writer may know.

There is also a breakdown in syntax in S21 as Sharron grapples with a complex sentence involving the co-ordination of dependent clauses (see Quirk *et al.*, 1972, pp. 720-3). Having negotiated her way down to the third level of clause structure she 'forgets' that it is the object at the second level – *them* – which syntactically fits the empty subject slot in the co-ordinated clause *go into space with them*, and *me* is called upon to serve as both the object of the first clause and the elided subject of the second (see Quirk *et al.*, 1972, pp. 342 ff.).

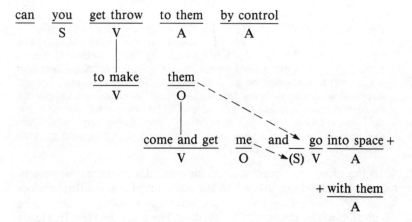

Only rewriting will put this right; there is no way of turning it into a grammatical sentence by the insertion of a full stop.

As Kress demonstrates, it is the development of the child's concept of the sentence as a linguistic unit that is crucial to the development of writing, and not the orthographic conventions that are used to mark sentences. If it is true that teachers' diligence in adding full stops and capital letters to children's work is, in Kress's view, 'to some measure beside the point' (1982, p. 70), and if at the same time the concept of sentence is crucial to the learner's task, then it is important that teachers be less vague in their understanding of the term, and more alert to the problems it presents for the learner writer.

Spelling (4)

Teachers demonstrate a variety of strategies for dealing with spelling mistakes: they may ignore them, correct them, underline them, cross them out, put a ring round them, or write 'Sp' in the margin. Where reference to spelling appears in a final comment, it may be to give specific advice - perhaps a reminder of a spelling rule, or an example of a misspelt word in context, such as 'Think about the difference between "were" – The boys were playing and "where" – I do not know where to find them. Where is a place word.' The poor speller is frequently exhorted to make a positive effort to improve: 'Really think about your spelling'; 'Your spelling needs working at very hard'; 'Concentrate on spelling'; or she may be asked to learn a particular word: 'Try and learn how to spell *finish*'. More often than not, the comment serves simply to point out to the child that mistakes have been made: 'Your spelling is very weak'; 'A lot of careless spelling mistakes in this, M.'; 'Spellings'. The child with a spelling problem is likely to be all too aware of it, and there can be little value in constantly pointing it out. Many teachers are sensitive to this, and go to some lengths to offer positive help to the poor speller, even if, at times, their advice may be misguided: for example, 'Try to whisper each word to yourself and check that you have each sound in your writing.' The implication here is that there exists an exact correspondence between sound and symbol: between the phonetics of speech and the graphetics of writing. This is often quite misleading, especially where words occur in the context of other words. For example, in the phrase *a hundred pounds*, the final *d* of *hundred* often assimilates to *b* in rapid speech, as the lips close in anticipation of the following *p*. In some contexts, sounds may be omitted altogether, as with *t* in *most people*. (Further examples may be found in Brown, 1977).

An examination of the text to which the above quote relates shows five misspelt words underlined by the teacher: *happenped*, *diccied* (decided), *goodby*, *frighted* (frightened), *noiseies*. Unmarked mistakes are: *cept* (kept), *nexted* and *beatting*. It is possible that, in some instances here, it is precisely because the writer has attempted to reproduce the sounds of speech that the errors appear. In the spoken realization of *happened*, for example, /p/ is often glottalized; /n/ assimilates to /m/; and the lips remain closed until the first sound of the next word is formed – in this case the /t/ of 'to'. (Try saying *happened to you* quite rapidly.) Seen in this way, the intrusive 'p' becomes not a random error, but a resourceful attempt to reproduce the properties of the word in writing. The 'ed' may have been added, not because the child hears it, – there may be no perceptible difference between the present and past forms of *happened* in rapid speech – but because she knows the regular past *-ed* rule. If this is so, we might infer that the writer has drawn on both sound and knowledge in arriving at this spelling.

In the case of *diccied*, the 'i' is surely motivated by the sound of the word but, again, sound is unlikely to account for the whole word, or we would expect to find 'ss' rather than 'cc'. It seems that the writer knows that 'c' is involved somewhere so, in this case too, both sound and knowledge may be providing clues to the spelling. 'Whispering the word' is offered by the teacher as a way of checking the spelling but it is unlikely that this process would reveal, for example, the final 'e' of *goodbye*. There are several possible explanations for *frighted*. It could be a 'slip' that the child might remedy by listening to herself saying the word, but since this spelling closely approximates to a very common child pronunciation of 'frightened', it seems more likely that the error is fundamentally grammatical. We have to bear in mind dialectal and social variation in relation to the sounds of words and we cannot, of course, rule out the possibility of adenoid trouble, which could certainly sabotage spelling based on the 'say it to yourself' principle!

With *noiseies*, the writer has tacked on an ending which is the appropriate one for other words that sound like 'noises' – *daisies*, *posies*, *babies*. It happens to be the wrong rule which applies to nouns ending in 'y', and she has forgotten to delete the 'e', but it is nevertheless a predictable error where sound provides the clue. It is interesting too that she produces *hitting*, *waiting*, and *beating* in their correct forms, but also *beatting*, unmarked by the teacher. This suggests that she is well on the way to knowing the rule that two 't's follow a short vowel, and one a long, but that she can still slip up over this. Whether or not the teacher chose deliberately to overlook the mistake in this instance, it is probably a wise strategy where there is evidence, as here, that the writer has almost mastered the rule for herself.

So spelling mistakes may occur for several reasons: the writer may be misled by the sounds of words, or she may attempt to apply inappropriate or partly learned rules. The cause may even be 'psycho-linguistic' – consider the omission of the final 'ed' in *diccied*. The brain moves ahead of the pen, and it could be that the pen is forming the 'ed' of *diccied* as the brain is forming the 'ed' of *decided*. Thus the first 'ed' is perceived as representing the second, and the word is finished short. A similar explanation could also be offered for *frighted*. It seems reasonable to infer that the teacher's advice to 'whisper each word to yourself and check that you have each sound in your writing' was motivated by these two words in particular, or might she not just as well have written 'Check that you don't have any extra sounds in your writing' (*happenped, beatting, nexted*)? It is perhaps easier to describe errors in terms of 'bits missed out' than to describe what has happened when 'eci' becomes 'iccie', and it is interesting to speculate what advice might have been offered had the child produced 'diccieded' and 'frigtened'.

The main point here is that this teacher has not simply settled for writing 'Spelling' on the child's work, but has attempted to offer some practical guidance. Less helpfully, she fails to discriminate between the mistakes that she singles out, and offers advice that is for the most part inappropriate. Had she a more principled understanding of spelling problems, and the time to analyse more precisely the problems of this particular writer, her efforts to help might well have been more successful.

Before leaving spelling, we might do well to reflect on the different responses elicited by two writers of widely differing spelling competence. 'You have taken a lot of care over spelling' was noted on one perfectly spelt script. On another, a veritable lattice-work of crossings out and mistakes, the same teacher had written the clearly unnecessary reminder 'Spellings'. Perhaps the child who earned the teacher's praise is usually careless, and this particular story represents a special effort on her part. In general, however, the good speller is fortunate in not having to try: for her, good spelling comes naturally. The poor speller may or may not persevere in trying, but the text marked 'Spellings' here contains ample evidence that the writer is trying very hard indeed. One example among many more shows her attempts to arrive at a satisfactory spelling of *who*:

oʜw

hẃo   ho

oẃh

You can hardly take more care than that, even if in the end you still get it wrong.

Grammar (8)

Many of the problems that appear in children's writing at a grammatical level are marked with such comments as 'Does not make
sense' or 'Muddled'. In such cases, if often seems that the marker
recognizes that something is wrong, without being able – or without
having the time – to work out exactly what. James's downfall, for
example, is a sentence containing a dependent clause with another
dependent clause embedded in it, and along with the comment 'Does
not make sense' is a cross against each of the three lines that the
sentence occupies. Here is the sentence:

> When the box and polystyrene which kept it neatly packed there in
> front of us stood a six foot robot, he had shrunk without the packing.

By the time he has got as far as *packed*, James has forgotten that he
now needs a verb. A possible explanation is that he began to write
When the box . . . was opened, but lost sight of the beginning and proceeded as if the sentence had begun *When we had opened the box . . .*
If this is so, then the added complication of the passive construction
would make the task even more unwieldy.

Mistakes like this are commonly made as young writers become syntactically more adventurous, attempting to handle increasingly complex relationships with correspondingly complex linguistic structures.
Such 'not quite sentences' might more positively be seen as evidence
of the development of competence, rather than of incompetence or
just plain carelessness. It seems to me, incidentally, a flaw in the APU
system of assessing grammatical competence that they award a full
five points for a text having no grammatical errors in the first twenty
lines, decreasing to nought for a text which has no grammatically well-
formed sentences. This means that a text comprising a series of main
clauses conjoined by *and* would score more highly than one which
contains imperfect attempts at the kind of complex structure that
James is juggling with here. To dismiss such attempts as James's with
comments like 'Does not make sense' makes very poor sense itself;
for, however true it may be, it is not a response likely to encourage
young writers to persevere in their attempts to master the structures
of mature writing.

The same comment, 'Does not make sense', appears in the margin
of Mary's story next to this sentence, reproduced here with the
teacher's correction:

> The ten*s*ion of the balloon drifting far far out to sea felt very relaxing.

In this instance, the problem is not structural, but lexical, involving

Mary's choice of the word 'tention'. However, the teacher fails to point out why the sentence does not make sense, and re-reading is unlikely to help. Moreover, she effectively obscures the error by bracketing the whole sentence and correcting the spelling of 'tension', suggesting that the word itself is acceptable in its correct form in this part of the sentence. Yet it is the word itself which is inappropriate; either the child does not know its true meaning, or what she intends is 'sensation', a word she may have heard, but not seen written down. In any case, the teacher's strategy is worse than unhelpful here.

One feature of narrative which teachers do identify specifically is **tense** – perhaps partly because it is a term they know and feel confident in using, and partly because temporal relationships seem particularly difficult for young writers to handle linguistically. However, the observations that teachers make concerning tense are frequently ill-founded, the reasons being that they have neither a clear insight into the exact cause of the writer's difficulty, nor a sufficient understanding of the tense system in English. It is widely believed that tense is synonymous with 'time', whereas this is not the case: tense is a grammatical category, whilst time belongs to the real world. Although tense is used to signal time, it has other functions too, and there are other ways of referring to time which do not belong within the tense system at all. These are realized by members of the large and complex class of adverbials, and it has been argued that the adverbial element is in some contexts more important than tense in denoting time (Crystal 1971, pp. 97–8).

Although children do make errors in their choice of tense, it is more likely to be their handling of time adverbials that breaks down in their writing. Andrew is well on the way to using these appropriately, but he has still not quite got it right:

> On Friday the fair came it was Witney feast. There were a lot of things that came including the zipper, the orbitor, the dodgems and the cage. When I went to the fair next day I watched them put the rockets up. Now the fair next day was built, so it would be on tonight. As soon as I got out of school that day I biked as fast as I could to get home.

We cannot fault Andrew's use of tense here, and the references to *next day*, *that night* and *on Friday* show that he is learning how to use the appropriate adverbials to denote the relationships between past events, and between past events and the time of writing. But we cannot be certain on which day the fair was actually built, nor which night the writer went to it, as the repetition of *next day* makes it unclear whether two or three days have been accounted for at this point. There is also a problem with the future-in-past, as *that night* becomes 'tonight' and the story takes on a present orientation.

Joanne meets a similar problem in recounting the events of her holiday:

> It was Friday evening. The following day we were going on holiday . . . The following day we got up at 7 o'clock . . . That evening we all went up to the ballroom . . . That night it was all dancing, but tomorrow night was in fancy dress.

Although she is able to express both past and future-in-past time by the use of *the following day*, *that evening* and *that night*, she too slips into the present with her references to *tomorrow*.

The use of direct speech may add to the writer's difficulty. In Neil's story, the juxtaposition of past and present reflects the conflict between an intention to report thoughts as they occurred at the time, and the consciousness of the fact that the story is located in the past:

> Throughout the year I watched the houses . . . Then at last people started moving in and best of all a family moved in my house. This means fun I thought and that night following means real fun. That night . . .

Notice that it is not the tense of the main verb that is wrong here, but the past significance of *that night following*. Later in the same story, however, Neil shows that he can select the appropriate adverbial to set the direct speech form in its narrative context:

> The next morning I crept through a wall and entered the dinner room where they were eating I thought no I'll save it for tonight. And then that night I changed myself into a glowing mist . . .

Yet as the plot thickens, and Neil struggles to establish the increasingly complex relationship between the events in his story, the adverbial again eludes him:

> The next day the family went out for a day recovering I think from last night.

But Donna, in her story, has managed to secure it:

> On the day of the horse show I got up at six o'clock . . . Then my mum came down and brought my saddle which I had cleaned the previous night, ready for the horse show the next morning.

and Janet really has events under control, along with the conventions of punctuation and paragraphing:

It was the night before the day we were going on holiday. Mum was packing the case while I was getting the clothes together.

At last we had finished and the time was 9.00 at night. Mum said, "Come on then you had better go to bed early tonight, because we have got to catch the aeroplane to the Canary Isles in time," I said, "Yes we don't want to miss it do we?" That night I couldn't get to sleep as I was so excited, But in the end I did. At 7.30 in the morning the alarm went off.

But even at this level of competence, time related concepts may still prove to be a problem, giving rise to some infelicitous if not ungrammatical constructions:

The hour till when we actually got on the aeroplane went very quick . . . the flight itself took us about 2½ hours to get there.

It seems that children have less difficulty with tense than teachers' attention to it suggests, and that, where mistakes are made, they are more often than not triggered by the misuse of an adverbial. An example of this may be seen in Ruth's story about a horse show, which receives the comment: 'Tenses. Narrative/thoughts muddled'.

Here is the story, with the verb phrases italicized:

A DAY AT THE HORSE SHOW
When I *go* to a show I always *have* a bath which Rachel and Ruth *give* me.
After they*'ve finished bathing* me they *plait* my mane and tail and then I*'m* all ready to go to the show.
The show they're *taking* me to *is* northleigh and i*'m* very excited because I *meet* lots of other horses.
We*re* nearly ready to go.
We *are going* with my friend Champ. Rachel's *hurt* her leg, so she *can't ride* so Ruth *is going to ride* me, and I *think*, we *are going to go* in the clear round.
She always *takes* me in that.
Oh good we *are* off.
I *hope* it*'s* not too hot because if it *is* I *will sweat* a lot and it*'s* uncomfortable if you*'re sweating* and you*'ve got* a saddle on.
We*'re* nearly there now and i*'m not sweating*.
There*'s* a big hill *coming* now I*'ll* probably *sweat* now.
We*re* nearly up the top.
I *can see* lots of horses now and i*'m* very excited so *is* Champ. We *are* here now and Ruth *is going to take* me into the clear round. We *are going to have* a look at the jumps, they*re* quite big but I *can jump* them Rachel*'s put* Ruth's name down and she*'s put* Sheila's name down.
It*'s* my turn now Ruth*'s going to trot* me round to warm me up.
We*'re* at the first jump then the second then third fourth fifth sixth yes a clear round. and I*'ve got* a rosette for a clear round it *is* red and white

with northleigh horse show round the out side and in the middle it *said* clear round in gold lettering on it. It's Champs turn now and Sheila's *going to warm* him up as well he's *coming* to the first and he's clear then the second the third, fourth, fifth, sixth, yes a clear round so he *got* a rosette as well.

By the time we *finished* that it *was* dinner time so we *went* over by the hedge and Rachel *took* my tack off and Sheila *took* Champs off and *let* us have a drink while they *ate* their dinner then after that Rachel and Sheila *took* the food back to the car which mum and dad *had come* in while Ruth *held* Champ and me. there *was'nt* much to do in the afternoon so we *stayed* a little while then *went* home. And when we *got* home we *had* a roll and all the mud *stuck* to us because we *were* sweaty.

To discover what the teacher might mean, let us begin with her remark 'Tenses' (for a useful discussion of tense and time see Leech and Svartvik, 1975, pp. 63 ff.).

Tense can frequently relate the meaning of the verb to a time scale, and *present* and *past* tense – the two forms available in English – often signal present and past time respectively. However, each verb form may serve other functions. For example, they may be used to denote a point in time other than that suggested by the name of the tense: the present tense verbs in statements like *We leave on Friday* and *Mavis retires next year* refer to a point in the future. But tense can also have an attitudinal rather than a temporal function: the past tense verbs in *What was it you wanted* and *I wondered if you'd mind answering a few questions* convey politeness or tentativeness towards the audience.

Most mature native speakers are able to exploit (apparently effortlessly) the wide range of meaning potential of the several forms of present and past tenses. However, it is probably true that comparatively few of us are able to explain exactly what it is we are doing when we select one tense in preference to another, as our knowledge of the tense system does not exist independently of its use. What we are lacking is the descriptive apparatus necessary for making that tacit knowledge available for inspection. Where this is true of teachers, it is difficult to see how they can be in a position to advise children on the management of tense when they are themselves without conscious access to the underlying principles of the system. The response to Ruth's story seems to demonstrate this rather well, when we consider it in the light of what the writer actually does with tense. In Table 7.1, column A sets out the forms of the present and past tenses used in the story, column B the various functions that each form serves in its contexts, and column C the specific items that realize them.

It may be seen that the writer uses five forms of the present tense and two forms of the past to serve several different functions. In some

Table 7.1 *The Management of Tense*

A *Form*	B *Function*		C *Items*
	1	*Present Tense*	
1 Simple	i	Universal time statement	's (uncomfortable if you) 're sweating (and you) 've got
	ii	Habitual time statement	go; (always) have; give; plait; 'm (all ready to go); meet; (always) takes
	iii	Contemporary state	's (northleigh); 'm (very excited); 're (nearly ready to go); (I) think; are (off); hope (it's not too hot); 're (nearly there); 're (nearly up the top); 'm (very excited); is (Champ); are (here); 're (quite big); 's (my turn); 're (at); 've got; is (red); 's (Champs turn); 's (clear)
	iv	Future state	's (not too hot because if it) is
2 Progressive	i	Contemporary event	're sweating; 'm not sweating; 's (a big hill) coming; 's coming
	ii	Future event	're taking; are going
3 Be going + Infinitive		Future event	is going to ride; are going to go; is going to take; are going to have; 's going to trot; 's going to warm (him)
4 Perfective	i	Habitual time statement	(After they)'ve finished bathing
	ii	Contemporary relevance	's hurt; 's put (Ruth's name); 's put (Sheila's name)
5 Modal + infinitive			
a) Will		Future event	(if it) is (I) will sweat; (I)'ll (probably) sweat
b) Can		Contemporary state (ability)	can't ride; can see; can jump

(Continued)

Table 7.1 (*continued*)

	2 *Past Tense*	
1 Simple	State/event with definite past time reference	said; got; finished; was; went; took; took; let; ate; took; held; wasn't; stayed; went; got (home); had; stuck; were
2 Perfective	Event with past-in-the-past reference	had come

instances, the function of the tense form is simply to locate the action in time − for example, *said* (past), *'m excited* (present), *are going* (future). But there are more complex meanings too: the function of the present perfective *has hurt*, for example, is to indicate the continuing relevance of an event that has already taken place: the actual injury to Rachel's leg happened at some point in the past, but it still has a bearing on current events, that is, *so she can't ride*. The function of the past perfective *had come* is to locate a past event further back in the past, relative to another past event: *Rachel and Sheila took the food back to the car which Mum and Dad* had come in *while Ruth held Champ and me.*

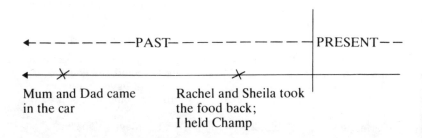

As well as functioning to locate particular events in time, and to show the relationship between events, there are instances in the story where tense is used with no specific time reference. The function here is to denote what are often referred to as 'eternal truths'; there are two types, and both are exemplified in Ruth's story. A **universal time statement** relates to something that is everywhere and always the case, and here it is the fact that *it is uncomfortable if you're sweating and you've got a saddle on*. **Habitual time statements** have more to do with events than states, and so there is often some kind of adverbial element to denote when the event habitually occurs − *every day, on*

Saturdays, once a year. In Ruth's story, the habitual time statements all relate to the adverbial, for example, *When I go to a show.* All these examples have to do with the complex relationship in English between tense, mood and aspect, terms which it is not possible to explore at greater length here (a full account may be found in Quirk *et al.*, 1972). Even so, we can see from this brief discussion the wide range of meanings that Ruth is able to convey in her story, largely through her management of tense.

This is further illustrated in Figure 7.1. The headings in this refer to real time, and the arrows map the development of time reference through the story. The table shows that the writer has sufficient skill in handling tense, mood and aspect to achieve successfully numerous time shifts within the formal framework of the present tense. The problem comes when she starts to veer off into the past and, although she twice manages to set the story back on to its temporal track, a third derailment leaves it finally in the past. It is perhaps significant that the shift is triggered in two places not by the tense of the verb, but by that notorious trip-wire, the adverbial – here the conjunct *then*.

That Ruth manages to sustain the form of a commentary as far as she does is no small achievement, especially as she has to remember that she is telling the story from the horse's point of view. (And notice that she only lapses once in this respect, in her reference to Mum and Dad!) It is unlikely that the meaning of 'Tenses', obscurely noted at the end of the story, is intended to be favourable. It presumably does not mean anything like 'Well done – you have successfully manipulated five forms of one of the two tenses in English to develop your story along several temporal dimensions'. It can only refer to the final paragraph, and yet why does the teacher choose to single out, from a text which positively demonstrates the child's competence in handling this feature of narrative, the point at which it breaks down? It is possibly because the teacher herself is not equipped to recognize the extent of the writer's linguistic competence, nor to identify the real cause of her problem.

By 'Narrative/thoughts muddled' the teacher may be attempting to distinguish between the final paragraph – 'Narrative' – and the rest of the story. Yet, despite the fact that the writer has cast herself in the role of the horse, there is surely some sense of audience here. Apart from the echoes of the television commentary *he's coming to the first and he's clear then the second the third, fourth, fifth, sixth yes a clear round*, the informative opening of the story would be redundant without the presence of a listener. Thus 'Tenses. Narrative/thoughts muddled' is itself rather vague and unilluminating, with the teacher again relying on the oblique to hint at a relationship which she is unable – or has not the time – to identify more precisely.

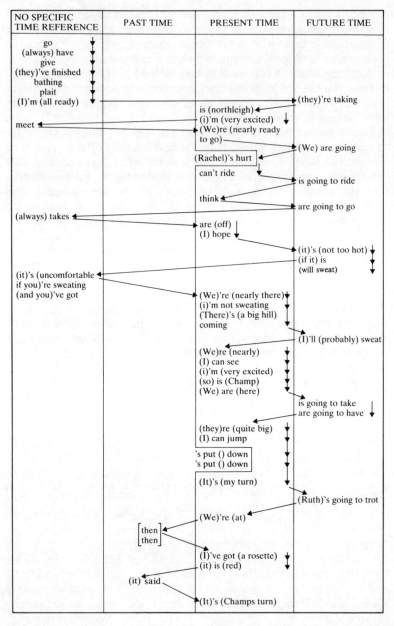

Figure 7.1   *The development of time reference (only prominent adverbial elements are listed).*

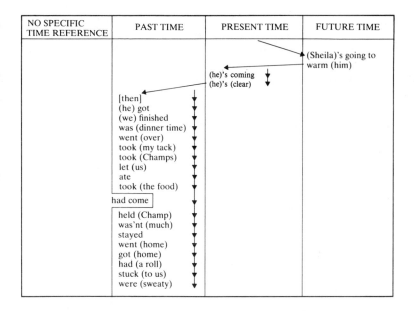

NO SPECIFIC TIME REFERENCE	PAST TIME	PRESENT TIME	FUTURE TIME
			(Sheila)'s going to warm (him)
		(he)'s coming (he)'s (clear)	
	[then] (he) got (we) finished was (dinner time) went (over) took (my tack) took (Champs) let (us) ate took (the food)		
	had come		
	held (Champ) was'nt (much) stayed went (home) got (home) had (a roll) stuck (to us) were (sweaty)		

Conclusion

I have attempted to show in this discussion of these categories of teachers' comments that the use of a principled framework based upon linguistic description is helpful in identifying the precise nature of the strengths and weaknesses in children's writing and in clarifying the meaning of the comments themselves. I am aware, also, that the discussion has implications that relate to teachers' knowledge of language and, more mundanely, their use of time. These I shall briefly comment on in conclusion.

The Bullock Report (DES, 1975, Chapter 11) makes a useful distinction between the use of language and the study of language, suggesting that for teachers the latter is helpful in reinforcing and clarifying aspects of the former, particularly when evaluating and/or responding to children's writing. Teachers are, of course, effective users of language themselves. But to be an effective user of language does not automatically imply that one is, therefore, able to teach others to use language effectively. *Being able to do* is not the same thing as *knowing about*. As, for example, with someone who knows how to digest food but who may well know nothing about the digestive system. Equally, if we have something wrong with our digestive system we would not think of consulting someone whose expertise consisted simply in the possession of a digestive system that was in excellent working order. We have a right to expect that the expertise would involve a detailed knowledge of anatomy and physiology and the ability to use this knowledge in diagnosing our problem. In the same way children should not be expected to bring their writing problems to a teacher who knows nothing about the anatomy and physiology of language: problems which, as we have seen, are not necessarily errors but valuable explorations towards a higher level of competence.

Such conclusions, as Dunsbee and Ford (1980) point out, place an overwhelming burden on the teacher. Pressures are exerted by parents, headteachers and often the children themselves who all seem to expect a liberal use of the corrective red pen. Being selective in the interests of diagnosis *can* seem to others like negligence. But is this reason enough for continuing a practice that appears both time-consuming and largely ineffective? We need to break this 'circle of expectation' and create a systematic way of responding to children's writing (whether orally or by written comments) that is, at the same time, selective in the types of problems that are given attention at any one time. To do this we need a principled framework, as I have argued above. We might also decide that to pursue such a policy carries with it the requirement that we are similarly selective about the amount, type and purpose of the writing we set.

Acknowledgement

I am indebted to Michael Newby and Talbot Taylor, my colleagues on the 'Structural Analysis of the Language of School Age Children' Project of Westminster College, Oxford, for agreeing to this material being used in this chapter.

Suggested Further Reading

Cooper, C., and Odell, L. (1977), *Evaluating Writing* is a collection of articles on different approaches to the evaluation of writing.

Dunsbee, T., and Ford, T. (1980), *Mark My Words: a Study of Teachers as Correctors of Children's Writing* is a very readable and informative discussion of the different responses to children's writing that teachers make.

Leech, G. M., and Svartvik, J. (1975), *A Communicative Grammar of English* provides a useful complement to *A Grammar of Contemporary English* (Quirk, R. *et al.*, 1972). In particular, it has useful sections on time and tense, and linking signals in connected discourse.

Shaughnessy, M. P. (1977), *Errors and Expectations* is a very practical guide for the teacher to the difficulties students encounter in writing, looking at syntax, vocabulary, spelling, punctuation and handwriting. This book has much to offer the teacher at both primary and secondary level.

8 Readings of Children's Writing: a Case-study

SEMINAR DISCUSSION

Introduction

What follows is an edited version of a one-day seminar held at Newman College, Birmingham. The aim of the seminar was to bring together a group of people who are, from a variety of perspectives, all engaged in the task of analysing texts and also concerned with education, to see what might emerge from discussing some pieces of children's writing that would illustrate the value of a linguistic perspective in reading children's writing.

The Participants

Margaret Berry	: lecturer in the Department of English, University of Nottingham
David Brazil	: lecturer in the Department of English Language and Literature, University of Birmingham
Mike Convey	: was senior lecturer in English at Newman College, Birmingham and is now a member of Her Majesty's Inspectorate.
Nicola Coupe	: lecturer in English at Newman College, Birmingham
John Harris	: principal lecturer in the Department of English and co-ordinator, Language Development Centre, Sheffield City Polytechnic
Michael Hoey	: lecturer, English Language Research, University of Birmingham
John Sinclair	: Professor of Modern English Language at the University of Birmingham (general editor *Aspects of English* series)
Jeff Wilkinson	: senior lecturer in the Department of English, Sheffield City Polytechnic

The writing selected was done by two top junior pupils, Rosalind and

Ben, and is of three different types – story, topic and an invented game with instructions for playing. The topic writing arose from a visit to a sixteenth century manor house in the Midlands. The class went there for a day visit and was asked to investigate certain aspects of the history of the house and, in particular, to concentrate on any aspect that was of personal interest. It was noted by the teacher that the children did not approach the task of the topic writing with the same enthusiasm they brought to the task of story writing or creating a game. These latter tasks arose in similar ways to each other. The games constructing was a piece of work that occurred towards the end of term when children had brought in some games to play. The teacher started talking to the class about games and how they were constructed. It seemed logical to see if the class could actually construct some games of their own and write the rules for them. The stories were written after a lengthy class discussion about what kind of stories the children found interesting to listen to. The task was framed in this way: the children were to imagine that they were writing a story for 'Jackanory' that they would like to hear and that they thought other children would like to hear.

The Texts of the Stories

BEN

It was nine o'clock. Peter was sitting in front of the television. Peter was thirteen he had brown eyes and fair hair. He was trying to watch the television but he was worrying about his parents they had gone in the car to a meeting a there work. Before they had gone they had had a row about whether or not to go to the meeting. Sudenly he heard the noise of a police car, it became louder and louder sudenly it stopped then he heard his doorbell ring he got up walked through the hall and opened the door. There stood a police he said "can I come in sonny" Peter said "yes of course you can". The policeman came in and said "We are sorry to imform you that your mother and father were just involved in a car acident". Suddenly Peter felt sick then he couldent breath he fell over and felt somthing like a hammer hitting his head then it all went black. When he work up he found it was morning he sore he was in a hospital a nurse came up to him and said "I expect you'll be wanting to know what happened" "yes please" said Peter "Well when you fell down You knocked your head against your stairs" She left his breakfast on his bed and went away. Peter was eating his breakfast when he heard the nurse saying to the policeman "Peter can go out tomorrow to his aunty margret" Peter felt sick again his aunt never liked children and him especily. She always made him do all the work. So then he made up his mind he was going to run away. He fell asleep again and when he woke up it was midnight. He got out of bed and got his clothes and changed into them. Then he climbed onto his bed opend the window and clamberd out he walk away. Seven days later he had reached his desdination witby were his grandad lived he was walking along the cliff edge when he fell of he plunged into the water he could swim but he paiked a speed boat came up to him and the fisherman said "who are you" "My name is Peter bishop Whats yours" "Edward bishops.

ROSALIND: THE BLACKSMITHS BOY

Long ago there lived a blacksmith with his family. He lived with his wife and his only son named Caine. Every day Caine would help his dad in the forge and watch and lean, for Caine wanted to do the same work as his dad. The forge was divided into two parts, half was where Caine helped to serve, and the other half where his father made horseshoes and other thing's. After that Caine would play with his friend's as normal and have his dinners. When it got dark Caine went into the house to have his tea in the best room. In this room there was apinewood table with a pine cabinet and chairs. Then after an hour's reading and writing it was Caine's bed time, he climbed the wooden stairs with a candle in his hand lighting the way, for it was very dark up those stairs. But as he reached the landing there was a wide window letting in the moon light. The next thing that happen something was shining in his eyes. It was only the sun beaming through the window, as it was already morning. Caine got washed, dressed and went downstairs into the kitchin where the kettle on the stove exploded with a whistle. After Caine's daily lesons and playing with his friend's he asked his dad if he had got any book's about hero's. His dad asked him why. Caine explained to his dad that it was a topic at school. Caine's dad agreed and he told him it was a ledgened book aswell. That night Caine woke up, but where was he. He seemed to be in a valley some where. Caine looked around him and there in the distance he saw a castle "ah" he said "I'll ask them where this place is." He aproched the castle cautiously just incase there might be a trap. Fineally Caine got to the door and rang the bell, he waited and waited and waited, Until he invited him self because he was getting board. There was a long hall way, and then at the side of that there was a staircase Caine climbed the stairs until he met the butler the butler explained that everyone had gone out. "Out where?" asked Caine "A hunting my dear fellow". After everyone had come back they invited Caine to stay for tea, they had cakes, sandwiches, jelly and hotdogs. In the castle their lived a king a queen and of course a princess. After tea Caine and the princess walked in the gardens, for it was a warm night. As they walked Cain fell into one of the gardeners dragon traps the princess said she was very sorry but Caine had fainted. The princess called and called Caine but in his mind her voice was getting fainter and fainter [word itself fades]. Just then everything went cold he woke up it was his mother pulling of his bed clothes. It was all a dream but it did relate to a ledgend.

The End

The Texts of the Topic Work

BEN: CHESS

There is an argument whether chess origanated from Old persia in the seventh Century or it origanated from India in the fifth or Sixth Century. The game is supposed to represent an imaginary battle between two armies. The peices were made to look like men of a battle feild, elephants, horses, chariots and foot soldiers. From were ever it origanated it spread very slowly taking hundreds of years. It was brought over to west europe by the moors. Nowadays chess is played in every country. It had come to Britain in the eleventh Century in king Canutes reign. One day King Canute was having a game of chess with an earl when the King took back a move. the earl was so outraged that he tipped the board so King Canute had the earls head chopped off.

The different chess sets there have been include A Medievel A Carved African set. A Reynard set. A lewis set and A queens bests set.

The designs in the Medievel German set are of king, queens and bishops with elaborately carved backs and warrior musisians as rooks. The designs in the Carved African set is for the knights they have giraffes for the pawns they have monkey and for rooks the have mud huts. The Reynard set peices are of all the chariters of Reynard fox stories. The designs of the lewis are of no pawns but instead they have tombstones and the reast is the same as nowadays. The designs of the queens beasts set is of heraldic beasts including the lion of England the red dragon of Wales and the unicorn of Scotland.

The Medieval German set is made of wood. The african set is made of thornwood and ebony. The Reynard set is made with wood. The lewis set is made with walrus tusks. The queens beasts set is made by resin.

The lewis set has a story behind it this is it. In 1831 a Scottish peasant in an underground chamber at androil on the west of the Isle of Lewis found figers which then turned out to be chess pieces.

ROSALIND: HOUSES 16th–17th CENTURY

A farm house in the sixtenth century was built with wattle and dawb. Wattle consisted of wickerwork frame for the dawb, which was made out of mud. Most times hazlel branches were used for the wickerwork. But as wood was scarce in those days, they started to use wattle and stone. When they got well into the sixtenth century they started to add chimneys to houses. The inside walls were made of alternate lines of plaster and wood and for the roof they used very heavy beams to support it. They made the floor by using stone flags with rushes spread over the floor. The rushes were used like a sort of mat or carpet to give a bit of bounce underneath feet. The furniture was made by the village carpenters or craftsmen. They would have an open fire in the main of the house. On the back wall of the fire was an iron fireback to protect the walls from damage. Staircases had only recently been built into houses (before they had used ladders). To sleep on people had to put up with hard straw pallets which are some sort of matress. The previous house had no glass so instead the people had drafts. Also the people had no cushions for comfort or benches they didn't even have proper chimneys. The bedrooms contained a wall cupboard for clothes, a heavy stool, a chest for valuables and perhaps for a little chest of money. The floor in the bedroom would again be covered with rush mats. They would make bedsteads (frame of bed) out of heavy and solid oak. Round the bedstead was some very long curtains which when drawn gave warmth. In a town house they had about and had had great numbers of gardens which a farm house would not have but insted have a yard. These gardens cosisted of many faintains and statues with flower beds in geometric patterns. The three types of materials use mainly for building was timber, brick or stone. Inside the house in one of the halls are some tables, benches and chairs with the odd bookcase here and there. The servents rooms were usually placed at the other end of the house to where the owners rooms were. As in a farmhouse they didn't even have servants. A staircase in a town house would be wide and they would have more than one as for a farm they would only have one staircase which wouldn't be in good condition.

The Games Instructions

BEN

1 The tombstone moves either two squares forward one square to the wide or one square diagnally forward tombstone canot move backward.
2 The phantoms can move up to 5 squares diaganally. Unlike the tombstones the phantoms can move backwards.
3 Poultergeists can move up to seven squares vertically and up to 5 squares horizontally.
4 The witch moves like a knight in chess

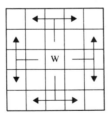

5 two people play it.
6 You take it in turns to move.
7 To win you have to get the oponents two keys and then get two of your players in the same room as the person.
8 To take peices you have to land on there squares. You canot take two peices at once. The only time you canot take a peice is when

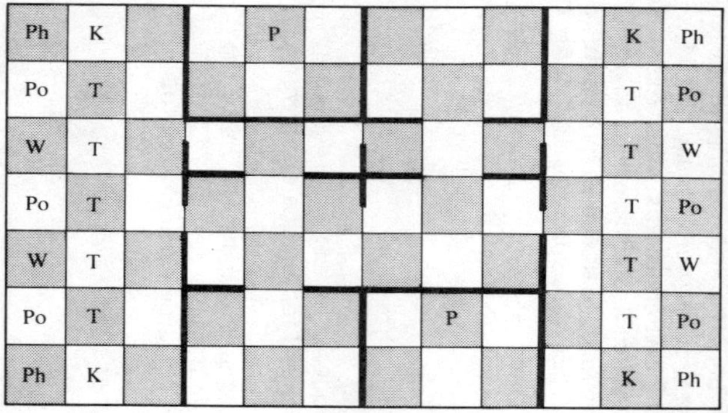

peiceshape	name	name on board	number of peices	value of peice
	tombstone	T	5	1
	phantom	Ph	2	2
	poultergiste	Po	3	3
	which	W	2	6
	person	P	1	12
	key	K	2	19

Figure 8.1 *Ben's game.*

that peice has just took a key. Also when you take an oponents tombstone the peice that took it go's back to its origanal square if there is one of your peices there it is taken of the board.

9 You canot miss a turn.
10 There are two peices that canot move these are keys and people.
11 You are not allowed to jump over your oponents peices or your own.
12 Whites go first allways.

ROSALIND: RULES

1 You have a card each with a colour on, what ever colour you have, you go to the square with the name on it – eg Europe
2 Each player shakes the die in turn And moves the number of squares shown on the dice.
3 When you land on a coloured square the same colour as your card, you are allowed to go 5 spaces forward.

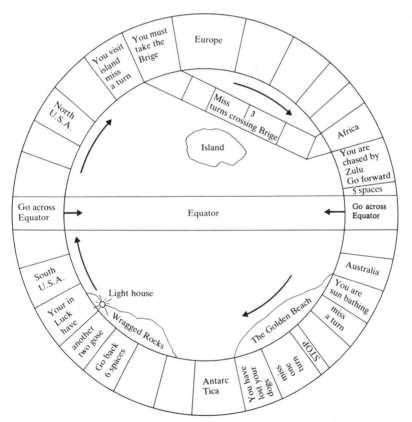

Figure 8.2 *Rosalind's game.*

4   If you come to a square with yellow lines you just stay there and do nothing until your next go.

5   When you land on the yellow squares you go a cross the Equator.

6   When you land on a square with instructions *you have to* obay them

7   When you come to STOP , *You* must stop and follow the Instructions

Approaches to Analysis

Note: quotations from the children's texts occurring in the discussion have been left in the form cited by the speakers.

JW   One of the things that we're interested in exploring is how linguists approach a text and seeing if this might be beneficial for teachers. Do you look at what interests you in the writing first of all in terms of how you respond to it as a reader; or do you say, for instance, as a linguist. 'I am interested in subordination. I will, therefore, look at all the subordination elements in the text'?

MB   Initially, I scanned through the texts, gaining intuitive impressions and then read them through again more carefully to see if I could account for my initial intuitions. So that would be point one. And point two would be that when trying to account for my intuitions, I worked 'top-down' rather than 'bottom-up',[1] that is I started by trying to look at overall, narrative structure in the stories, and global structures of some other kind in the other texts. I first concentrated on the semantic organization of the texts, then I moved on to the more formal features and the smaller units after that.

JW   So, it's that sort of progression. The majority of studies of children's writing over the past thirty or forty years have tended to work in the opposite direction, from 'bottom-up', from clause structure and what have you.

JH   I was also fitting it in with my knowledge of features I would expect in writing at this stage of development, but working very much, like Margaret, from 'top-down'. What was interesting to me was the temporal ground plan of the stories and looking at them in terms of setting, events and so on; then going on to things like complex relationships coming in which you can identify syntactically. Then down to more detailed items, but fitting those within the overall structure.

NC   My approach is, perhaps, not quite so ordered. I tend to start at the top, read through and see what leaps out of the page at me, looking at it feature by feature, possibly on several different levels. I don't start by looking at, say, all the time features. I look at what comes up all the way through and then go back and focus on one area and go through again and take it feature by feature.

JW Is this a general approach, then, because in recent discussions by linguists of children's writing it seems to have been done very much the other way round? Certainly in the past and in some of the current publications linguists have tended to look for the structural elements such as words, phrases and clauses and define them as accurately and precisely as they can.

JS I think, certainly from the point of view of the tradition that most of us here have grown up in, that Margaret's statement is fairly classic. First you take your subjective 'fix' on the text and, in fact, it's probably rather hazardous to poke around in the structure initially. As you go into it in more detail you are relating this not just to your initial impressions but to fairly measured opinions. I personally took a rather different approach because I find that at any given time a linguist is always more interested in some aspects rather than others — so you have the 'hang-up of the moment'. I was quite consciously looking for an awareness on the part of the writer of what was going on, because I happen to be working on this at the moment. I don't think any linguist is likely to approach a text with a completely balanced perspective.

JW I feel relieved at this because I think that linguistics as a study has been done a great deal of disservice by the sort of approach from the 'bottom-up' that concentrates on lower level aspects only. It seems to me that the kind of approach where you start with your intuitions and develop from them is much more valuable for teachers than, for instance, the approach of Gannon and Czerniewska (1980) which is to identify the structural features and say what's wrong with them and how they need to be developed.

MB Ought we to distinguish between different kinds of linguists? When you say that you specify intuitions and then account for them, then that is general to linguists, but the particular intuitions *you* are interested in are not general to all linguists. Certainly the 'top-down' approach wouldn't be general to all linguists by any means though it is pretty common among text linguists and discourse analysts. I think one needs to be a bit cautious of talking about 'the linguist' and 'the linguistic approach'.

JW But in terms of what is published on children's texts it seems to me a useful corrective because so much analysis of children's texts has been from 'bottom-up'. The 'top-down' approach is one that I think teachers would find much more useful.

JH And it is a perspective which enables teachers to contribute something.

JW Exactly – because you start from the same point as the teacher. You don't start with a jargon which is alien to the teacher. You start at exactly the same point, which is how he or she responds personally to a text.

MC I think it is particularly important because the teacher is the child's reader, probably the only one sometimes.

JS Yes, perhaps a point to come back to is the very curious status of the reader of these texts, as possibly having an effect upon the structure.

Summary: Approaches to Analysis

(1) The approach to analysis adopted by the contributors is basically one of starting from perceptions of a text as a whole then moving on to look at lower rank features. It is not an approach that has been widely used in looking at children's writing.

(2) This approach is consistent with the recent tradition of discourse and text analysis, but is not common to all linguists. It may, indeed, be doubted whether there is such a thing as 'the linguistic approach'. Linguists tend, in any case, to approach texts in the light of their own current preoccupations.

(3) However, the 'top-down' approach is seen as having a lot to offer teachers. Because it starts from intuitions about texts based on close and careful reading it does not immediately create a sense of excluding those without specialist knowledge.

Discussion on the Story Texts

Ben's Story

JW Let's look at the texts in detail, the stories first.

MB Ben's story just knocked me backwards, that was my initial reaction. It's a very powerful little story – and I think you mentioned that there is a personal history behind it, which I had actually guessed. But I think it is a very well constructed and economically written story in that everything in it is functional and purposeful.

MH It struck me as being a rather sophisticated piece of writing until very near the end. As a discourse it didn't seem to me significantly different in type to something that an adult might have written, though there are clearly differences at a lexical choice level. I tried to analyse it in terms of two things – the way in which the problem/solution patterns [see Chapter 5] operated in it, and also the way in which time is stretched out along the line. He has, initially, established a broad situation in the first three lines and an expectation of an answer to the question 'is there anything to worry about?' in the third. This isn't technically a problem but it's something akin to a problem. To have a sense of its being a complete discourse we'd need to find out whether this worry was groundless or not. We then reach a resolution of this worry – we have an explanation as to why there's a worry, answering the question 'why worry?' in the statements about the parents. They've gone to the car and they've had a row.

We reach a resolution of this first tension in the form of a policeman saying 'We're sorry to inform you that your mother and father were involved in an accident'. That resolves the worry but sets up for the reader two further questions: first of all 'What's happened to them. Are they seriously injured or are they O.K?; and the second 'What's going to happen to Peter as a result?'. Peter evaluates this internally; the narrator doesn't do it directly but through Peter's reaction, 'Peter felt sick'. We then have these major questions: 'What's happened to the parents?'; and secondly, 'What's going to happen to Peter?'. This question is apparently answered by the nurse coming up and saying, 'I expect you'll be wanting to know what happened', and, crucially, the wrong answer is given: 'Well, when you fell down you knocked your head against the stairs' – which is not an answer to the question that an adult reader has in mind. We don't need that spelt out; we need, but never get, an answer to our other question about the parents: are they dead? are they seriously injured? or whatever. But almost immediately a new problem is set up without having resolved the earlier one and we have a resolution to the question of what's going to happen to Peter in the form of 'Peter can go out tomorrow to his aunty margaret' which is negatively evaluated by Peter – he felt sick again. Then, in true classical problem/solution pattern, we have a negative evaluation of a solution reinstating the pattern so that you now expect a further solution to this new problem of the aunt. The negative evaluation is followed by a reason for the negative evaluation: 'His aunt never liked children, and especially him. She made him do all the work.' So we have this new problem to be solved. There's a possible response – 'He made up his mind he was going to run away'. Then that's actualized; 'he got out of bed, got his clothes and changed into them. He climbed out of his bed, opened the window and clambered out. He walked away.'

What was the result of this? 'He had reached his destination' and this is the part where it seems to me to go substantially wrong. Instead of then evaluating this solution or providing the evaluation of the result – was this the result he wanted; did grandad welcome him; did he send him straight back to aunty Margaret, saying rotten little Peter? – Ben loses confidence in his story at this point and introduces a new problem/solution element. So we have the situation (walking along the cliff edge), the problem (when he fell off, plunged into the water), and the possible solution which is immediately dismissed, (he could swim, but he panicked). Immediately then a new solution is needed because that one has been dismissed (a speedboat came up to him) and there is an assumption that that carries within it a positive result ('and the fisherman said, who are you, my name is Peter bishop, whats yours, Edward bishops') which doesn't give us an evaluation of whether his solution of running away worked; nor have we had any final conclusion to the question of whether his parents are O.K. What I'm saying, I suppose, about the story is that it's quite sophisticated in its organization, but it's the end that shows him up as being not yet a fully skilled storyteller. He doesn't know how to finish a story; therefore, instead of finishing it, he switches into another story.

JW   Is it possible, Margaret, to look more specifically at some of the devices that you found in the light of your initial reactions to the texts?

MB   I looked particularly at transitivity and theme[2] in the Halliday type of analysis and both of them seemed to account for my earlier intuitions. In terms of transitivity, there is some kind of development in the story. You have relational processes in the early part, where you'd expect them: 'was nine o'clock', 'was sitting', 'was thirteen', and so on. Then you have a preponderance of mental processes in the next section of the story, and then in the last section you find a preponderance of action processes. I'm not saying that this works all the way through exactly, but you find them in chunks. They tend to cluster so that you feel there is a structure to the story and that there's a progression going on. Whereas in Rosalind's, they seem to me to be haphazardly mixed all the way through. We get mixes of relational processes and action processes and they appear to be quite haphazard. There is no sense of movement or progression.

JW   This would suggest that Ben has a tight hold on his story, of where he wants to go and how he wants to develop it, whereas Rosalind is wandering, not knowing precisely where she's going with it. It seems that the choices children are making from those three areas, relational, mental, and action, are in fact crucial to how a story gels. What you seem to be saying is that it's the selection and grouping of these elements that make it work.

MB   You remember we did some work on transitivity in our project (see Harpin, 1973) and what we seemed to be discovering was that younger children made a random selection so that you had mental/relational/action processes more or less haphazardly turning up next to each other. Whereas older children tended to be much more selective so that you would find whole groups of one, then whole groups of another, or sometimes a whole piece of writing which was almost entirely in terms of one or other of these three.

JH   This would suggest, then, a more self-conscious approach and also the ability to select.

MB   Yes, what you're getting is latent patterning with the older children, where it isn't just a random selection but where you find a higher than average frequency of another selection somewhere else.

JW   It's related to gradual awareness of what they're doing with a text?

MB   It would seem to be.

JH   I was looking at this text more at sentence level. What interested me was that in Ben's you find a lot of the piling up of co-ordinated clauses that Kress (1982) points out is indicative of a stage of junior writing. But what is also interesting is that there is a greater sense of the sentence as a syntactic unit, both in Ben's orientation rather than in the narrative and also in Rosalind's.

NC   Yes, initially Ben's sentences are very short and simple, and you also have the repetition of 'Peter' in the third sentence. When I first read it I thought, 'ah, that's an immature form, normally you'd be substituting a pronoun', yet reading it again it seems right somehow. It fits in with the style: 'It was nine o'clock. Peter was sitting in front of the television. Peter was thirteen.' It seems to fit in with the scene-setting. If he had 'he' there, it would put too much emphasis on the fact that he was thirteen, as though this was something significant, perhaps his birthday.

JH   I wonder if it's because he's setting his scene because, apart from that, he works the pronominal reference perfectly well. I think that the 'Peter' is repeated because there is a sense of parenthesis — as if he's saying 'Oh, there's a bit of information that you need and I'll put it in'. He thinks of it as a separate unit within his text. It's almost like a fresh start.

NC   That's right. If he'd put a 'he' instead of a 'Peter' it would have carried on. It wouldn't have been parenthetic.

JW   Could you just pursue the argument a little further about Ben's use of sentences?

JH   My point is a comparatively simple one. It starts from the punctuation. I think it's interesting to trust the child, and not to say he can't punctuate, but to ask what does the punctuation actually tell you. You have a mixture in Ben's story of punctuation that is actually marking off syntactic units, but more frequently it seems to be marking off what I would call 'event stretches'. You find a much higher incidence of syntactic units in Rosalind's story punctuated as such, yet one can chunk Ben's story with reasonable certainty, I think, in terms of the punctuation, as each time involving a new stage, and within each stage there are several bits of action that are realized in co-ordinated structures. Sometimes he just misses out the co-ordinating adjunct and you get simple sentences or clauses strung together. I think you have to see it as a child would see it. You sometimes get children stringing together ten, twelve clauses that consist of a coherent episode in the story. Then you get a full stop, a sentence boundary. Then you may get another few structures which represent the next sequence. It doesn't always work consistently in Ben's story, but it tends to be a very good indicator of how he is actually using sentence structures to chunk the episodes of the story.

MB   Actually, that does raise something else that I started looking at, which was to try and look at Ben's sentence units and at the same time look at the thematic coherence, using Daneš's three types of thematic coherence.[3] In the first type, the rheme of one sentence becomes the theme of the next. In the second, the theme stays the same in two adjacent sentences, but a new rheme is added to it. In the third type you have some kind of proposition which entails a lot of other propositions. It's the first two types that are relevant here because it looked to me as if the sentence units were more or less corresponding with the occasions on which the themes stayed the same and it was the occasions on which the rheme of one turned into the theme of the next that a sentence boundary was put in.

JS   It happens very nicely in 'Suddenly Peter felt sick', and then 'When he woke up'. It's still 'he', but there's a change in the time orientation.

JW   Do these points link up with the perspective of the writer's awareness of what he's doing in a text?

JS   Yes, they do, although tangentially from my point of view. In a fictional narrative, your judgement of it and your interpretation of it depend in great measure on how far you trust the author. It's always a problem with a 'novice' author as to how far you can trust him. I trust Ben very much at the level of keeping things tidy as he goes along. It makes sense, there's nothing missing. It's quite elaborately supported. On the other hand, I don't trust him in terms of the inevitable predictions one makes about what is going to be important and what is going to be referred to again and how his proportions are; that is, the amount of words that are devoted to a particular part of the story. In a narrative which you trust you assume that any of these things, colour of hair or whatever, is there for some particular reason. If he spends three lines on something, then this is a kind of biggish event, and in that respect I don't trust him. I don't know if it's fed back to the children that the number of words you spend on a particular bit should have some relation to the importance of that bit to the story as a whole.

JW I have the impression from those first bits of Ben's story that he's not using them for any specific information purposes. It's not important to know that he's thirteen, he's got brown eyes, he has fair hair. I suspect that he's using those to build up to the 'suddenly he heard the noise of a police car' bit, that he's using this as a deliberate device to set up the shock of the police-car arriving. So it isn't an important piece of information in terms of what it is, but in terms of what it's doing at that particular point in the text.

NC I wonder just how much is deliberate in this piece. I have the feeling that its effectiveness is largely accidental all the way through. How perfect, for instance, is the ending: 'my name is Peter bishop, what's yours Edward bishop'? We can infer that it's his grandfather, we don't need any further information. But how far is this an intentional stylistic device, and how far is it just forgetting to tell us? Don't forget we have the point further back, which Mike pointed out, where we're not told what happens to his parents.

MB Which is very similar again; we're left to infer.

NC Yes, again, does he realize that? I suspect that he's just forgotten that we don't know.

MB Though at least he's consistent, isn't he? At both the most dramatic points in the story he's leaving us to infer. That seems to me to be clear.

NC But on the next to bottom line we have 'a speedboat came up to him and the fisherman said' and we have no previous reference to a fisherman, and yet he seems to assume that we have because of the use of 'the' rather than 'a'. And, had it been a fishing boat, that would have been O.K., but it's a speedboat.

MB That's just something a bit odd about his knowledge of the world, isn't it? I mean, he thinks you catch fish with speedboats.

JH Yes, there's a difference of opinion here, isn't there? I can see from one point of view that the end part of the problem/solution pattern is not fully realized. But I feel that the ending is interesting precisely because it is implicit.

MH Yes, I suppose I'm not giving him the benefit of the doubt in the way I would do if I'd encountered that same ending in a piece of adult writing. I would have seen it as a manipulation of the familiar pattern. It does seem to me that there is always a danger in evaluating as successful the inadequate management of a pattern because it looks identical to the skilful manipulation and playing on expectations set up by the pattern.

MB How do you know it's one or the other? I mean, he's innocent until proved guilty.

MH You don't know — sure! I admire Ben as a storyteller. I think he shows all the signs of being a thoroughly good storyteller but I don't see enough indications that Ben is in total control elsewhere to allow me to evaluate positively a considerable divergence from the typical pattern.

JW Yes, I think the variance of opinion over something like the ending of Ben's story is a fairly crucial point because it does raise the whole business of what you expect children to write and what they're capable of writing.

DB And it raises the ultimate question of what the child thinks he's doing. It seems to me that a thing like this must be evaluated against some notion of the child's own perceptions of the text. My reading of this suggests to me that he is actually midway between two quite different kinds of storytelling. There is the sophisticated, highly dramatized sequence of events and then there is the social anecdote of which the ending 'my name is Peter bishop. What's yours. Edward bishop' is a splendid example. That is the end to the sort of pared-down social anecdote which throws away all unnecessary detail. You can talk an awful lot of nonsense about kids' writing, if you're not careful, but the fact that he kills his mum and dad off in mid-story, and it doesn't seem to matter, could be seen as indicating that it is totally subordinate to the point of the story.

Summary: Ben's Story

(1) The immediate response to the story was positive. It was felt that it communicated effectively. The intuition that the story was well

structured, by and large, was supported by following through the problem/solution pattern and the transitivity choices.

(2) Ben's use of sentences and punctuation indicate that he is at a stage where he tends to work in time or event units rather than, as yet, perceiving the sentence as a syntactic unit.

(3) Opinion about the ending of the story was divided. Some regarded it as stylistically sophisticated because crucial information was left to be inferred, while others saw it as not wholly satisfactory, suggesting that Ben was not fully in control of his material and had moved from dramatic story structuring to social anecdote in which the implicit is appropriate.

(4) Underlying much of the discussion was the question of trust in the writer. There is never any certainty with immature writers whether effects are intentional or not.

Rosalind's Story

JW   How does Ben's work as a storyteller compare with Rosalind's?

DB   My feeling was that this was not so much a story as a series of events, only very loosely connected.

MH   Yes, I would accept that. It seemed to me that Rosalind's story is somewhat far from the adult model which we are, for the moment, assuming that they're striving to imitate. In terms of the same analysis that I applied to Ben's story, in terms of questions and expectations that are set up, Rosalind is constantly surprising one's expectations but in the wrong way. All the time you have this question of what aspect of the situation is the motive for telling the story and we keep waiting for that. At one point it looks as if it might be the pine: 'in this room there was a pine wood table with a pine cabinet and chairs'. Now could this be a sort of 'Master Humphrey's Clock', you know, which we're going to open and find interesting things inside – but no, it's lost, and so we wait. Then we reach the window, and we feel confident about the window because it's actually set in this moment in time and then we're told that something's shining, but again we're let down on that one – it's the sun. So we wait for the next time round: 'he asked his dad if he'd got any books about heroes'. Ah, we say, this is going to be it, it's going to be something to do with heroes. Then we have, 'His dad asked him why' which actually spells it out, why? Then the answer: 'Caine explained to his dad that it was a topic at school' which is a let down. Rosalind seems to have a talent for the banal.

JH   It's actually a superb message for teachers, isn't it? All that build-up of mystery ends in being a topic for school.

MB   I liked the beginning and the end of Rosalind's but I wasn't so happy about the middle. Bearing in mind what stories on 'Jackanory' are probably like, I think she's caught the kind of beginning I would expect here with the way of introducing the characters and putting them in their setting. Then the final section of the story, the actual dream and waking from the dream, I think is well carried out. But I was very much in two minds about the bit starting from 'After that Caine would play with his friends as normal and have his dinners', going on to the day when he wakes up and goes down and asks his dad if he'd got any books. In Labov-Waletzky terms (see Chapter 3) I wasn't sure whether that was meant to be orientation, whether she was still setting the scene, or if the story had actually started.

NC   Yes. She begins by setting the scene and you have 'every day Caine would help his dad'. There's this 'would' setting the habitual scene and then 'the forge was divided into two parts, half was where Caine helped' and here she seems to lose track of what she is doing in terms of setting the scene. If she had said 'half was where Caine would help' she would have preserved that scene setting, but she doesn't. She goes into the simple past there and again with 'made horseshoes'. Then the 'would play' comes again, so we are back into the scene-setting. The 'as normal' seems to suggest a problem here, as though she's trying to say 'usually', 'generally', but the 'as normal' indicates something that is happening now so she's just falling in between. Then 'have his dinners'; the fact that she's put that in the plural suggests to me that she's trying to make it general but hasn't perhaps managed it. Then she seems to go into specific time, 'and when it got dark'. I think if this was a fairy-story what you'd expect here is something like 'one day, when it got dark' to bring them to the action. So she seems to be trying to set the scene, then to go into the 'one day' but she just keeps hovering.

JH   Yes. I started also by looking at it in Labov-Waletzky terms, and came to the bold decision that the orientation or setting went right down to 'very dark up those stairs'. But I agree with Nicky that she seems to want to make it a generalized statement but something breaks down in terms of actually realizing it in the surface features. You have the uneasy arrangement that as he goes up the stairs it's a part of the generalized setting but also it is the primum mobile for the events that follow. But something strange happens to the first event. It seems that the cost of transition from generalized – what he does during each day – to the particular occasion of the story does create problems.

MC She seems to have a conception of time in terms of days, doesn't she, and this complicates the orientation very much because she has to work through two 'day sequences' in order to get to the point where she says 'that night', which is really the substance of the story. I think she works through a different kind of day, as it were, in order to reach the dream and so there is a double orientation towards the dream sequence.

JW In your experience of looking at children's writing, John, is that sort of difficulty of moving from an orientation to an action a very general problem or one specific to Rosalind?

JH No, I don't think it's a specific problem. But there is possibly an exceptional point because with Rosalind's story the emphasis on the setting, or orientation, is much greater than one would normally expect with children of this age. There is an elaboration and a complexity at a structural level and in terms of the syntactic features that is unusual. But generally wherever there is a move from the setting into the action, I think that in terms of the actual realization one is likely to find problems.

JS There's an ungrammatical sentence at the core, I think: 'as he reached the landing there was a wide window letting in the moonlight'. I don't know if it's ungrammatical or un-narrative, but you can't have a 'there was' following a sequential time expression because 'there was' is background. Then she can't be quite sure what to do next because she uses 'the next thing that happened', so she obviously went a bit off beam there.

JH But she is trying to build-in time lapses, isn't she? The other place she does that is 'that night Caine woke up but where was he?' and 'that night' seems to indicate that a day has elapsed which she has chosen not to talk about. You've a similar jump in the time scale with the going upstairs and the light coming in and that somehow coincides with next morning and the moon becomes the sun, so the light's still there. It's strange.

MB And the bit John described as ungrammatical is actually a narrative device where she's changing persona, as it were. She's stepping out of straight narrator's role into seeing things through Caine's eyes in which case 'there was' becomes much more explicable.

JS In terms of the children's awareness of how these things are constructed, I don't know if they ever get told about narrative. The simple past tense is unmarked narrative form and so once you've set a basic ground with your 'would haves' and so on, then you can go into simple past and it's maintained until you make a change, and it's all assumed to be under the orientation. You must specifically make a break and indicate that you have finished the orientation and are now into sequential narrative which Ben does very well indeed. He has a brief but fairly complex piece of orientation and then he wades in and very clearly marks the boundary, whereas Rosalind doesn't. As John says, possibly because of an over-elaboration of the orientation, she gets tangled up in it.

JW   Is it, perhaps, also that Rosalind is using the style of the fairy-tale where you have obvious markers which indicate that this is the fairy-tale beginning of a 'long ago there lived ...' sequence?

JS   Is anyone going out to bat for that curious first episode in Rosalind's story about the moonlight and the sunshine as having some kind of structural role – in that it suggests this bloke has amnesia, patches of blackout, so he doesn't know where he is – or whether it's a kind of false start? It's very difficult to know whether it's intentional, whether in her mind you had to go through this part in order to understand the dream sequence later on, or whether she tired of that approach and realized she hadn't brought in the heroes and the legends, and, so to speak, had to go back round again.

MC   She's very concerned with light and dark, isn't she? There's a candle lighting the way, there's a moon, then there's a shining and then there's the sun. Her introduction to the dream is very much in terms of light and dark. It seems too much to be accidental really.

JH   My first intuition was that there was a false start. When I first read it I said to myself, 'Is she more interested in the typical day of this blacksmith's boy?' And I had a strong sense that she was, because she seemed to have spent a lot of time and effort on it. Then I wondered whether the story wasn't something of an imposed task. Perhaps she really wanted to write about 'A typical day in the life of a blacksmith's boy', but then realized she had to write a story and didn't get into it properly.

JW   In other words, she's changed her mind. This is a characteristic, isn't it, of writing the story off the top of your head. As you say, she starts off by writing about a typical day in the life of a blacksmith's boy, and then she says, 'Oh well, this isn't a story, we'll move it into the story about the legend and so on'.

JH   That was an intuition but when I looked at the difficulty she had moving from the orientation into the first event it seemed to confirm it, or to support the theory, at least.

MC   I wonder to what extent, in Rosalind's story, conventions such as the 'long ago' and 'of course a princess' and various others suggest that she's playing around with the conventions of these stories but not actually seeing it as something to be told to someone else – unlike Ben – because the more conventional the phrases, the less information they carry. Is she, perhaps, playing games with certain tasks that children are required to do, that is presenting certain devices? Whereas Ben is doing something quite different because he is actually trying to explain what has happened to him. Consequently he uses far fewer of these almost cliché devices like 'long ago'.

MB   Is one allowed to know how much of Ben's is autobiographical? I am wondering how much it is structured for him and how much he has structured it. Rosalind obviously hasn't anything available that structures hers for her.

JW   Ben's story has some autobiographical elements but it's not altogether so.

MB   So he's not just rehearsing events as they occurred.

JH   There's another thing that follows on from what you've been saying. I've been noticing recently how most analyses of children's stories tend to lump together fantasy stories and personal narratives. It seems to me one has to make a very clear distinction between them because there are some very striking differences. Often these affect the organization of events, the sense of audience, reader consideration, and so on.

MB   I wonder if there is only one sort of thing that can count as a story. Mike mentioned the 'adult model' just now, but what sort of adult model? This is a dream story. And the whole point about dream stories is that things happen in a haphazard sequence and you don't expect one thing to lead to another.

JH   Whereas Ben's is a personal narrative.

MB   Exactly.

DB   This would be my feeling, really. The point that I was making earlier was that the happening in Rosalind's story is far too gross and does not provide a sufficiently clear indication from the child's work of what she's supposed to be doing.

MB   Unless she's mixing up three literary genres? She's mixing up stories about heroes, legends, and dream tales – but even so one doesn't expect a sophisticated understanding of these three genres.

DB   But there are three things here, partly identifiable as genres, that are not entirely successfully kept apart. One is the opening, which seems to me to be a recollection of the opening of many a story that she has either read or had read to her – give or take blacksmith for cobbler or something like that. There are certain predictable features. Then there's the 'a-hunting, my dear fellow' part, which comes from another sort of story, and the other piece where she is obviously trying to make something of her own knowledge of the world - the 'cakes, sandwiches, jelly and hotdogs' bit, and other things like this that strike one as being very incongruous. This seems to me to be a classic example of the pen-chewing exercise where she writes a little, then chews her pen and says, 'now what can I do next?' It's the sort of serially-produced effort in which in the beginning there is no anticipation of later events.

MB   Well, that's what I was suggesting. That, in fact, it fell into three parts which didn't hang together, but that the first and third parts each have some kind of internal consistency; but I entirely agree with you about the three parts not fitting together.

JW   Then the title would refer to the first part of the story – because she put the title first and then started.

JS   But doesn't she need to introduce, about the sixth or seventh line, a statement like, 'Strange things used to happen to Caine at night'? Then that would provide an organizational framework to pull the whole thing together.

JH   That type of comment in a narrative, or in a text where an author is actually revealing intentions or structure, seems to me something of a difficulty with primary-aged children – the sense of being in overall control of how you make a text. I think it often leaves one with a feeling of the text being out of focus because you lack these purposive statements within it.

JS   Yet it's amazingly difficult to write the simplest narrative without them. They're crucial, because otherwise you would have to write down everything. You can't even skip a little unless you have control over organizing too, which Rosalind hasn't.

Summary: Rosalind's Story

(1)   It was difficult to see the main motive for Rosalind's story. The intuitively-felt lack of organization was supported by more detailed analysis of the narrative structure. Indeterminacy over parts of the structure was related also to tense choices.

(2)   It was suggested that there were crucial differences between personal anecdotes like Ben's story and the type of fantasy that Rosalind was attempting. Fantasy stories rely to a greater extent on conventional elements. The real-world events help to structure personal stories.

(3)   Rosalind's story was felt to be a hotchpotch in which different influences were discernible but had not been welded into a consistent whole. This was felt to be the product of writing without a clear sense of purpose.

Discussion on the Topic Work

Ben: Chess

JW   Could we turn now to the topic writing and look at Ben's piece first. Are the same types of analysis useful and do similar problems emerge to those we found in the narratives?

MB   I tried applying Daneš' thematic progression type analysis, and it's very easy to do with Ben's piece; you can see exactly how he gets from one sentence to the next, by turning themes into rhemes and so on. For instance, we have 'There is an argument whether *chess* originated from old Persia in the seventh century or it originated from India in the fifth or sixth century. The *game* is supposed to represent an imaginary battle between two armies'. So we've taken the theme there from the theme of the 'whether' clause in the previous sentence. Now we go on from wherever it originated '*it* spread very slowly' – we're still with chess. 'Nowadays *chess* is ... *it* had come to Britain'. We've mainly kept the theme the same so far. And we get '*it* had come to Britain in the eleventh century in King Canute's reign'. We now find it as a rheme in 'One day King Canute was having *a game of chess*' – the theme turns into the rheme – 'with an earl when the King took back a move'. Now the earl was part of the rheme in that sentence, and the earl now turns into the theme of the next one, 'the earl was so outraged that ...' So, in the early part of that paragraph, the theme stays constant; in the later part of the paragraph, you have rhemes turning into themes. Then what happens next is the third type of Daneš' progression. You then have different chess sets, 'medieval German, etc.', where you have a whole succession of things mentioned in the rheme, each of which turns into a theme for the next paragraph. Also, for that paragraph about the designs, you could provide a proposition which would be entailed by all of the things in there, that is, you could say something like 'The designs of each set are special', and that's entailed by all the things that are said in the rest of the paragraph. Then, similarly, in the next paragraph each set is made of something. It may not be a very profound proposition, but it is the underlying proposition that links all the propositions in that paragraph together. Then the last paragraph is something special. It picks up one of the themes in the earlier paragraph, it has a story behind it, and then all the rest of that paragraph is actually the story. So you can trace the thematic progression through and he's using all three types of Daneš' thematic progressions, and they're in chunks again. They aren't just coming haphazardly.

JH   Much of Ben's piece is what Britton would call 'low level analogic' – a sort of cataloguing. But there are problems, I think, where he is describing the differences between the chess sets. This is implying a comparison between the norm and what he perceives as deviance from the norm of chess sets. That sets up problems in terms of his actual resources for realizing the comparisons. It's interesting from an organizational point of view that he hasn't inserted any propositional statements like 'there are these different types of chess sets. In terms of design they differ' – adding some such overall structuring sentences and then giving the details of how they differ.

MB   Something he has done, though, is to try and vary the style. In the long middle paragraph about the designs, that kind of thematic structure does turn into a catalogue unless one varies the start. He does it rather clumsily but he is attempting some kind of stylistic variation to offset the catalogue effect.

MH   But the problem is that he's answering two questions simultaneously; in fact, he's answering three. In the first paragraph he has the first thread of 'where did chess come from?', which he starts in the first sentence, picks up again in the fourth, in the fifth and in the sixth possibly. Then there's the second thread of 'what is chess?' and 'what do the pieces look like?' which is going to become the main theme of the second, third and fourth paragraphs. Finally you have an interference of time sequence so that, having received an answer as to where it started from, you get 'it had come to Britain in the eleventh century'. Then, instead of doing as an adult would do there, that is, supply some evidence for saying so, he launches without warning into an anecdote. He prepares us better for the anecdote when he reaches the Lewis set. It's a perfectly reasonable and proper thing to say 'The Lewis set has a story behind it, this is it'. That's fair enough.

NC   It seems almost as if he's picked out the facts from his source book, whatever it was, flicked backwards and forwards, and put them all together. It's as if most of the sentences are lifted straight out: for instance, 'there is an argument whether chess originated'; 'the game is supposed to represent'; 'the earl was so outraged'; all this is lifted straight from the book. Yet, in the third paragraph, he's either tried to paraphrase it, or he already has it as his own knowledge, because syntactically it's far less sophisticated than the first. His problem is that he starts every sentence but one with 'designs', which is probably the most difficult way into these sentences. The second one is typical of the kind of devices children employ to get themselves out of this syntactic tangle: 'The designs in the carved African set is for the knights.' They introduce what they're going to talk about and then they start again, and talk about it, which is a characteristic means of getting over a complex syntactic problem. I think there's a great contrast between the first two paragraphs.

JW   In fact, I think that Ben's one step ahead of all of us in this respect. I don't think the stories came from the source books he was using at the time. He just happened to know them, because he told me once, when I was in the classroom, the story about King Canute and the business about the Isle of Lewis figures. What I suspect is that he's got used to a style of 'topic' presentation, in which you have organization of a general type, but, at times, you put in a snippet of a story.

Summary: Ben's Topic
(1)   Overall this piece of writing was felt to be competently organized but lacking 'signpost' statements to make the organization clear to the reader.
(2)   Ben was seen as being influenced by his sources in the first part of his piece, and writing with less complexity at sentence level but with more directness in the last part where he was drawing on his own knowledge and interests.

Rosalind: Houses 16th – 17th Centuries
JW   How does Rosalind manage this type of writing?
JH   I became very involved in Rosalind's topic work. What interested me was that there seemed to be a fundamental problem in her treatment of time. That was my first intuition. I didn't know where she was referring to early sixteenth, late sixteenth or seventeenth century houses. I think one can trace through the problem of the time scale as being one reason why it is a very difficult text to read, even verging on the incoherent in some ways. The other thing that I found interesting was that there seemed to be a series of comparisons implied. You have an underlying comparison first, in terms of time between sixteenth and seventeenth, or early and late, depending on how you want to describe it. Then, later on, there is a comparison between the farm house and the town house. Also there seems to be implied a comparison of the sort of materials used early and the sort of materials used late. I think that many of the points of ambiguity that one can trace to specific sections of the text relate in fact to that overall structure which seems to me not to be clear in her mind.

JW   This perhaps comes from the nature of the task in the sense of picking bits of information from different sources. If you're presented with a series of sources to look at in terms of houses of the sixteenth and seventeenth century without any sort of framework for organization you will tend to pull in things in a fairly haphazard way.

NC   Yes, you don't know what the time sequence is in which she starts, because the title is the sixteenth and seventeenth century. When she starts you're not quite sure whether she's starting right from the beginning, 'wood was scarce in those days, they started to use wattle and stone'. So you have some movement, presumably through the sixteenth century: 'When they got well into the sixteenth century they started to add chimneys.' The real difficulty comes halfway down, where she says, 'The previous house', and after this you really don't know which part of the time scale she's talking about.

JH   And, in fact, if one goes back to 'Staircases had only recently been built', that's just a comparative time scale, because you don't know where your base line is.

MB   If you assume we're gradually moving through, we're told they started to add chimneys early on, but further on in the passage we're told they didn't even have proper chimneys.

JS   Also they have beds on the floor at one point, and then they have bedsteads.

JW   Does that then square with your point earlier on, Margaret, about the use of the transitivity system, in terms of options in the transitivity system, and chunking and grouping of those options? Does this mean that in Rosalind's topic work the selections she's making are not readily apparent?

MB   I don't think transitivity has much to say here, but the more general point about chunking and grouping of options is relevant. There just seems to be no overall form or organization in the piece.

MH   I look at this piece rather differently. Until about halfway through it seems to me that it's a very well organized piece of writing. She's basically answering, in the first third of the thing, the question, 'how did they make houses?', and she masters levels of detail, it seems to me, extremely well. There are problems with these, but then there are problems because it's a much more difficult type of writing to master. Plenty of undergraduates can't cope with these sorts of problems. Your first sentence answers the question, what's a house made of? It's 'wattle and daub'. O.K., what's wattle made out of? It's the 'wickerwork frame for the daub'. What's the daub? It's 'made out of mud'. And then having got the wickerwork, it's not immediately clear; so we need to know what wickerwork is made out of: 'Most times hazel branches were used for the wickerwork.' So we've got our hazel branches. She now turns to an alternative method, 'wattle and stone'. Now there is a problem here because she makes it seem as if wood is scarce, so you'd expect to have daub and stone. It's a major problem and for a while it worried me more than the overall pattern, then I realized that the overall pattern is pretty impressive and that it is a serious defect within it, but nevertheless I'll forgive her.

JH But that seems to me to be part of an ongoing problem, because she has no temporal ground plan and this leads to a whole sequence of confusions.

MH I take your point. It ties in with the idea that the handling of time is not particularly sophisticated in her narrative. She doesn't have that sense. But if you ignore the next sentence which is an abortive time scale one, 'when they got well into the sixteenth century', we then reach the next point. You've explained what a house is made of, you then look at parts of a house. The walls, the inside walls; what they are made of – plaster and wood. They don't need explaining, so you move to the floor; the floor was made 'by using stone flags'. She works diagrammatically.

JH O.K. I would grant a lot of your defence, but it seems to me that embedded in the text there are other dimensions, and one of these is the time dimension. When you find expressions like 'the previous house' and before that 'only recently' and 'before they had used', it seems to me that there is a suggestion of progression in terms of the type of building and the type of furnishing and so on that's not made clear. Also there is an underlying juxtaposition of the farm house and the town house which again is not made clear. She doesn't start off by saying 'houses in the sixteenth century were built of wattle and daub', but 'a farm house was'. Later on she's comparing that with the town house. Although I can accept this nice tour round the walls, the roof and the floor as having a degree of coherence, it seems to me that in terms of overall coherence the text does not answer the questions posed by the implicit dimensions of time scale and contrast between farm and town houses.

MH I entirely take your points. It does seem to me, though, that to organize on three dimensions, which is what she is by her topic forced to do, to organize on the dimensions of the spatial or the constructional, the time one, and the contrast between town and country, is to have a very complete sense of the overall. It's a far, far harder writing exercise than writing in narrative. I am interested in this in my son's writing. He tells me very good stories, but he finds it far harder to write topics because he hasn't a model. Even if he had a model, the model's much less

reliable because there are always different dimensions. I do
think we have to encourage teachers to be more charitable
about this sort of writing just because the task is that much
more difficult, and because the models are that much less
available.

JH   On that we're in complete agreement!

Summary: Rosalind's Topic

(1) Initial reactions were that this piece was adversely affected by
Rosalind's inability to organize her time scale and articulate at
surface level the implied comparison between farm and town
houses.

(2) There are, however, some aspects of organization discernible
even if these are not sustained throughout.

(3) It was made clear that the organizational demands of this type
of writing are far greater than those of narrative. Models are also
less reliable. Teachers, therefore, need to be aware of this in their
response to such writing.

Discussion on the Games Instructions

JW   Perhaps we can say something about the games, that is the
instructions for playing the games. Is there a different type of
organizational ability required in this type of writing?

JS   I think it's a higher level of organization in the games.
Sentences themselves are fairly easy. But you have cohesion
problems with rules; for example, getting a reference right, for
which player, which piece, and so on.

DB   A numbering device would solve a lot of these problems.

JS   Yes, but even with numbers you still need the higher level of
organization – you still need cohesion. In games you have to
cope with items like 'the previous player', and so on. You have
to be able to control quite a lot of condition rules, haven't you?

JH   There's a good example of the cohesion point in rule seven,
with the mention of 'the person'. The person can only be inferred by referring to the diagram.

JS   Yes, the person is missed out of the first bit; but, again, as we
have said before with Ben, you feel that he has some idea of
how to sort something out. He says: 'to win you have to do
this'; 'to take pieces you have to do this.' He's grouping. And
you feel this chap could be knocked into shape – as we felt
about his other two pieces – whereas you just would not know
where to start with Rosalind.

DB   It struck me that the instructions for Ben's game have a logic that is not necessarily the logic that we would expect, but it's a justifiable one because he first of all tells you the game and then tells you about playing it. At number five we have 'two people play it', which anybody else would put at the front, I suppose.

JW   It comes after what he's said the object of the game is.

MH   No, it doesn't. If it did, I'd feel happier. The object of the game comes in number seven, if you're talking about the object in terms of winning, rather than playing. He's telling you how to play, how to move the pieces, then he tells you the general things, and then he goes to the purpose of playing. He really leaves it to a fairly late stage.

DB   Yes. You need to know these things about the game before you start, then you need to know how many people you need to play it and how to organize the moves, and then you need to be told what is your object, what is your aim.

MB   What do instructions for games look like? I'm afraid I paid less attention to the games than I did to the story and the topic, because I felt that I had some adult models for stories and topics which gave me a way into looking at children's writing. But I haven't made a study of instructions for games, so I don't have any sort of adult models to bear in mind. Does anyone know?

JH   I checked last night with one or two of the ghastly games we have at home, and also with one very good game, and all of them started off 'the purpose of this game is'. I think that's your point, isn't it, Mike? You must start with some overall notion of why you're playing the game, and then something about how you move the pieces and how you end.

JS   They often say 'a game for two, three, or four players' even before that. Those two vie for being first, because those are the two things that are most important. What you must basically have is who are the people in the play, and what are they trying to do.

DB   Yes, I accept all that. Assuming that this clearly doesn't follow that sort of ordering, we either have to assume that it is completely randomized – that he hasn't thought about it at all – or else that he's following some other sort of order that is logical enough to him. It seems to me that in introducing you to a game, I could very well say: 'Now these things move this way, and those things move that way. If you do that with that one it has a certain effect; if you do it like this it has another effect. Now, there are two of us, you take first turn and I'll take second turn. What you have to do is to get that one over to there.'

MH　In your terms, rules eight to eleven in fact represent the compulsory points whereas one to four represent the options available. It's as if he's saying: 'You're not allowed to do this, and you're not allowed to do that, and you've got to do that.'

DB　Yes. It seems to me there is a sense in which it follows a conceivable procedure in playing the game.

JW　So the procedure is not, in fact, fixed. You can have different procedures, or ways of going about presenting the instructions.

DB　Yes, this seems to me, at least, a justifiable procedure. Going back to where we were a minute ago, if one did, in fact, devise a special list of rules to put on the outside of the box, they would by no means be in the order in which you would present them if you were actually telling somebody how to play the game. You would say 'Get out the draughts game. You don't know how to play it? Right, well, two players, two people can play, now rule two . . .' and so on.

MH　Yes. You're quite right. Something I'm aware of when I'm teaching my children to play games is that the natural way with children is to take the board out, open it up, and start them on a dummy go; so that they learn as they go through the moves. The instruction writing has clearly been influenced by the types of game the children have played up till now. Ben's failure to produce a workable set of rules for his game is somewhat more understandable than Rosalind's, because what Ben is trying to do is create a version of chess, and trying to explain to anybody the rules of chess is a murderous task. Therefore, it's not all that surprizing that he fails with his kind of 'para-chess'. Rosalind, however, has taken a very simple board game – you go round a route, you have short cuts on the route, and there are squares on which you stop and perform the instructions written on them. It's the kind of game you find on the backs of cornflake packets every now and then, and, as such, her failure to find a purpose, a beginning or an end, is more worrying. As far as I can see, once you start playing Rosalind's game you are doomed to it eternally.

DB　Interestingly enough, it's the one kind of game for which no instructions are necessary; the game is self-explanatory.

MH　Again, I feel strongly that, as with the topics, the degree of ambition in what is being attempted must be taken into account in examining the language that's being used to achieve it. It's the problem of Rosalind's topic, if you like. She's being moderately ambitious in the way she writes and organizes her rules and is, probably rightly, regarded as not having succeeded terribly well. But she makes a reasonable stab. Ben, however, is trying to do something very difficult in his game. I have a feeling that I'd probably quite enjoy Ben's game, if Ben had only managed to communicate to me how it was played – but I wouldn't want to play Rosalind's.

JW   I think it's also a problem that they haven't had time to fully work the games out or to revise or edit them, or to see the consequences of what's happening.

Summary: Games Instructions

(1)   The organization of writing instructions requires a high level of competence since there are complex problems of creating inter-sentential cohesion. The children had not coped with these successfully.

(2)   The children's attempt to write games rules does not follow expected models. However, it was suggested that there was a logic, possibly derived from the likely sequencing of oral instructions given to someone on a 'dummy run'.

(3)   It was pointed out that the two games are at very different levels of complexity as games and that this needs to be taken into account in considering the success of the instructions.

Teaching Implications

JW   Could we, finally, turn our attention to a wider issue? In looking at these pieces of writing what points of value have come across about the teaching aspect? Are there things that we can comment on that would be useful for teachers?

JH   Do you know anything about the actual circumstances of the writing? Did the children use jotters? Is their work first or final draft writing?

JW   What they've been doing with the class teacher is not on the basis of jotting or revisions. It's writing off-the-top-of-the-head. It's the normal type of writing activity found in the classroom. They write stories straight off and that's how they approached all these pieces of work. The only one where they did do some revising was the game, because it was more immediately apparent to them that there was a problem of communication. I managed to see part of that lesson, and they were saying, 'Well, I can't write it like that because it doesn't make sense', and they were actually looking at each other's writing. But the other two pieces were done on their own in a fairly conventional way.

JH   They didn't, for example, look at the rules of published games as a model?

JW   They did do some research on that. They had to, simply in terms of trying to find out how rules are presented. But I couldn't guarantee that everybody approached the task in that way.

JS   Could I attempt to summarize my feelings? I think the topic pieces are highly revealing of the children's lack of organization. I think in Ben's piece, although the structure is quite coherent and well-prepared, he doesn't express the structure where he needs to express it. Where he does express it, it is quite often misleading. At the end, for example, he says that there is a story about the set, but he doesn't tell it. Also in the King Canute part, he switches, as Margaret has said, into a narrative using a different theme/rheme structure, but he doesn't tell you what the point is of King Canute and the earl. One would have expected a mature writer to say something like, 'it was important, it was quite a big element in the culture of the eleventh century'. But there's nothing at all, just 'bang' into narrative! Rosalind, on the other hand, attempts a much more tricky business – a comparison – and she hasn't really got what we call the 'metalanguage', but it's not that really; it's that a properly constructed piece of writing must be on two levels. There is the level of the propositional content and there is the level of explicit organization, which doesn't need to be wholly explicit. But there are certain points where, unless you're writing a deliberately obscure piece, you would have to look to your junctions and your changes. Ben's ability to organize material, just like his ability to organize the steps of his narrative, seems to me to be highly sophisticated, but his ability to express the organization is extremely limited. I think that the key to the whole problem is John's interest in the fact that they were not encouraged to revise; that and not being made aware of the need for a self-evaluation, both in terms of reading their own work and thinking, 'Is it doing what I want it to do?', and also making it fairly explicit for the reader. There's no sense of reader at all, in any of these six pieces.

JW   Isn't it related to the school situation and the nature of writing tasks in general, with topic work and with the game? It seems to me they've interpreted the game work in a similar way to the topic work. They don't really see that it's for any purpose other than to satisfy the teacher. They've just got to do the exercise.

MB   But they must understand what the exercise is.

JH   Doesn't it also reflect the extremely narrow writing curriculum that you find in primary schools? There is not seen to be a range of communicative purposes for writing, and, in fact, most of the writing in the primary school is not really communicative at all. What would be interesting with the games would be to give them to a parallel class and ask them to play them; and then that class could tell the inventors what's wrong with the instructions. Then you'd actually get somewhere.

MC I'm surprised that they took it so far and didn't actually do that.

JH That's because writing is perceived as being for the teacher only.

MB What's more, it's seen as a one-stage process. John was saying they aren't encouraged to revise. I should think they're also not encouraged to pre-plan because, it seems to me, that (to go back to the topics) Ben and Rosalind are very different in this respect. Ben might well have been encouraged to read through what he'd written and revise it, but I don't think that would have helped Rosalind. She'd have had to start all over again, to write the whole thing from scratch to produce a coherent piece of writing. So what she should have done is have pre-planned it. Really, in terms of offering practical advice for teachers, writing ought to be seen as a three-stage process: planning, writing, and revising.

MC I think that's often said. What I suspect we're trying to get at is the teacher's understanding of the organization of a text. I think it's that level that we're trying to operate at, rather than giving teachers tricks. This understanding is a necessary preliminary stage to advising the children.

JH Yes, and certainly in terms of non-narrative. For instance, it may not seem to be a very deep perception to say that there are elements of comparison involved in Rosalind's topic about houses. Yet I've found on in-service courses that this is a fundamental sticking point. Teachers need to develop an awareness of what the organizational demands of a particular task are. Until you reach that stage you're not really able to help children pre-plan. I very much agree with what you say, Margaret, but teachers have also to be able to perceive the demands of a task that they set. And for that they need the support of the right sort of initial training and in-service courses. It's not their fault as things stand if they don't have that understanding.

JS I'm at the moment involved in constructing a course on advanced writing for overseas students; we've been thrashing it out over the last couple of years. We've certainly come up with the kind of proposals that Margaret's making − that there should be an elaborate pre-planning stage where drafts are circulated. So, with the rules of the game, you'd come right up against it in terms of whether someone could play the game, and then you'd get some feedback, re-cycling and so on. Each communicative activity is part of a total cycle, so you can see, from beginning to end, the place of your part in it. Then there are three stages of revision, so to speak: proof-reading, revising in the sense of 'Is it doing what we want it to do? Are the right things in the right sequence?' and then overall 'Is it having the sort of maximum possible effect?' We've worked these things out from piloting material in actual situations for students who are, shall we say, technically fluent, but lack these organizational commands that we've been spending a lot of time on today.

MC   I think the last point you mentioned is something that's not very well understood. I suggest that after the child has produced what he thinks is the best version and it's been handed in and marked, and there has been a response, then — at that stage — you start talking about re-drafting, making it something better than you thought it could be. I don't know whether that coincides exactly with the last of your statements but it does have to do with effectiveness, doesn't it, and whether a piece of writing is doing its job? I think that's not widely practised.

JW   Or even if it's done it's done within an atmosphere where children are very reluctant to change in any way what they've written, because of the setting. They say, 'What do I have to change this time?' There isn't an attitude of revising for communicative purposes.

JS   You need motivation. I think that if you're going to have, as we do in the course I was mentioning, over 70 per cent of the actual class time spent, not in writing but in the talk that is involved in the preliminaries and follow-ups and so on, then you're going to have to motivate.

JH   Yes, motivation's a big problem also because of how writing is habitually perceived within our education system. The other problem is that, with children of this age, you're up against concentration span. It seems important for a teacher to be able to differentiate between different sorts of writing tasks to determine in which ones they can lead children on to revision, and how habitually they do it. There's a delicate balance. If a child is still very much at the stage of being a reactive writer, of just getting something down on paper and lacking the ability to cast back as well as to project forward in a text, then he's going to find it extremely difficult to make revisions.

DB   Nearly everything we've said here seems to me to be indicative of the type of tasks that are being set. 'Topic' to me suggests that it is the kind of enterprise where kids are turned loose in the library to look up all they can about sixteenth and seventeenth century houses. They make a lot of notes and then go back and somehow or other weld them into a piece of consecutive prose. Given those circumstances, it's pretty unreasonable to ask kids to produce prose organized on two, three or whatever dimensions. If they were writing out of their own internalized thoughts and had some organized knowledge of sixteenth century houses you might expect something different.

MC   Yes, there's an indigestion of information, isn't there?

JW   And why give a child this particular task?

DB   Yes, there is the very basic question of what they are actually asking the kids to do.

MB   Or how they're asking them to do it. Isn't that a more important question?

DB   Well, I think the writer needs to know what he's doing. Unless he does, he doesn't know how to do it.

MB   What I mean is that collecting, distilling and then reformulating information is an extremely important and difficult thing to do. And that is essentially what they are being asked to do. One has to see this as a multi-stage operation, where they collect the material first and then they plan their essays according to whatever dimensions they select.

DB   I would go further and say that they then live with it for three or four years. I know that's an exaggeration but, surely, this business of expecting people to digest information and immediately turn round and re-present it as something that is intelligible is imposing impossible strains. I couldn't do it.

MB   We all have to, don't we?

DB   No, I couldn't open a book about something I knew nothing about and make notes on a chapter.

JH   It's the time scale for writing in school that's so frightening, isn't it? There is no time for a process of internalization. There's no time for gestation.

DB   And there's no pre-existent background to which to relate these tasks. It's a question of what use they are able to make of anything they find in books.

MB   But, surely, learning to make use of what they find in books is one of the main skills that a school ought to be teaching children.

DB   I would agree, but I don't think it's an immediate X–then–Y process. It's much more complicated.

MH   Yes, that's right, and it seems to me that of the three pieces, the topic has the most purposeless language. Don't misunderstand me. I'm not saying that there aren't important roles to be played by this type of exercise. But I think it's important to see that when the child has a story to tell it's something new for the teacher and there's genuine communication taking place. With the games, however unsuccessful those are, they have a game they've invented, and they're trying to communicate what they've invented. In the case of the topic, this is the first piece of a whole series they're going to do — right until they finish university perhaps — where they're going to be talking to people who are more knowledgeable than they are. They're communicating the known to the knower. It's a curious exercise and it's one that we can't expect people to do well to begin with.

JW   Yes, I think one thing that came out for me was that, in looking at children's writing, people have tended to look at the problems the child has. But really what we're looking at rebounds upon the teacher. It's what you can get out of a piece of writing that will then give clues about how the teacher approaches the task — the relationship that the teacher sets up with a child in terms of the kind of writing and the purpose of the writing — that's an absolutely crucial thing.

MC   Teachers need to be told about this more frequently when they're being trained.

JS   It seems to me that there are two major problems. First of all, there isn't any perception of development in seeing a child's writing as being a stage in a process, where you can ignore this part, concentrate on that part. Also there are fundamental things which appear to be completely missed in the setting-up of the exercises. Every piece of writing must be located somewhere in the world and it is one side of an interaction in some sense. There are different ways of seeing it, and it must have some target value to the writer which can be somehow expressed and evaluated. If those basics could be got across, then the task set might more realistically reveal stages in development to the teachers. I think they started off from the wrong point.

MB   I agree entirely, and might one also capitalize a little more on the enjoyment a child can take in his own writing? Presumably, if a child paints a picture, he takes pleasure in its design, the pattern as it were, and I'm not sure enough is done to encourage children to take a similar interest in their own writing. I suspect Ben already does. I suspect he already can see that he's imposed some kind of pattern on the material that he's been dealing with and that he can enjoy having created that pattern out of it. I wonder if this is a different kind of motivation, oneself as audience, as well as other people as audience.

DB   It seems to me that the great fallacy of recent years has been to assume that enjoyment in writing comes only from personal, emotional writing, where sincerity is said to be the key. I think kids get at least as much, if not a bigger kick, out of mastering technicalities, which will enable them to do a job in different ways. There is an issue bubbling under here which I'd like to bring to the surface, and that's the relationship between personal and public writing. It seems to me that part of the difficulty is that personal writing is basically what they're getting practice in and what they're getting good at because it's also what they're getting a lot of, the story telling and verse-writing. I think there is a case for saying that the type of writing that the science student in the secondary school needs is so totally different from the type of writing that the personal writing tradition represents, that when a child is being encouraged, for the first time, to produce factual writing, whether it be historical sixteenth or seventeenth century houses, or whether it be an account of chess, or whatever, that this should be done as a group. They should go through it together as a very carefully planned process over a period of time in the way John was describing, in overt recognition of the fact that the type of work that is being demanded of them is almost entirely different from the type of things they've done up to that point. The only thing they have in common is that they still have to construct sentences. I think that the mistake comes from hoping that public writing will grow naturally out of personal writing. I don't think it does.

Summary: Teaching Implications

(1) Two major problems emerged from the discussion of the children's work. They both had considerable problems with organization and with the conscious articulation of that organization. There was also a failure to evaluate for themselves their performance in the sense of being able to consider whether the piece of writing was in fact doing what they wanted it to do.

(2) Both these problems could be related to the practice of writing in the classroom in that children were neither encouraged to pre-plan nor to revise their writing. There was little sense of being engaged in a genuinely communicative act.

(3) It is apparent that teachers need to be more aware of text features such as organization.

(4) If writing, particularly of the more difficult types, is to be attempted with a chance of success children need to be motivated to sustain their effort over a period of time to allow for pre-planning, writing and revising. Enjoyment of writing is important and it should not be thought that personal writing is the only sort to afford pleasure to the writer.

(5) The value of the type of tasks represented particularly by the topic work could be questioned since these might well entail

children absorbing for instant regurgitation knowledge from source books that is totally external to their existing knowledge. Writing involved in these types of task can be classified as public writing, which is not the same as personal writing and the one does not emerge naturally from the other.

Notes: Chapter 8

1 The notion of **top-down** and **bottom-up** approaches to analysis can be simply illustrated. Language is organized hierarchically in levels as follows:

(1) Discourse/Text	(4) Group
(2) Sentence	(5) Word
(3) Clause	(6) Morpheme

A bottom-up approach would look first at a lower level feature such as word or group and then move up to sentence level. A top-down approach considers the text at discourse level initially and then relates analysis of discourse structure to specific features at lower levels.

2 Halliday (1970) outlines a description of language which reflects how we, as individuals, perceive and represent our experiences of processes, persons and relations in the world both around and inside us. The **transitivity system** is one category used to account for just one part of this perspective and, in its analysis of clause/sentence units, focuses particular attention on the nature of the **verb** and its relationship to other parts in such units. In providing such a perspective on how language organizes, and is organized by, our view of the world, *three* different types of process are identified:

1 **Action processes.** These processes involve the participation of animate or inanimate beings. For example:

> Joan coughed loudly.
> The volcano erupted violently.

2 **Mental processes.** These processes are related to either internalized (liking, seeing, perceiving, and so on) or externalized (saying, shouting, uttering, and so on) ways of interpreting the world and may express:

(a) perception, e.g. She looked at the book
(b) reaction, e.g. They all liked ice-cream
(c) cognition, e.g. He was firmly convinced of this
(d) verbalization, e.g. He spoke about this at length

3 **Relational processes.** These are processes which reflect the relation in the clause or sentence between one participant and another. For example:

> She is a civil engineer.
> He seems desperately ill.

3 Daneš (1974) identifies, in terms of his analysis of a sentence into parts, what he calls a **functional sentence perspective**. This, as the label implies, offers an analysis of that clause/sentence in terms of its function in the text as a whole. He divides any sentence into two identifiable (but related) parts: **theme** and **rheme**. Theme is that part of a sentence which is selected to occupy the initial position, thereby giving it some kind of prominence as an item of information. For example:

> *George* slew the dragon   (subject theme)
> *Down the road* they marched   (adverb theme)

Rheme is the remainder of the sentence after the initial theme has been identified. For example:

> George *slew the dragon*   (rheme)
> Down the road *they marched*   (rheme)

In terms of how theme and rheme relate to each other both **internal** to the sentence structure (as in the above examples) and **external** to the relationship between one sentence and the next (see Chapter 6), Daneš identifies *three* types of functional sentence perspective based on the notion of **thematic progression** (that is, what particular 'topic for discussion' holds a functional prominence from sentence to sentence).

It is these three types that Margaret Berry uses as a basis to identify cohesive features in the writing of Rosalind and Ben. By focusing on thematic progression she is essentially exploring text organization in relation to **coherence** and **evaluation**.

What follows is a simplified summary of Daneš' three types of thematic progression (for a more detailed study, see Morgan and Sellner, 1980).

1 **Simple linear progression.** Any text has a simple recurrent theme/rheme structure, where the original rheme of the first sentence becomes the theme of the second sentence. This, in turn, takes on a new rheme which subsequently becomes the new theme for the third sentence, and so on. For example:

> George smote the dragon. The dragon fell to the ground and the earth trembled at the impact.

2 **Thematic progression with a continuous (constant) theme.** Again, the first sentence in the text has the simple theme/rheme nexus, but, this time, the same initial theme is taken up in subsequent sentences, but with new rhemes. For example:

> The explorer is constantly fascinated by travel. He has an almost boundless energy and he evidences a determination to succeed at all costs.

3 **Thematic progression with derived themes.** Similarly, the initial sentence has a theme/rheme structure, which consists of a **hypertheme**. All subsequent 'new' themes, however, in successive sentences, can be regarded as **sub-themes**. For example:

> Blackpool is one of England's most popular holiday resorts. The tower is one of the most recognizable features of its landscape. Thousands of people are attracted by its lively and breezy atmosphere.

Suggested Further Reading

Cowie, H. (ed.) (1984), *The Development of Children's Imaginative Writing* is a series of articles on the writing of young children which look at the nature of the writing process and offer many practical suggestions for teacher response.

Crystal, D. (1979), 'Language in Education – a Linguistic Perspective' is an article which, although initially considering the relationship between linguistics and language in education in general terms, illustrates the argument well by focusing on the cohesive devices children use in their story-writing.

Dixon, J., and Farmer, I. (1981, 1982). The Bretton Hall Language Development Unit has published a useful series of booklets on different aspects of children's writing development. Topics include developing children's storytelling techniques and establishing a policy for writing development.

Harris, J., and Kay, S. (1981), *Writing Development* considers many aspects of children's writing in the eight to thirteen age range and offers much practical advice for teachers on initiating and developing writing of different kinds.

9 Classroom Implications

JOHN HARRIS and
JEFF WILKINSON

Evaluating Writing

In the 1940s Flesch developed a formula for the objective measurement of readability (interpreted by him as 'comprehension difficulty'), based on a statistical count of the number of words per sentence; of the number of affixes present; and of the number of references to people. The texts he investigated covered a wide range of types, from scientific writing to fiction, from academic articles to comics. On the evidence of this analysis, he concluded that 'conversational quality' and 'story interest' are of prime importance in judging writing effect: 'It seems hardly necessary to prove the importance of human interest in reading ... That people are most interested in other people is an old truism' (Flesch, 1948, p. 227). In terms of 'reading ease' he argued that the scientific and the academic caused the greatest difficulty; and fiction and comics the least. From a human interest angle, scientific articles and trade journals are 'dull'; whereas newspapers and fiction are 'dramatic'.

Obviously, we all respond to different kinds of writing in different kinds of ways; it would be unwise to assume that we all love reading stories, but hate non-fiction. Nevertheless, Flesch's research does draw attention to our responses to the written word in a way that is reflected in much of the approach adopted to textual analysis described in this book. Writing, of whatever kind, needs to be seen more clearly in the context of its interest for the reader and the nature of that interest more carefully defined. Key elements, therefore, for the teacher in judging the effectiveness, or otherwise, of writing types are: an awareness of the nature of the writing process (the way in which written work is produced); the identification of organization in any text (explicit analysis of discourse features); and understanding of the relationship between writer and reader. In fact, Bereiter sees an important element in the developing maturity of the writer as 'the discovery that writing can be used to affect the reader – that it can direct, inform, amuse, move emotionally, and so on' (1980, p. 89). For this to be achieved, increasing attention needs to be paid to the writer (rather than the writer's product) and text organization (awareness of writing as 'a complete whole'). Certainly, much of the motivation to write in the first place arises only from the writer's projected sense of reader-reaction. Perhaps, it is possible to maintain that narrative texts have more immediate 'impact' in this respect. Children's stories abound with actions and participants. For example, the text of *Rosie's Walk* by Pat Hutchins consists of a single sentence: 'Rosie, the hen, went for a walk and got back in time for tea'; but the colourful drawings, in sequence, reflect a series of problem–solution episodes at the heart of all adventure stories:

    1 Fox attacks Rosie – Fox treads on rake
    2 Fox attacks Rosie – Fox falls in lake
    3 Fox attacks Rosie – Fox falls in hay
    4 Fox attacks Rosie – Fox is covered in flour
    5 Fox attacks Rosie – Fox lands on cart
    6 Fox in trouble   – Fox chased by bees

The situation is finally resolved when the pattern is broken for the last episode, but the fact that each successive episode is 'halted' between *problem* and *solution* by the turn of a page heightens excitement over story outcome.

Stories of this kind (not far in *form* from the similar attractions of *Indiana Jones* or *Dallas*) have an obvious immediate appeal, and children enjoy both reading and writing them. Events and participants are fast-moving and prominent. This is ten-year-old Lee's contribution to the genre:

THE LOST COIN
One day a man was out walking and there was an hole in his pocket but he didn't notice and a coin fell out. Suddenly the coin came to life and ran away when a dog came rushing towards it suddenly. But luckily the coin dodged it and fell down the drain. Unfortunately he coulden't swim a piece of paper floated by and jumped on to it When he met a rat. when a log stopped them but cleverley he picked up the log and hit the rat with it but while they were doing it a water snake came up behind them but they got away in time they sailed on a bit more when they saw a light in front of them they thought it was the sea but it wasnt they started going faster but it was a pirranha with his mouth open and he swallowed the coin and carried them into the sea not knowing what was going to happen there just suddenly they rocked it was the suirs getting thinner when they stopped and was coughed out then finally they was at the sea and they swam home.

Episodes happen thick and fast and events take precedence over participants:

    1 Man has hole in pocket   – Coin escapes
    2 Dog attacks coin   – Coin escapes

3	Coin falls down drain	— Paper rescues coin
4	Rat attacks coin	— Coin defeats rat
5	Water snake attacks coin	— Coin/paper escape
6	Piranha swallows coin/paper	— Coin/paper coughed out
7	Coin/paper at sea	— Coin/paper swim home

One teacher's evaluation of Lee's work was to suggest that he rip it up and start again! Yet, as could be seen when Lee read this to some of his friends, there is much in the successive actions to interest both teller and audience. As children move through the primary and, eventually, the secondary school where an increasing variety of writing demands is made on them, what must be encouraged is an 'active' awareness of the responses to many different types of writing — an understanding of both signal senders and receivers. Success in writing (both narrative and non-narrative texts) would best seem to be achieved by the pupil who most takes account of the communicative relationship necessary between writer and reader.

This, of necessity, must focus both the child's and the teacher's attention on the writing task and the situation in which it is produced; and many of these constraints have been raised and explored in this book. For instance, the teacher needs to clarify the writer–reader relationship so that the pupil is aware of both *how* and *why* the reader is responding in the way he does (Chapters 5 and 7). The exact nature of what is being evaluated has to be made very clear, so that writing demands may more effectively promote learning skills. There are, also, difficulties involved in trying to relate *form* to *content*; non-time-related organization is, in many ways, more problematic for the pupil to handle than is time-related material (Chapter 4). A related question is a much commented upon aspect of children's work: the degree of 'trust' a reader has of a writer (Chapters 3 and 8). This, it would seem, has to involve the teacher 'in dialogue' (both oral and written) with the pupil; it also involves the pupil in self-evaluation of his material (planning, drafting, revising, and so on). Teachers also need to acquire a more precise method of analysing the texts they are evaluating and nowhere is this more evidently imperative than in the classification of lexical items (Chapter 6).

What is being advocated is that, within the communicative context as a whole, there are many aspects of language study worthy of attention (phonological and graphological; grammatical; lexical; and organizational) — all contribute to the 'effect' a piece of writing has on a reader. Lee's text, for example, contains much, at several of these levels, that provides an insight into the way he set about the writing task:

(1) **Phonological and graphological** — the relationship between spoken and written story-telling.

(2) **Grammatical** – the use, for example, of 'when' as 'then'; confusing pronominal references (for example, 'he' and 'they').

(3) **Lexical** – the sequential off-the-top-of-the-head writing indicated by word repetition: 'suddenly'.

(4) **Organizational** – the fast episodic nature of the narrative; the introduction of different thematic elements; the title reflecting only the first part of the story, and so on.

It is hoped that language features described in these chapters will provide readers with sufficient background to apply the descriptive models to a wide variety of children's texts (of all kinds); above all, it is hoped that such a framework will provide the teacher with a 'rationale' for evaluating texts which will allow him to consider: the reasons for writing in the first place; the process by which the pupil organizes the writing; and, more precisely, an awareness of teacher response. All these issues ultimately demand a holistic response to writing and they all assume that any of the considerations listed should be borne in mind in relation to the *development* of the child's competence in writing.

A linguistic approach to the study of children's writing can provide a useful insight into, and model for, an analysis of reader response; but it must also provide some suggestions for the devising of practical activities for subsequent writing development. One such approach is to develop explicit awareness of the way in which both narrative and non-narrative texts are organized. Much publicity has been given recently to the introduction of 'language awareness' courses at upper junior and lower secondary level (Forsyth and Wood, 1977; Aplin *et al.*, 1981; Saunders, 1982; Hawkins, 1983), where pupils are consciously encouraged to describe, as explicitly as possible, the range and variety of language use (dialects; registers; notions of correctness; spoken and written features; and so on), by way of introduction to their English teaching and foreign-language courses at secondary level. The success of these approaches is, we suggest, largely dependent on considering the study of language in relation to situation; there is very little value in returning to 'grammar' lessons *for their own sake*. Much that is of direct relevance in the study of lexical and grammatical features of the language is so only when it is seen in context.

For example, the exercises advocated by Fraser and O'Donnell in *Control and Create*, where language structures are manipulated in a variety of different ways in de-contextualized situations, might be more effectively carried out in specifically identified contexts. For instance, 'story-so-far' texts for comics and magazines can be interestingly constructed from 'the necessary information to be included'. In this situation, pupils have to consider not only *what* to include but *how* to organize content in such a way that the message is understood, and yet economically conveyed. Similar 'operations' can be performed on telegrams; selected paragraphs from newspaper articles; appropriate dialogue in plays and stories; arguments reorganized to express a differing viewpoint using the same information; texts explaining diagrams; instructions for games; and so on.

Text manipulation of this kind can be both stimulating and rewarding, for it not only makes pupils aware of the different ways there are of representing and organizing content on paper, it also draws attention to the 'impact' this has on the reader. Writing is then considered 'in action'; it starts to be seen, not as a private and solitary act, but one that, collaboratively, pupils can engage in themselves for their mutual benefit – as a means of understanding the process of 'effective' writing.

So much for a consideration of activities which illustrate the 'potential' that language has for selection and organization: but what about identifying such exercises within the framework of a developmental programme? It is in this area that language work can so easily degenerate into a series of repetitive and predictable tasks. An assumption made by all the contributors in this book is that it is possible to teach effective writing skills for differing occasions; and that teaching is partly developing a conscious awareness of text organization in pupils. It should be possible to devise materials for many writing types. Here, there is only room for one illustration: story-writing and its development (for more detailed information on this particular approach, see Wilkinson, 1985).

The following units, in the order in which they are presented, were introduced to pupils at upper junior and lower secondary level as a means of drawing attention to the way stories are organized. Much of the material is based on ways of describing oral narrative discourse outlined in Labov and Waletzky, 1967; Labov, 1972; and Peterson and McCabe, 1983.

Stage 1
Introduction to the ways in which stories are organized as a whole by means of 'sentence-sequencing' exercises which consider story-line and how it may, or may not, develop (see Chapter 3).

Stage 2
The 'sections' that stories may be divided into and the functions such units might have: such as part one (description) – part two (actions) – part three (result).

Stage 3
Identification of these three elements in greater detail:

Part 1 — focusing on character (who) and place (where).

Part 2 — given the beginning and the end, is it possible to construct 'what happened'?

Part 3 — given the beginning (description) and the middle (actions), is it possible to construct an end (result)?

Stage 4

A further overview of the three sections, linked to the crucial 'evaluative' element: who? what? where? This was achieved by the introduction of random selecting from three bags, each of which contained a 'who' (character such as magician); a 'where' (place such as airport); and a 'what' (characteristic such as nervous). Pupils had then to construct a possible story based on these elements.

Stage 5

The reorganization of the narrative in different ways:

(a)   increasing the number of action episodes; for example, serials.

(b)   withholding certain of the who/what/where elements; as in mystery stories.

(c)   re-ordering the three sections; for example, action → description → result.

(d)   changing 'point of view'; for example, the same events seen through the eyes of two different participants.

All these activities encourage children to understand, and comment upon, how different types of stories might, ultimately, be written. Not all (in fact, very few) might lead to the actual writing of a full story; much of the work is designed to encourage drafting, note-taking and discussion of ideas; and teacher—evaluation of pupils' work took the form of teacher—in—dialogue—with—pupil, both orally and in written terms. What is crucial to the whole approach is, that by a conscious understanding of the effectiveness of varied story structures, children might eventually see writing as being genuinely communicative and be motivated by this understanding to a more active involvement in trying to realize this effect. It is in the spirit of such work that a principled framework for the evaluation of teacher response might be best realized.

Teaching Writing

In the second part of this chapter we group together a set of classroom implications that are concerned with the pedagogy of writing. We are here making two assumptions: first, that the teaching of writing is not an end in itself but is related to learning in all the areas of the curriculum at both primary and secondary levels; and, second, that 'teaching' is understood in a wide sense and not restricted to notions of direct instruction or exposition. This is an important assumption since it is likely that the most powerful and effective means of teaching writing are those that are, to a greater or lesser extent, incidental.

One clear conclusion from the rather depressing research evidence surveyed in the opening chapter is that few pupils are likely to receive consistent and structured help with writing. Yet the other chapters have all from their different perspectives established an overwhelming case for the need to teach writing; the argument is that it is not simply a matter of providing an initial stimulus or imposing the requirement for a certain writing task to be done and leaving it at that. The reasons for this state of affairs are undoubtedly complex. However, we can, perhaps, suggest three important factors:

(1) the rival and usually dominant claims of subject learning, particularly at secondary level;
(2) the widespread lack of understanding about the nature of writing and the intrinsic demands of specific types of writing;
(3) an assumption that writing competence develops simply through practice; that, in effect, we learn to write by writing.

Each of these points should be borne in mind as we develop the discussion of strategies for teaching writing. By design we are pitching this discussion at a generalized level, wishing to avoid any suggestion that some practices should be restricted to either junior or secondary level.

1. Creating an awareness of text types and text organization

Although it will be apparent to readers of this book that describing text types and their organization is a complex and far from fully determined activity, it will, nevertheless, also be apparent that teachers need to develop their own awareness so that they can offer informed and appropriate help to their pupils. The problems from a teacher's point of view are formidable. There is no ready-to-hand language in which the discussion can be couched. The conceptual and linguistic requirements are great. Teachers, therefore, will need to do a great deal of background work themselves before they are in a position to help their pupils.

However, we would emphasise that we are not here advocating 'taught courses' in text analysis but, rather, a raising of consciousness in pupils that can best be achieved through discussion of their writing both in the process of its creation and at the initial stage of planning.

This raising of consciousness can also be developed through the sentence scrambling and 'cloze' exercises described above and in Chapter 3. Reading supported by discussion either as a class activity or, possibly more usefully, in small groups of three or four pupils has an important part to play. And in making this last point we are very much aware of a happy co-incidence of interests with the Schools Council Project 'Reading for Learning' (see Davies and Greene, 1984; Lunzer and Gardner, 1984). Although the analytical approaches adopted by the project team differ in some respects from those presented in earlier chapters here, the emphasis on looking at both content *and* structure of texts is in accord. In both publications cited above there are useful examples of how to prepare texts for activities designed to improve the effectiveness of reading and increase awareness of text structures.

Closely related to such activities should be the reading aloud by the teacher of various types of texts associated with particular areas of the curriculum. It is generally acknowledged that the amount of fictional narrative (stories, legends, folk and fairy tales) that is read aloud (or re-told) to children in the early years of their schooling helps, in part, to create a generalized model of narrative organization upon which they are able to draw in generating their own narratives. This provides the foundation on which a more sophisticated knowledge of story structure can be built. It is, therefore, important that the practice of reading aloud by the teacher should be extended to include other text types (expository, persuasive, theorizing, and so on), thereby helping pupils to acquire generalized models of how these possibly less accessible texts are organized.

It needs to be asserted emphatically that time spent on reading aloud is not time wasted but time needfully devoted to part of the incidental pedagogy of writing that we are advocating. It also follows that at secondary level this should be the concern of all subject teachers, not merely the teachers of English.

2. Setting up writing tasks

There is, of course, much that needs to be said about the initiating of writing from an educational perspective. Factors such as purpose, the quality of the learning experiences and stimuli provided and the realism of the task are all highly influential on the success of the writing outcomes. For our present purposes, however, we want to raise three issues that are complementary to such concerns but relate specifically to the emphasis we are placing on text organization.

The first point is to reiterate what was suggested above in Chapter 4. There it was argued that a simple categorization of school writing into time-related and non-time-related types enables teachers to work through in their heads writing tasks they are proposing to set. In this way they should be able to anticipate some of the likely pitfalls of a task from a text organizational perspective. This is a necessary preliminary to the second point; and this is that when initiating a writing task it is important that the intrinsic requirements of the writing need to be made explicit and, of course, matched to the pupils' stage of development.

In his discussion of lower secondary science writing Hoey (Chapter 5) shows strikingly that the careful instructions given by the teacher relate to the task as a scientific investigation not as a writing task. As he points out, some of the texts can be seen as examples of 'undeveloped discourses' precisely because their organization is related to the teacher's questions. Similar comments apply to the history essay outline cited in Chapter 1 taken from *Aspects of Secondary Education* (DES, 1979). The carefully structured help in both cases is directed at 'content' not at text organization. If pupils are to be assisted in the creation of developed discourses then part of the pre-writing guidance given by the teacher needs to focus on this aspect.

A similar point can be made about topic writing at junior level. While not wishing to engage in a general discussion of the value of this sort of work, it can, nevertheless, be said that if, as reported in Chapter 1, much of the writing is merely copied from source materials, there is an urgent need to re-think the ways in which this sort of writing might be initiated. If, for instance, Rosalind expresses an interest in writing about town and farm houses in the sixteenth and seventeenth centuries (see the discussion of her text in Chapter 8), it would be helpful for her to undertake some or all of the following activities before writing a final text:

(1) making notes (in rough and in her own words) on what she has seen and read;
(2) creating a time-scale of development, possibly presented in the main visually with sketches of those features that were added at different stages − the features would need to be listed in two columns or on separate sheets, one for town, the other for farm houses;
(3) listing, again in rough, the main differences between the two types of houses at given points of time using the information in (1) and (2).

She would then be in a position to attempt an initial draft of a discursive piece of writing on her chosen subject and the teacher could concentrate *at this stage* on helping her with the problems of the writing itself, since the content is already taken care of, so to speak.

The third point concerns the typical nature of class discussion prior to writing. Bennett *et al.* (1984) report that in the writing lessons observed with six- and seven-year-olds the most common activity prior to writing was a class discussion in which the teacher drew up a list of vocabulary items related to the subject in hand. Subsequently the children were encouraged to include these words in their writing. As the observers comment, the texts produced had an artificiality and uniformity that was at odds with the teachers' expressed aims of encouraging the child's individual response and creativity. As has been shown earlier (see Chapter 6), vocabulary development is not simply a matter of encouraging children to use 'good' words. Vocabulary is one level of language organization and it needs to be related to overall text organization. In the approach observed by Bennett and his colleagues, then, the teachers were imposing organization at one level (perhaps unwittingly) and failing to relate it to organization at other levels or to text type. The discussion prior to writing, in this instance, may well have been detrimental to the writing itself.

A similar comment applies to the type of pre-writing activity observed by the Scottish Council for Research in Education team (Spencer, 1983a). The common form of preparation for an extended piece of writing in one of the subject areas of the secondary curriculum, so they report, is a question and answer routine led by the teacher to revise the content required for the essay. We have argued that revision of content in itself is not enough to help pupils develop well-organized texts. It may well be that this type of preparation through discussion is again positively unhelpful to text creation. Sinclair and Coulthard (1975) have shown that the usual form of teacher-led discussion is a series of exchanges each with this pattern:

    Initiation   (teacher's question)
    Response   (pupil's answer)
    Feedback   (teacher's confirmation or rejection of response)

This is, of course, a grossly simplified account of their model of classroom interaction yet it serves to highlight that it is the teacher who frames the questions – a feature also noted in other researches into classroom discourse. The significance of this for writing is clear. A major problem for *all* writers is that they have to generate questions as well as supplying answers (see Widdowson, 1983 for an engaging and perceptive discussion of this point). The I–R–F pattern of classroom interaction in which the teacher does all the initiating does not allow pupils opportunity for the rehearsal of questions – and, it may be suggested, it is the generating of questions, not the supplying of answers, that is at the heart of the difficulties experienced by novice writers.

3. The Writing Process

We have argued that many of the problems to do with school writing stem directly from the habitual demand for 'off-the-top' writing. The requirement that pupils should create a finished piece of writing at first attempt − or, conversely, that their first attempt should be treated as a finished product − is highly damaging and inhibiting to the production of well-organized texts.

As noted in the opening chapter of this book teachers have good instincts about how to approach a writing task themselves. They naturally distinguish between writing that has a formal requirement and writing that does not. They realize that the former needs to be planned in whatever way they find most helpful and that an initial rough draft follows. It is likely that they will invite others to comment on this draft as well as reviewing it themselves. When a final draft is achieved − and there may be further interim drafts − they will proofread it prior to publication in whatever form that takes. With informal tasks, however, they may well be content with some rough jottings and no more.

These processes reflect an intuitive awareness that pieces of writing have a different **status** and this is evidenced in the degree of revision or polish lavished on them. The notion of status is one that urgently needs to be incorporated into classroom practice.

Implicit in the idea that writing has a range of statuses is the assumption that more formal or public forms of writing require an extended process for their successful production. It is significant in this respect to recall how frequently in the preceding chapters comments on texts have indicated that as a first draft they may be acceptable but that they need to be taken further through another stage of revision informed, ideally, by discussion with the teacher and/or other pupils before they could be regarded as fully developed and adequate texts. This suggests dramatically that although pupils spend a lot of time writing, as was noted in the first chapter, the time is not apportioned adequately to the business of text creation. It is not a matter of spending more time in total on writing but of ensuring that the time spent, at least with selected pieces of work, allows for pupils to engage fully in the extended process of planning, drafting and revising.

Recent work on the process of writing (see, for instance, Emig, 1971; Britton *et al.*, 1975; Cooper and Odell, 1978; Gregg and Steinberg (eds), 1980; Smith, 1982) acknowledges that evidence is not easily accessible or verifiable since it can be made available only through introspection or question-based protocols. Nevertheless, there emerges a broad consensus as to what a model of the process should be like. At a simple level three stages can be identified as follows:

(1) Pre-writing	(2) Writing	(3) Revision of text
or	or	
composing ideas	transcribing ideas	

Some comments can be made on each of these relatively self-explanatory stages.

Stage 1: Pre-writing or Composing Ideas

There needs to be some initial stimulus or invitation to write. How far the task proposed by self or an outside agency (teacher or publisher, for instance) fits in with the writer's existing knowledge and interests will determine the subsequent activities within this stage. If the task makes demands that are beyond the writer's existing store of knowledge, then a lengthy period of research follows. If, however, the task fits well with the writer's existing store of knowledge, detailed planning follows more immediately. It should be noted that the nature of this detailed planning is highly variable. Individual writers plan in different ways – using key-words, diagrams, flow-charts, detailed notes or even entirely 'in the head' – and the same writer plans differently according to the task. It should, therefore, be noted that stereotyped plans or outlines imposed on a class of children may be more of a hindrance than a help. Nevertheless, it is clear that time is required for 'gestating' the topic and planning the approach. As has been argued earlier (see Chapters 4, 5 and 8) the nature of the task also carries organizational demands that will influence the fluency of the planning process.

Stage 2: Writing or Transcribing Ideas

Writers differ in their habits. Some tend to write slowly at this second stage, gradually fashioning a reasonably finalized text; others work quickly to produce a draft which may then need extensive re-writing. One of the problems that children face in writing at school is the constraint of a timetable which usually imposes a demand to write at speed. Another problem is that they do not see the need (unless it is pointed out to them) to cast back to the already-written portion of their text as they proceed.

Stage 3: Revision of Text

At this stage a writer needs once more to call upon existing knowledge as at Stage 1. Revisions may involve a radical recasting of the text to account for the writer's perception of readership; they may involve resequencing to articulate the argument more clearly; or they may be in the nature of attention to surface features such as spelling and punctuation. Often revision may involve all these aspects.

The simple model proposed so far carries with it a suggestion that each stage is completed progressively. However, it is generally recognized that the model is recursive, that is, at any stage a 'mini-process' may occur. This gives us a much more flexible though complex model – see Figure 9.1. In this model, adapted from one developed by Hayes and Flower (see Gregg and Steinberg, 1980, p. 11), the bold arrows indicate the main dynamic of the writing process – from task to pre-writing, to writing and finally to revising. The single arrows indicate that the writing and revising stages are both interactive with the text whether partially or fully drafted. The broken lines emphasise that both task and the writer's knowledge (of content, readership and of how a particular text needs to be shaped) impinge on all other stages of the whole process.

It should be noted, however, that any two-dimensional representation of a complex cognitive process may fail to reveal adequately the nature of the complexity. Smith (1982, Chapter 8) prefers a linear representation with lines of thought stretching along the whole period of writing, feeding into spasmodic writing episodes (short periods of actual text creation) that are themselves interactive with the text so far produced.

Before we leave this crucial question of process it may be helpful to look at a text produced by a top junior pupil in which we can see the value of revision. The report is of some traffic census activities.

Traffic Census Report   Teresa (J4)
First draft
A foggy day on the A57
   On the 7th November our class went down to the A57. It was a foggy day but it didn't matter for our group because we were studying visability and traffic lights. There were three groups one group was counting cars and lorries, and the other group were counting car and lorries who went North to South.
   When our group got to the cross roads we got in to two's or three's one person has a stop watch and we timed how long red was on and so on. We

                              X

[At this point she put a cross to show that she didn't like what she'd written and turned over the page and started again.]

Second draft
A foggy day on the A57
   On the 7th November our class went down to the A57. My group went with Mrs Vollans and we studied visability and traffic lights. It was a foggy day so it made it more interesting for the visability bit. There were three groups our group had eleven people in.

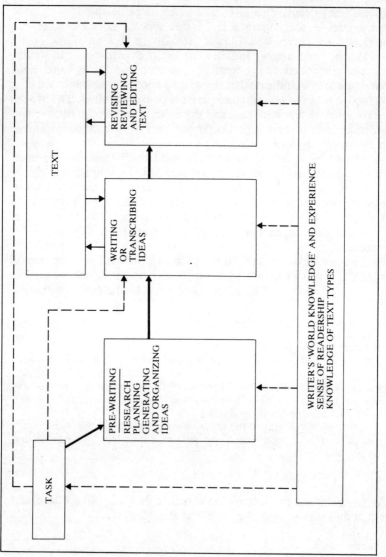

Figure 9.1 Model of the writing process.

Our group went to the crossroads first and we got in to pairs and one person had a stopwatch and we were timing the sequences of the traffic lights.

We crossed the road and two boys took a tape measure and marked 10 metres from the traffic lights with chalk on the pavements they did this until they reached the garage then we stood on each chalk line and wrote how good you could see cars, people, lorries and the traffic lights.

We did three recordings on each light and all of the recordings were different. Red and green were on for the longest.

We found out for the visability that you couldn't see the people at 160 metres, and cars at 170 metres, and at 190 metres the lorries had disappeared but at the end of the path the traffic lights were very faint.

[After reading through their first attempts, the teacher called the group together, and asked each child to read aloud to the group the introduction to their report. They then talked about relevant and irrelevant information in writing a report of this kind, and listed what was relevant to the introduction and identified what was irrelevant in their first draft. They then re-wrote the introduction, read it aloud again to the group, and discussed each other's work with reference to relevance. Then in groups of three they continued with the next section of the report.]

Third draft
A Report
On the 7th November 1984 at 11.15 am our class went down to the A57 to time the sequence of the traffic lights and the visability of the drivers and pedristrains. It was foggy so it made it more interesting for the visability. I expected the traffic lights to be at random times and visability to be bad.

We got into pairs and one person had a stopwatch and we timed the sequence of the traffic lights three times to see if the recordings were the same. Then we timed ourselves how long it took to cross the road. Two boys from our group took a tape measure and marked a chalk line on the pavement every ten metres from the traffic lights and carried on until they reached Wain wrights garage then we stood on each line and looked back to see how well you can see the cars, lorries, pedristrains, and the traffic lights.
[A table of results follows]

A detailed commentary on these drafts would be superfluous since the main features are readily identifiable. However, the move from the chatty, relatively non-selective nature of the first draft to the tighter propositional coherence of the unfinished third draft is notable. Mention of the activities of the other groups has been deleted; the purpose of the activity has been clarified; the method of the investigation elaborated. It is also interesting to see (in a school where the practice of drafting has been encouraged for a few years) how far the writer has progressed from first to second draft without the teacher's intervention. The teacher's well-judged intervention has helped to sharpen up perceptions already made by the pupils. It should also be noted that the sort of process illustrated here is far removed from the mechanical and tedious practice of doing a rough version and then writing it up neatly 'in best books' that is still found.

4. Collaboration in Writing

Writing is normally a solitary activity. In part the difficulties novice writers face are to do with the isolation in which a writer habitually operates. This isolation means, as we have seen, that writers have to anticipate the questions that a reader asks of a text; they have, also, to project for themselves the extent of knowledge and cultural background shared with their readership. Solitariness, too, cuts off writers from the supportive mutuality to be found in conversation (see Chapter 4). It may well be, therefore, that providing opportunities for collaborative writing in school will be beneficial.

We accept that writing by committee has something of a stigma in the world at large because it can often entail a loss of individuality and a consequent blandness. Nevertheless, for novice writers needing to puzzle out questions as well as answers, to sort out sequencing and to judge the effectiveness of their texts, working in pairs, for example, may be helpful in sustaining endeavour through the stages of text creation. It will also provide a *modus operandi* that individuals can apply when they have to write by themselves.

Obviously this form of pair or group writing has to be restricted to writing that is not, by its nature, of a personal type. It is not, for instance, appropriate for autobiographical writing. We have, however, found that it is an approach which can overcome the natural reluctance some pupils have over revising their own work and it establishes a habit of exchanging pieces of writing with friends to get their reactions and comments to assist in the process of revision. Pupils, in short, can help each other by writing together from time to time and by becoming readers of each other's writing.

5. Planning development in writing

It is evident from our experiences on in-service courses that planning for development in writing causes teachers much anxiety. Yet it is an aspect of the pedagogy of writing that is clearly important. Teachers have, for example, reported when looking at the types of writing task set in their junior schools that identical tasks are set at J1 and at J4 levels. This can, of course, be justified on the basis that the response to the same question can be expected to be increasingly sophisticated. However, it also suggests that more structured planning for development in writing is needed. It may be useful, therefore, to suggest an outline strategy for a non-fictional area of writing since examples have already been offered in relation to story writing. In choosing letter-writing we are aware that it is, at the same time, one of the more routine aspects of writing at junior level, often made a lot of in course-books, and one where the need for genuine communicative contexts is paramount. The creation of such contexts will necessarily be the concern of the teacher. What we can do here is to sketch out a developmental sequence.

Letter-writing – a developmental sequence

General dimensions of development in writing can be identified as follows:

(1) audience-awareness
(2) relevance of content
(3) sequencing of information
(4) degree of formality
(5) purpose of communication
(6) conventions of a particular type of writing (letters, it should be noted, can take a highly conventionalized form).

In each of these aspects we would expect that increasing demands should be made on pupils but not, of course, all at the same time. We can suggest, therefore, a progression along these lines roughly divided into four stages.

Stage 1
(1) emphasis on letter writing as a communicative act;
(2) expectation of audience-awareness will be low initially;
(3) initially degree of formality to be expected will be low and there will be little emphasis on conventions of lay-out, and so on.

Stage 2
(1) introduction of some degree of formality;
(2) imposition of need to consider a remote/impersonal audience but combined with personal (anecdotal) subject matter;
(3) extended, informal communication to peer-group audience;
(4) introduction of simple elements of conventions.

Stage 3
(1) demand considerable degree of formality;
(2) expect sophisticated awareness of remote/public readership;
(3) impose need for selection of information relevant to purpose of communication;
(4) require use of necessary conventions in lay-out, and so on.

Stage 4
(1) introduction of notion of letter-writing as a means of influencing behaviour and attitudes in society at large;
(2) introduce tasks that require a letter to be drafted and revised, and so on; also to re-sequence information into acceptable order;
(3) expectation of considerable sophistication and precision in projecting into a reader's needs.

In tabular form the progression is as follows:

Aspect of Writing	Stage 1 ⟶	Stage 4
Formality	low	high
Conventions	not important and idiosyncratic to an extent	conforming to socially established precedents
Audience	known (seen particularly in the degree to which experience, knowledge or attitudes are shared)	unknown/public
Sequencing and selection of detail	personal and arbitrary	dictated by conventions, purposes of communication and needs of readership
Aims/purposes	of immediate relevance and related to peer group experiences	related to a wider social setting and to the individual's participation in it

Following through this progression we might suggest these sorts of writing activities at each stage.

Stage 1
(1) secret notes — such as invitations to classmates to join a secret society, explaining nature of society and time, date and place of meeting.

(2) rescue notes — where you are and why you need to be rescued (like the hapless Piglet's 'HELP! PIGLIT (ME)' and, you will recall, on the reverse side of his note 'IT'S ME PIGLIT, HELP HELP!').

(3) complain — holiday postcard to relative about funny or disastrous holiday experiences.

(4) requests — filling in details on form for ordering 'special offer' product.

Stage 2

(1) party invitation — not formalized but still requiring details of time, date and place and expecting a reply, which involves giving the address to which reply has to be made.

(2) cheering-up letter — to friend in hospital.

(3) requests — ordering something relatively straight-forward from mail-order catalogue.

Stage 3

(1) requesting information — seeking information when planning a class trip to local castle, etc., about opening times, catering facilities, etc.

(2) complaints — letter to travel agency about badly organized trip.

(3) apologies — letter to your friend's mum apologizing for bad behaviour at party and/or for breaking window while playing football.

(4) requests — as in Stage 3 but selecting goods from mail-order catalogue that require precise details (e.g. shoes and/or clothing) and arranging details of payment.

Stage 4

(1) persuasion — letter to company persuading them to trial a new computer or board game that you have devised.

(2) complaint — to local authority about lack of provision of play areas or community facilities for old people.

(3) public debate — response to abusive letters in the press about children's behaviour in public.

(4) request   – letter to local coach company setting out details for a school trip with all logistics pre-planned and explained.

Conclusion

Much of the 'message' of this book may seem to imply that teachers need to become expert writers and expert text analysts, as well as practising their skills as teachers. There is, of course, a realistic level that has to be set to these expectations. Increasingly, it seems, teachers are required to know more and more about more and more. Obviously one line of development that would be encouraging would be to see elements of initial teacher education language courses designed to create awareness of text organization. Such an approach might usefully link description to pedagogic issues of both reading and writing. There is a similar need for in-service courses.

Many teachers, however, may well be on their own in coming to terms with the issues to which we have addressed ourselves in this book. What we have been discussing is one aspect of writing – one that we feel to be important and, hitherto, neglected – but that is not to suggest that there are not complementary issues. To provide some guidance, a list of selected reading follows each chapter which, it is hoped, will be useful to those readers who wish to explore further both the linguistic and educational aspects of text organization.

Acknowledgements

I should like to convey my many thanks to Ann Darnton and to the children and staff of Bromford Junior School in Birmingham for all their help and enthusiasm in devising, commenting on and revising ideas for the story-writing activities suggested in this chapter.

J.W.

I should like to record my gratitude to Joyce Vollans of Hillcrest Primary School, South Anston, Rotherham, for permission to use the traffic census material.

J.H.

Suggested Further Reading

Calkins, L. McC. (1983), *Lessons from a Child* is a detailed and highly informative examination of the writings of one particular child and offers useful advice on revising work and writing for real audiences.

Gregg, L., and Steinberg, E. (eds) (1980), *Cognitive Processes in Writing* contains many interesting articles considering writing as a process which involves planning, drafting and revising.

Widdowson, H. G. (1983), 'New Starts and Different Kinds of Failure' again succinctly identifies the difficulties involved in coming to terms with writing for a particular audience.

Bibliography

Andersen, E. S. (1975), 'Cups and glasses: learning that boundaries are vague', *Journal of Child Language*, vol. 2, pp. 79–103.

Anglin, J. (1970), *The Growth of Word Meaning* (Cambridge, Mass.: MIT Press).

Aplin, T. R. W., *et al.* (1981), *Introduction to Language* (London: Hodder & Stoughton).

Asch, S. E., and Nerlove, A. (1967), 'The development of double-function terms in children: an exploratory investigation', in de Cecco, J. P. (ed.), *The Psychology of Language, Thought and Instruction* (New York: Holt, Rinehart & Winston), pp. 283–90.

Assessment of Performance Unit (1981), *Language Performance in Schools: Primary Survey Report No. 1* (London: HMSO).

Assessment of Performance Unit (1982a), *Language Performance in Schools: Primary Survey Report No. 2* (London: HMSO).

Assessment of Performance Unit (1982b), *Language Performance in Schools: Secondary Survey Report No. 1* (London: HMSO).

Assessment of Performance Unit (1983), *Language Performance in Schools: Secondary Survey Report No. 2* (London: HMSO).

Ballard, D., *et al.* (1971), 'The deep and surface grammar of interclausal relations', *Foundations of Language*, vol. 7, pp. 70–118.

Beard, R, (1984), *Children's Writing in the Primary School* (London: Hodder & Stoughton).

Beekman, J., and Callow, J. (1974), *Translating the Word of God* (Michigan: Zondervan).

Bennett, N., *et al.* (1984), *The Quality of Pupil Learning Experiences* (London and Hillsdale, NJ: Lawrence Erlbaum).

Bereiter, C. (1980), 'Development in writing' in Gregg, L., and Steinberg, E. (eds), op. cit., pp. 73–93.

Bloomfield, L. (1933), *Language* (New York: Holt).

Brautigan, R. (1963), *The Revenge of the Lawn* (New York: Simon and Schuster).

Britton, J., *et al.* (1975), *The Development of Writing Abilities 11–18* (Basingstoke: Macmillan).

Brodkey, L. (1983), 'Flapping ghosts humming in jazz: reading a child's writing', *Text*, vols. 3–4, pp. 327–45.

Brown, G. (1977), *Listening to Spoken English* (London: Longman).

Brown, R. (1973), *A First Language* (Harmondsworth: Penguin).

Brown, G., and Yule, G. (1983), *Discourse Analysis* (Cambridge: CUP).

Brumfit, C. (1981), 'Being interdisciplinary: some problems facing applied linguistics', *Applied Linguistics*, vol. 2, no. 2, pp. 158–64.

Calkins, L. McC. (1983), *Lessons from a Child* (Exeter, NH: Heinemann).

Carter, R. A. (1982a), 'A note on core vocabulary', *Nottingham Linguistic Circular*, vol. 11, no. 2, pp. 39–50.

Carter, R. A. (1982b) (ed.), *Linguistics and the Teacher* (London: Routledge & Kegan Paul).

Carter, R. A. (1982c), 'Language, literacy and assessment of language', *British Educational Research Journal*, vol. 8, no. 1, pp. 85–90.

Carter, R. A. (1984), 'Lexical associations, lexicography, and the foreign language learner', *Journal of Applied Language Study*, vol. 1, no. 3, pp. 37–52.

Carter, R. A. (forthcoming), *English Vocabulary in Use: An Applied Linguistic Introduction* (London: Allen & Unwin).

Channell, J. (1981), 'Applying semantic theory to vocabulary teaching', *English Language Teaching Journal*, vol. 35, no. 2, pp. 115–22.

Chatman, S. (1978), *Story and Discourse: Narrative Structure in Fiction and Film* (Ithaca NY: Cornell University Press).

Cleland, W. P. (1976), *English for Primary Schools* (London: Nelson).

Convey, M., and Wilkinson, J. (1977), 'Grammatical analysis of children's writing', unpublished mimeograph, Newman College, Birmingham.

Cooper, C., and Odell, L. (eds) (1977), *Evaluating Writing: Describing, Measuring, Judging* (Urbana, Ill.: NCTE).

Cooper, C., and Odell, L. (eds) (1978), *Research on Composing: Points of Departure* (Urbana, Ill.: NCTE).

Cowie, H. (ed.) (1984), *The Development of Children's Imaginative Writing* (London: Croom Helm).

Crystal, D. (1971), *Linguistics* (Harmondsworth: Penguin).

Crystal, D. (1979), 'Language in Education – a Linguistic Perspective', in Cashdan, A. (ed.) *Language, Reading and Learning* (Oxford: Blackwell), pp. 13–28.

Crystal, D. (1984), *Who Cares About English Usage?* (Harmondsworth: Penguin).

Daneš, F. (ed.) (1974), *Papers on Functional Sentence Perspective* (The Hague: Mouton).

Davies, F., and Greene, T. (1984), *Reading for Learning in the Sciences* (Edinburgh: Oliver & Boyd).

de Beaugrande, R. (1980), *Text, Discourse and Process* (London: Longman).

Department of Education and Science (1975), *A Language for Life* (The Bullock Report) (London: HMSO).

Department of Education and Science (1978), *Primary Education in England* (The Primary Survey) (London: HMSO).

Department of Education and Science (1979), *Aspects of Secondary Education* (The Secondary Survey) (London: HMSO).

Dillon, G. L. (1981), *Constructing Texts* (Bloomington, Ind.: Indiana University Press).

Dixon, J., and Farmer, I. (1981, 1982), *Bretton Hall Language Development Unit Publications* (Wakefield: Bretton Hall Language Development Unit).

Donaldson, M. (1978), *Children's Minds* (London: Fontana).

Dunsbee, T., and Ford, T. (1980), *Mark My Words: a Study of Teachers as Correctors of Children's Writing* (London: Ward Lock Educational).

Emig, J. (1971), *The Composing Processes of 12th Graders*. Research Report no. 13 (Urbana, Ill.: NCTE).

Flesch, R. (1948), 'A new readability yardstick', *Journal of Applied Psychology*, vol. 32, no. 3, pp. 221–33.

Forsyth, I., and Wood, K. (1977), *Language and Communication* (London: Longman).

Fraser, H., and O'Donnell, W. R. (1968), *Control and Create* (London: Longman).

Galton, M., *et al.* (1980), *Inside the Primary Classroom* (London: Routledge & Kegan Paul).

Gannon, P., and Czerniewska, P. (1980), *Using linguistics: an Education Focus* (London: Edward Arnold).

Genette, G. (1980), *Narrative Discourse* (Oxford: Blackwell).

Graustein, G., and Thiele, W. (1980) 'Zur Struktur der Bedeutung von englischen Texten', *Linguistiche Arbeitsverichte*, vol. 26, pp. 12–28.

Graves, D. (1983), *Writing: Teachers and Children at Work* (London: Heinemann).

Gregg, L., and Steinberg, E. (eds) (1980), *Cognitive Processes in Writing* (Hillsdale, NJ: Lawrence Erlbaum).

Gregory, M., and Carroll, S. (1978), *Language and Situation* (London: Routledge & Kegan Paul).

Grimes, J. (1972), 'Outlines and overlays', *Language*, vol. 48, no. 3, pp. 513–24.

Grimes, J. (1975), *The Thread of Discourse* (The Hague: Mouton).

Halliday, M. A. K. (1970), 'Language structure and language function', in Lyons, J. (ed.), *New Horizons in Linguistics* (Harmondsworth: Penguin), pp. 140–65.

Halliday, M. A. K. (1975), *Learning How to Mean* (London: Edward Arnold).

Halliday, M. A. K., and Hasan, R. (1976), *Cohesion in English* (London: Longman).

Harpin, W. (1973), *Social and Educational Influences on Children's Acquisition of Grammar*, Research Report 757 (London: Social Science Research Council).

Harpin, W. (1976), *The Second 'R'* (London: Allen and Unwin).

Harrell, L. E. (1957) *A Comparison of the Development of Oral and Written Language in School-Age Children* (Chicago: University of Chicago Press).

Harris, J. (1980), 'Suprasentential organisation in written discourse with particular reference to writing by children in the lower secondary range' MA thesis (unpublished), University of Birmingham.

Harris, J., and Kay, S. (1981), *Writing Development* (Rotherham: Metropolitan Borough of Rotherham).

Hasan, R. (1980), 'The texture of a text', in Halliday, M. A. K., and Hasan, R., *Text and Context: Aspects of Language in a Social Semiotic Perspective* (Tokyo: Sophia University), pp. 70–97.

Hawkins, E. (1983), *Awareness of Language* (London: CUP).

Hoey, M. (1979a), *Signalling in Discourse*, Discourse Analysis Monographs no. 6, English Language Research, University of Birmingham.

Hoey, M. (1979b), 'Secondary writing', Appendix to *Block 6: The Language Curriculum PE232* (Milton Keynes: The Open University).

Hoey, M. (1983a), *On the Surface of Discourse* (London: Allen & Unwin).

Hoey, M. (1983b), 'The place of clause-relational analysis in linguistic description', *English Language Research Journal*, University of Birmingham, vol. 4, (1983–4), pp. 1–32.

Hunt, K. W. [1966], (1975), 'Recent measures in syntactic development' in Richard L. Larson (ed.), *Children and Writing in the Elementary School* (New York: OUP), pp. 55–69.

Hunt, K. W. (1970), 'Syntactic maturity in school children and adults', *Monographs of the Society for Research in Child Development*, vol. 35, no. 1, pp. 1–67.

Jordan, M. (1980), 'Short texts to explain problem-solution structures – and vice-versa', *Instructional Science*, vol. 9, pp. 221–52.

Jordan, M. (1984), *Rhetoric of Everyday English Texts* (London: Allen & Unwin).

Kress, G. (1982), *Learning to Write* (London: Routledge & Kegan Paul).

Labov, W. (1972), 'The transformation of experience in narrative syntax', in *Language in the Inner City* (Oxford: Blackwell), pp. 354–98.

Labov, W., and Waletzky, J. (1967), 'Narrative analysis: oral versions of personal experience', in Helm, J. (ed.), *Essays on the Verbal and Visual Arts* (Seattle and London: University of Washington Press), pp. 12–44.

La Brant, L. L. (1933), 'A study of certain language developments in children', *Genetic Psychology Monographs*, vol. 14, pp. 387–491.

Leech, G. M., and Svartvik, J. (1975), *A Communicative Grammar of English* (London: Longman).

Longacre, R. E. (1976), *An Anatomy of Speech Notions* (Lisse: Peter de Ridder).

Lunzer, E., and Gardner, K. (1979), *The Effective Use of Reading* (London: Heinemann).

Lunzer, E., and Gardner, K. (1984), *Learning from the Written Word* (Edinburgh: Oliver & Boyd).

Luria, A. R. (1972), *The Man with a Shattered World* (London: Jonathan Cape).

Lyons, J. (1968), *Introduction to Theoretical Linguistics* (Cambridge: CUP).

Lyons, J. (1977), *Semantics*, Vols. I and II (Cambridge: CUP).

Lyons, J. (1981), *Language, Meaning and Context* (London: Fontana).

McCarthy, M. J. (1984), 'A new look at vocabulary in EFL', *Applied Linguistics*, vol. 5, no. 1, pp. 12–22.

Martin, J. R., and Rotherey, J. (1981), 'Writing Project Reports: 1980 and 1981', *Working Papers in Linguistics*, nos. 1 & 2 (Sydney: University of Sydney).

Meara, P. (1980), 'Vocabulary acquisition: a neglected aspect of language learning', *Linguistics and Language Teaching Abstracts*, vol. 15, no. 4, pp. 221–46.

Milic, L. T. (1967), *A Quantitative Approach to the Style of Jonathan Swift* (The Hague: Mouton).

Morgan, J. L., and Sellner, M. B. (1980), 'Discourse and Linguistic Theory', in Spiro, R. J., Bruce, B. C., and Brewer, W. P. (eds), *Theoretical Issues in Reading Comprehension* (Hillsdale, NJ: Lawrence Erlbaum), pp. 165–200.

Nash, W. (1980), *Designs in Prose* (London: Longman).

Nation, I. S. P. (1982), 'Beginning to learn foreign vocabulary – a review of the research', *Regional English Language Centre Journal*, vol. 13, no. 1, pp. 14–33.

North, A. (1982), 'Children's written language', mimeo., Department of English Studies, University of Nottingham.

O'Donnell, W. R. and Todd, L. (1980), *Variety in Contemporary English* (London: Allen & Unwin).

Olson, D. (1977), 'From utterance to text: the bias of language in speech and writing', *Harvard Educational Review*, vol. 47, no. 3, pp. 257–81.

Perera, K. (1980), 'The assessment of linguistic difficulty in reading material', *Educational Review*, vol. 32, pp. 151–61.

Perera, K. (1982), 'The language demands of school learning' in Carter, R. A. (ed.) (1982b), op. cit., pp. 114–136.

Perera, K. (1984), *Children's Writing and Reading* (Oxford: Blackwell).

Peterson, C., and McCabe, A. (1983), *Developmental Psycholinguistics: Three Ways of Looking at a Child's Narrative* (New York: Plenum).

Propp, V. Y. (1958), 'Morphology of the folktale' in *International Journal of American Linguistics*, vol. 24, no. 4, Part 3.

Protherough, R. (1983), *Encouraging Writing* (London: Methuen).

Quirk, R., *et al.* (1972), *A Grammar of Contemporary English* (London: Longman).

Rosen, C., and Rosen, H. (1973), *The Language of Primary School Children* (Harmondsworth: Penguin).

Rudzka, B., *et al.* (1982), *The Words You Need* (Basingstoke: Macmillan).

Rutter, P., and Raban, B. (1982), 'The development of cohesion in children's writing: a preliminary investigation', *First Language*, vol. 3, pp. 63–75.

Sampson, O. C. (1964), 'A linguistic study of the written compositions of ten-year-old children', *Language and Speech*, vol. 7, no. 3, pp. 176–82.

Saunders, M. (1982), *Multicultural Teaching* (Maidenhead: McGraw Hill).

Schonell, F. J. (1942), *Backwardness in the Basic Subjects* (Edinburgh: Oliver & Boyd).

Shaughnessy, M. P. (1977), *Errors and Expectations* (New York: OUP).

Sinclair, J. McH., and Coulthard, R. M. (1975), *Towards an Analysis of Discourse* (London: OUP).

Smith, F. (1982), *Writing and the Writer* (London: Heinemann).

Spencer, E. (1983a), *Writing Matters – Across the Curriculum* (Edinburgh: Scottish Council for Research in Education).

Spencer, E. (1983b), *Written Work in Scottish Secondary Schools* (Edinburgh: Scottish Council for Research in Education).

Stubbs, M. (1980), *Language and Literacy* (London: Routledge & Kegan Paul).

Stubbs, M. (forthcoming), 'Language development, lexical competence and nuclear vocabulary' in Durkin, K. (ed.), *Language Development in the School Years* (London: Croom Helm).

Thornton, G. (1980), *Teaching Writing* (London: Edward Arnold).

Trudgill, P. (1975), *Accent, dialect and the school* (London: Edward Arnold).

Van Dijk, T. A. (1977), *Text and Context: Explorations in the Semantics and Pragmatics of Discourse* (London and New York: Longman).

Wallace, M. (1982), *Teaching Vocabulary* (London: Heinemann).

Wallwork, J. F. (1969), *Language and Linguistics* (London: Heinemann).

Werlich, E. (1976), *A Text Grammar of English* (Heidelberg: Quelle & Meyer).

Widdowson, H. G. (1981), 'Models and fictions', *Applied Linguistics*, vol. 2, no. 2, pp. 165–70.

Widdowson, H. G. (1983), 'New starts and different kinds of failure' in Freedman, A., Pringle, I., and Yalden, J. (eds), *Learning to Write: First Language/Second Language* (London: Longman), pp. 34–47.

Wilkinson, A., *et al.* (1980), *Assessing Language Development* (Oxford: OUP).

Wilkinson, J. (1985), *Developing Stories* (Sheffield: Language Development Centre, Sheffield City Polytechnic).

Winter, E. (1968), 'Some aspects of cohesion' in R. D. Huddleston, *et al.*, *Sentence and Clause in Scientific English*, OSTI Report 5030 (London: University College), pp. 560–604.

Winter, E. (1971), 'Connection in science material: a proposition about the semantics of clause relations' in *CILT Reports and Papers*, no. 7 (London: Centre for Information on Language Teaching and Research), pp. 41–52.

Winter, E. (1974), 'Replacement as a function of repetition: a study of some of its principal features in the clause relations of contemporary English', PhD thesis, University of London.

Winter, E. (1976), *The Fundamentals of Information Structure: A Pilot Manual for Further Development According to Student Need* (Hatfield: The Polytechnic).

Winter, E. (1977), 'A clause-relational approach to English texts – a study of some predictive lexical items in written discourse', *Instructional Science*, vol. 6, no. 1, pp. 1–92.

Winter, E. (1979), 'Replacement as a fundamental function of the sentence in context', *Forum Linguisticum*, vol. 4, no. 2, pp. 95–133.

Winter, E. (1982), *Towards a Contextual Grammar of English* (London: Allen & Unwin).

Names and Main Subjects Index

N. B. Italicized entries denote citation in 'Further Reading'

Index of Children's Texts

1. In order of occurrence

2. Alphabetically by author